Naples
An Early Guide

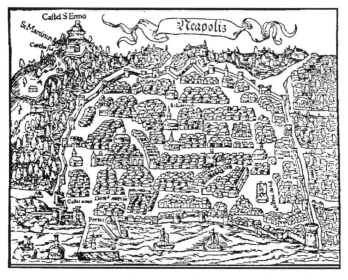

1. NAPLES. FROM SEBASTIAN MÜNSTER,
Cosmographia Universalis. BASEL, 1522.

Naples

An Early Guide

by
Enrico Bacco,
Cesare D'Engenìo Caracciolo
& Others

Edited & Translated by
Eileen Gardiner

Introductory Essays by
Caroline Bruzelius
&
Ronald G. Musto

ITALICA PRESS
NEW YORK
1991

Copyright © 1991 by Italica Press

ITALICA PRESS, INC.
595 Main Street
New York, New York 10044

Library of Congress Cataloging-in-Publication Data

Bacco, Enrico.
    [Descrittione del Regno di Napoli. English]
    Naples : an early guide / by Enrico Bacco, Cesare D'Engenio Caracciolo & others ; edited & translated by Eileen Gardiner ; introductions by Caroline Bruzelius & Ronald G. Musto.
      p.   cm.
"Translation of the Descrittione del Regno di Napoli ... this edition focuses on the first part of the book covering the city of Naples"--Pref.
    Included bibliographical references and index.
    ISBN 0-934977-20-8 (pbk.) : $12.50
    1. Naples (Italy) -- Description. I. D'Engenio Caracciolo, Cesare. II. Gardiner, Eileen. III. Title.
DG843.B2713 1990
945'.73--dc20   89-46222
                                                            CIP

Printed in the United States of America
5 4 3 2 1

2. Napoli la Gentile. Map of Naples by Nicolò van Aelst, c.1590.

3. VIEW OF NAPLES. Bastien Stopendael, 1653.

At center top Castel S. Elmo; at center bottom Castel Nuovo, flanked by Molo S. Vicenzo (R), and Castel dell'Ovo (L). At left, beyond Castel dell'Ovo, lay Chiaia, Posillipo, and Nisida (extreme L). Below the fumerole of La Solfatara, (L, distance), is Pozzuoli. Poggio Reale is at extreme R.

CONTENTS

Contents

ILLUSTRATIONS

4-1. NAPLES. *Tavola Strozzi*. 1464. Naples, Museo di Capodimonte. L to R
Pizzofalcone, Torre S. Vicenzo, Castel Nuovo, Molo Grande, Castel Belf

Tavola Strozzi. From L to R: The harbor, S. Maria Nova, S. Chiara, Lorenzo Maggiore, the Duomo, S. Agostino della Zecca, Castel Capuana.

5. MOLO AND TORRE S. VICENZO. DETAIL FROM *Tavola Strozzi* (Plate 4).
To the left, above Pizzofalcone, rises the palace of the Prince of Aragon.

PREFACE

Naples is one of the greatest cities of the world, and yet there is a serious lack of material in English for anyone wanting to look beyond the general guides and understand the city and its history. In 1671 there was a similar need for books on Naples, and the original authors of this *Descrittione del regno di Napoli* prepared yet another edition for the foreigners who flowed into the city. All the previous editions of this book had quickly sold out, and it was once again unavailable. In an effort to remedy our current lack of material we have turned to this book and present here for the modern reader the material that the traveller to this baroque city on ancient ground would need to understand the city in its historical context.

This book provides the information that a cultured Neapolitan, foreign official, or tourist considered necessary to appreciate the city. For us it provides a key to the way that both Neapolitans and foreigners regarded Naples. It tells us what they considered important, beautiful, and noteworthy.

As the modern reader might expect, the church was important to the native and foreigner alike. Today, one of the most important reasons for visiting this city is to see the treasures built by the church. But from the perspective of the seventeenth century, the church was not simply a patron of the arts. The Neapolitan church was its religious orders and houses, its populations of nuns, priests, and monks; and it was primarily the church institutions that provided sacraments and cared for the poor, the orphaned, the sick, the dying, and the dead. The Neapolitan church was also both the laity and the clergy.

Lay organizations, usually established in conjunction with the churches, performed charitable services, especially providing dowries for impoverished young women. Evidently Neapolitans also took particular pride in the popes and cardinals who could be linked to the city and kingdom of Naples and in their bishops and archbishops. The lists in this book indicate that the names of these men were considered well worth remembering.

We can also see from Bacco's *Guide* that although the Neapolitans built some of the world's most beautiful churches, these churches were not visited for their paintings and sculpture, but for their miraculous relics. There is obvious pride in the inventories presented here of the whole bodies and small fragments of saints, apostles, virgins and martyrs found in Neapolitan churches – things that modern guidebooks seldom dare to mention.

The physical description of the city often focuses mainly on the places for escape. The city must have been extremely busy and bustling, because our authors are constantly recommending the delights of gardens, fountains, and seashores, clean air and grand views. Interest is focused on ancient sites, especially when associated with great engineering feats, like the passages carved through rock to connect the Bay of Naples conveniently to surrounding pleasure spots. Virgil's tomb is also a source of great pride – no doubt, not unrelated to the pride in the relics of its saints.

This cosmopolitan, international center could hardly ignore all the various people who composed the population of the city – the Lombards, Greeks, Normans, French, Austrians, Florentines, Genoese, and Spaniards. The authors of this work considered this heterogenous heritage a key to the present. They constructed chronologies and lists of rulers, carefully acknowledging sources, noting where material was lacking, and preserving what was remembered. This history was an important part of the city for foreigners who wanted to navigate the waters of this complex society and provides us with a detailed political history. To help these foreigners further the authors provided lists of the nobility and the names and titles of powerful Neapolitans, which increased daily, as did the buildings and the general population.

*

The original *Descrittione del Regno di Napoli* was prepared by Enrico Bacco, Cesare D'Engenio Caracciolo, and others, printed by Ottavio Beltrano, and reprinted by Novello de Bonis in 1671, after at least six previous printings beginning in 1616. The original work is approximately three times the length of the present edition, because the present volume limits itself to the first part of the book, covering the city of Naples. The remaining book covers the kingdom of Naples and includes descriptions of the provinces of Terra di Lavoro, Principato Citra and Ultra, Basilicata, Calabria Citra and Ultra, Otranto, Bari, Abruzzi Citra and Ultra, Contada di Molise and Capitanata. It concludes with a census of households in the twelve provinces. Italica Press will consider making the second part of this volume available in the future.

In focusing on the city of Naples, this edition has reorganized the original material into four chapters, whereas the original authors amassed their information without necessarily applying a logical sequence to the distinct subsections. The density of the information in this volume would make extensive annotation almost impossible. Parentheses are used throughout the text to enclose all annotations to this edition and are used solely for these editorial notes.

Often the Greek, Latin or Italian form of a word has been retained. These words appear in italics and, when necessary, are defined following the first occurrence. Names of identifiable buildings, locations, and individuals have been standardized. The names of well-known and important historical figures have been changed to the predominant form in English. The names of all popes have been changed to the standard in English, which is often a Latin form. The names of saints who are well-known to English-speaking readers have been given in the English form; saints who are particularly Italian or Neapolitan retain the Italian form of their names. The lesser known and completely unknown figures have retained the names given to them in the text; no attempt has been made to standardize the spellings of these names, except among various appearances of the same name. The Italian forms of the names of all churches have been retained.

Bacco's sources, and hence his chronologies, were less than perfect. In editing the text all the names and dates in his chronologies have been verified against other chronologies. Annotations in parentheses correct many of the historical errors. Typographical errors have been silently corrected. This, however, has been a vast undertaking, and some of the original inaccuracies may have been carried over into the present text. In subsequent printings we will correct any that are identified.

Several important tools have been added to this edition to make this area of study, which may be new for many people, more accessible. The edition includes two introductions: one on the history of Naples and the other on the art, architecture and physical city. Both cover the period from antiquity to the the time of Bacco's *Guide*. A new series of maps, which are based on those of Bartolomeo Capasso and others, has been prepared especially for this edition. Churches, palaces, and other buildings are included on the particular map from the era in which they were built. All five maps, therefore, should be used to locate monuments that exist in the city today. References in the text to maps use roman numerals to indicate the map and arabic numerals to indicate the building, so that, for example, Castel Nuovo (III:14) is building 14 on Map III. The bibliography includes a wide variety of material on Naples ranging from specialized works in Italian to general works in English. As noted above, there is a particular lack of material in English on Naples. This has necessitated the inclusion of a great deal of material in Italian. The index should be a great asset, since it is extensive and reflects accurately the magnitude of information provided in the text. It should provide direct access to almost any person, place or building. For a better understanding of Naples, this text should be read with the help of works like *Naples e Dintorni* by the Touring Club Italiano, the *Blue Guide to Southern Italy,* or a similar volume, since it has been impossible to provide annotations to all the buildings mentioned in the text.

In addition to the new maps, the text has been embellished with a variety of illustrations, from details of the *Tavola Strozzi* to maps and views contemporary with Bacco's *Guide*. Some small illustrations from the original edition are included, such as the coats of arms of noble families. There exists at least one version of this work with a series of fold-out views, but it was unavailable in the United States. A second edition of this work may include those views.

Without the resources and the help of the staff of the Research Library of the New York Public Library this volume would not have been possible. In addition, Debra Aguece Ivarson of the Enrico Fermi Center of the New York Public Library provided great help with the illustrations to this volume.

Finally, this volume is designed as a modest contribution to the effort now being made by many scholars to bring the riches of this city to light to an English-speaking audience.

6. Castel Nuovo. Detail from *Tavola Strozzi* (Plate 4).
The Castle shows the modernization completed under Alfonso I.

AN INTRODUCTION TO
NEAPOLITAN HISTORY

RONALD G. MUSTO

Naples, and the kingdom that took its name, has long
been a neglected field of history in the United States.
There have traditionally been several reasons for this.
The first derives from the outlook of most historical
writing in this country: medieval studies have long focused on northern Europe, especially France, Germany,
and England; while Renaissance history, even of Italy,
has tended to focus on the northern and republican
centers of the period. This fit well with the liberal and
democratic tendencies of the students of the Italian
Renaissance in the United States through most of this
century. Naples, both the city as capital, and the Regno,
as the kingdom was called, were long associated with
royalty: with the new Norman dynasty, the imperial
dreams of the Hohenstaufen, the dynastic conflicts of
Angevins and the house of Aragon, and then with the
despotic monarchies of the late Renaissance and early
modern Europe, the Spanish under Ferdinand the
Catholic and his Hapsburg heirs.

Coincident with this has been the emphasis of
historians to examine the origins and development of
Renaissance Humanism as an expression of this same
urban and democratic culture, of a "civic humanism"
that expressed the desires and values of a bourgeois and
republican way of life. Thus, again, historians have
tended to concentrate on Humanism's northern centers:
Florence, Siena, Milan, Venice; and in the High

Renaissance, Rome. This tendency has been reinforced by the canons of artistic taste of this century and the legacy of Romanticism in the nineteenth, which tended to view first the Gothic of the North and of northern Italy, and then the flowering of Renaissance style in Tuscany and the north as the normative periods of Italian art. Naples, long associated with the glory of the baroque, shared the disdain of the century for its style and ethic.

More mundane reasons, of course, have contributed to this long neglect of Neapolitan history. Perhaps the most pervasive of these is the "tourist" image of Italy formed by Americans: with the end of the "Grand Tour" in the late nineteenth century, Rome, Florence and Venice have become the points of an ironclad triangle of travel, both for the obvious attractions and beauties of these cities and their environs, and for the cultural framework with which Americans have come to view Italy.

This attitude, moreover, belies another American outlook, one that is, unfortunately, still shared by a great many Italians and Europeans themselves: that the Mezzogiorno, the "South" of Italy, is a land of poverty, ignorance, backwardness, cultural deprivation: a region – and a capital city – beset by corruption, crime, and the stereotype of the *"far niente,"* or do-nothing southern Italian. This is an image reinforced in the United States by the daily occurrence of Italian dichotomies: the cultured art, literature, even cuisine, of the North, as opposed to the supposedly poor, immigrant culture of Naples and the South.

Such attitudes have long contributed to a certain shyness among Americans to devote much time and effort to the study of things Neapolitan: why contend with so many negative attitudes, such a relatively remote, and perhaps unrewarding, field of research when the bright cities of the North offer much better areas for study? Again, while the Neapolitan kingdom and city have witnessed many events and personalities that have been central to European – and Western – history, they have also suffered the repeated ravages to their historical records: from occasional loses of itinerant archives during the Middle Ages to the popular revolts of 1647 and 1701 against Spanish rule (in which tax, court, and other records were destroyed), to the most recent destruction of the State Archives on September 30, 1943 at the hands of the retreating Nazis that forever removed most of the records of the high Middle Ages and Renaissance in Naples.[1] Indeed, Naples never seemed to have recovered from World War II and the impoverishment of the city and its facilities that it brought.

Recently, however, much of this has begun to change. There has long been a tradition of serious Italian historical and art historical scholarship for Naples and the South. One need only consult the multi-volume *Storia di Napoli*,[2] the *Storia di Campania*[3] or the works of Capasso[4] and Gliejeses,[5] among many others, to get some idea of the very well developed field of Italian research here.

The classical heritage of the Bay of Naples, of Pompeii, Herculaneum, Baia, Cumae, Pozzuoli, and Posillipo and their treasures in Naples' museums have long been a central focus of classical studies, both in Italy and in the United States. For the Middle Ages studies have focused on the Two Sicilies, as the mainland Kingdom of Naples and the island of Sicily are called, on the history of the Normans in the south, on Naples in the Renaissance, and with renewed interest in the culture of the Baroque, on that period as well.

Indeed, the city and its cultural treasures have once again begun to attract both historians and art historians: the former to the age of the Aragonese monarchy in the Renaissance, the latter to the baroque. Even medieval

Naples has begun to attract its students.[6] The reasons are numerous: the broadening of the horizon of historical studies in the United States toward more "Mediterranean" fields, especially given the impetus of Fernand Braudel[7] and other members of the "Annales" school of France and their European followers, the search for new areas of fruitful scholarly investigation, now that the chief northern centers of Italian culture have been analyzed with such wonderful results for over a century, and an understanding that Neapolitan politics, culture, and economic life had profound influences on Italy and Europe into the modern world. These trends happily coincide with renewed development plans for the Italian Mezzogiorno by the Italian government and private groups, which though slow in materializing, point to the needs and potentials of the South and its heritage.

*

The following introduction will survey the history of Naples and place the following *Guide* in its proper historical context. It will discuss the periods of Neapolitan history from antiquity to the time of Bacco's edition in 1671; the development of its institutions – urban, governmental, ecclesiastical, and popular; it will view the city as a center of economic life: of trade, population, manufacture, finance, and consumption; and highlight the chief events, personalities, and social and political groups that formed it. While it will inevitably refer to the development of the city's urban fabric and to its artistic heritage, these topics are fully discussed in the art historical introduction by Caroline Bruzelius and will not be entered into detail here.

THE PERIODS OF NEAPOLITAN HISTORY

Ancient Naples (c.900 BC-325 AD)

Naples lies at the focal point between the fertile agricultural area of the Campania and the Bay of Naples – what may, arguably, be the best natural bay in the world. Its own immediate region holds some of the most fertile soil in the world: the volcanic slopes of Vesuvius to the east and the Phlegraean fields *(Campi Flegrei)*, the volcanic ring to its west around Pozzuoli; a region rich in minerals and light to the plow and driving root. It is a region where sun shines 230 days of the year and the median temperature remains about 60°, with annual highs of 78° and lows of 41°F. Lemons and oranges grow next to grapes, figs and olives, wheat, flax, and barley.

Yet it is also an area that has seen repeated destruction: from the earliest recorded eruption of Vesuvius in 79 AD, which buried Pompeii and Herculaneum, to the most recent in 1944; to the constant volcanic and seismic activity of the Phlegraean fields, where the two major seismic fault lines of Italy intersect, which has caused the coastline there to rise and fall nearly twenty feet since antiquity. Most recently, the earthquake of 1980 badly damaged much of historical Naples, caused the abandonment of Pozzuoli, and left 100,000 homeless. It is, therefore, a region that has brought millennia both of *otia* (leisure) and of destruction; and it has, meanwhile, formed the particular character of the Neapolitans: a remarkable sense of resilience, tenacity, and irony that runs throughout their history.

*

The earliest history of Naples,[8] like that of so many other Italian cities, is shrouded in legend, occasionally illuminated by archaeological or literary record. The first settlement of the area was probably in the ninth century BC by merchants from Asia Minor and Achaean Greeks who used the Bay of Naples as a staging area for trade in the Tyrrhenian Sea. They seem to have established an emporium at the mouth of the Sebeto River[9] (see Map II) near the eastern foot of the hill of Pizzofalcone, the area of Santa Lucia. By the seventh century BC Greek colonists from Rhodes, the island off Asia Minor, established a permanent city, also on Pizzofalcone, named Parthenope (Greek ΠαρΘενοπη) after one of the legendary Sirens who had tempted Odysseus.

By the sixth century BC Parthenope (Map II:A) was a busy trade and military port, often in competition with neighboring Cumae, settled by Greeks from Chalcis. The incursions of the Etruscans from northern Italy left Parthenope weakened, and c.550 BC the city was taken by the Cumaeans. Some time around 474 BC these Chalcidians, along with Greeks from Syracuse in Sicily, founded a new city, "Neapolis" in Greek, next to the site of Parthenope, which they then called "Paleopolis," or Old City. Around 450 BC Neapolis (II:C), attracted new Greek immigrants from Chalcis, Pithecusa, and Athens and soon outstripped the "Old City."

Neapolis remained a thoroughly Greek city, part of Magna Graecia, until c.400 BC, when the Samnites, an Italic tribe from the Apennines to the north and east, took both Campania and the city. Remains of the "Samnite" culture were still to be found in Roman domestic architecture at the time of the destruction of Pompeii in 79 AD. In 326 BC, after a two-year siege, Neapolis fell once again to another northern tribe, this time the Latin Romans, who incorporated the city and its territory, the Campania, into its confederation.

The Romans and Neapolitans seem to have made an easy alliance, both benefiting from the new trade and political ties. Thus during the Second Punic War (218-

201 BC), in which large parts of Campania, headed by neighboring Capua, defected to Hannibal, Naples remained loyal. It accordingly retained its equal stature as a confederate city-state. Naples and its environs remained a center of Greek civilization and, for a Roman republic eager for the culture of the East, a magnet for students, artists, writers and patrons of the arts.

Under both the Republic and Empire the city remained a "municipium," or autonomous city. It became noted for its schools, as well as for its gentle climate, fertile soil, and beautiful shores. Virgil moved there later in life; he wrote both the *Georgics* and *Aeneid* there; and his legendary tomb is still visible today. Horace and Ovid both stayed there. The poet Statius was born there c.41 AD; Pliny the Elder died there during the eruption of Vesuvius in 79; Silius Italicus committed suicide there in 101. Roman patricians, such as Lucullus and Vedius Pollio, and the emperors Augustus and Tiberius spent much of their time in the area.[10] Emperor Nero found his Roman compatriots too loutish for his poetic inventions; he preferred the cultured Greek ambiance of Naples and performed regularly in its Odeon (II:1).

The tendency of the ancient city to grow toward the sea[11] closely reflected the city's role as a base for commercial and arms manufacturing tied to the east via the Mediterranean. It had little connection to the hinterland and was closer to far-away Rome than, for example, to its neighbor Capua. The Social Wars, in which Naples sided against Sulla in 82 BC, brought his sacking of the city, execution of most of its chief citizens, and the elimination of its fleet: a disaster to its merchant classes that started its shift from a life based on trade and manufacture to a "service economy" as the leisure capital of the Roman aristocracy of the late Republic and Empire. It survived on their conspicuous consumption and on its reputation as a cultural and educational center, as maritime trade shifted more and more toward neighboring Puteoli (modern Pozzuoli, see Map II, inset).

During the fourth century AD, therefore, the city's role declined as Constantine took the imperial court, and much of its wealth and consumption, to Constantinople. At the same time the peninsula fell into a slow economic slump in both maritime trade and agricultural production of the Campania. Naples is literally the scene of the traditional end of the Roman Empire: in the Villa Lucullana, the site of present Castel dell'Ovo, Romulus Augustulus, last titular Roman emperor, died a prisoner of Odoacer the Herulian chieftain.

Early Christian and Byzantine Naples (325-568)

The Bay of Naples was one of the earliest parts of Europe to feel the impact of Christianity. St. Paul first set foot in Italy at Pozzuoli on his way to trial in Rome and supposedly found Christians already there (Acts 28:14). Naples itself soon became a leading center of Christian culture and art, as its many catacombs bear witness.[12]

In 410 the Visigoth Alaric, fresh from his sack of Rome, passed through the Campania on his way south, bringing destruction with him. Gaiseric and his Vandals soon followed in 455. Yet the first "Barbarian Invasions" changed the face of Italy very little. Aside from toppling already teetering regimes and ruling elites, their numbers were small, and they merely passed through the peninsula. By the sixth century, however, the Goths, a Germanic tribe from north and west of the Black Sea, had come to stay.

The city, as most of Italy, then fell under the control of Theoderic (493-526) and his Ostrogoths, until the Byzantine Emperor Justinian (527-565) launched the reconquest of southern and central Italy under

Belisarius.[13] A brilliant general, Belisarius took the city in 536 after a vain siege by land and sea for months by bringing an advanced guard in through a broken aqueduct. Belisarius' successes were his very downfall, and a jealous Justinian soon replaced him with Narses, perhaps as capable but not as graced. Amid raging war, depredation, and starvation across Italy, in the face of a Persian invasion of the Empire and of Byzantine court intrigue, Narses' efforts were neutralized. The new Gothic king, Totila (541-552), recaptured Naples in 543; and despite Belisarius' return to Italy and then Narses' reappointment, the city of Naples remained under Gothic control through most of these disastrous Gothic Wars. Then, just as suddenly as the Romans from Constantinople had taken southern Italy, they lost it to a new invasion: this time by the Lombards, a tribe originally from eastern Germany, under King Alboin in 568.

Ducal Naples (568-1130)

With the murder of Alboin that same year and then of his successor Cleph in 574, the Lombards in Italy decided to divide their newly gotten kingdom among thirty-six "Lombard Dukes." Much of their early history in the south was taken up with carving out their own early feudal states. The wars that created these devastated most of the South's old diocesan towns – the Roman imperial administrative centers and now the seats of Christian bishops – and urban life declined in all but the most prosperous agricultural or coastal areas. Most of the old rural settlements of the Campania disappeared as their populations shriveled or sought refuge in fortified hill towns. The large Roman fields of the Empire, and their *latifundia,* or plantations of wheat and other cash crops, disappeared into smaller, higher and less productive plots: sufficient only for local economies. By the ninth century, as well, the face of the

Campania began to be transformed by the introduction of the lemon and orange, imported from Sicily by the Arabs, who had brought them there.

By the beginning of the seventh century Naples was almost alone of the nominal Byzantine areas of Italy in its independence from the Lombards and its continuous tradition of civilian life. While Lombard "dukes" began actively controlling the city's affairs by the eighth century, Naples retained its Roman and, beneath that, its Greek language, character and culture. It was nominally, and at times directly, under a Byzantine *strategos;* it retained vestiges of a senatorial class and kept its *curia,* or ruling council, into the tenth century.[14] Political life resembled that of late imperial Rome or Constantinople, where political parties formed around the election of its bishops.

While that late Roman institution had collapsed in northern Italy under the Lombards and did not survive their conversion to Catholicism, in Naples the bishop held his active role in the civic administration. The city retained its status as a "civitas," a Roman administrative center, as the seat of the bishop. This centered around the Duomo (cathedral) dedicated first to the Savior, then to S. Restituta, and on the archbishop's palace next door (III:20, pls. 16-17).

While the bishops of Naples could not match those of Rome in the shear economic clout they held through their ownership of land both inside and outside the city, they remained among the largest landholders in a society where land meant wealth and power. By the ninth century this power had become hereditary among a small handful of families, one or two of whom controlled the office of duke as well. Some, in fact, actually held both offices at once.[15] Authority on all levels gradually shifted from a public office to a privatized contract between strong protectors and weaker clients: an ancient Mediterranean social relationship now increasingly influenced by the new feudal forms of the Lombards, Franks, and Germans.

The city seems to have escaped the general fate of most urban centers of Italy, especially of southern Italy, with the fall of Rome. Its population base remained firm, numbering about 40,000 by the mid-eighth century. While we know little of its extent, or even the circuit of its walls, during these centuries, we do know that the city was one of the few to retain its Roman aqueduct and, like many others, its forum and (converted) temples. As many of the older public buildings – the stadium, hippodrome, and others – fell into disuse their place was taken by new Christian institutions: monastic houses spreading upon the ruins of the Roman city. Among these were S. Maria a Circolo and, near the shore, S. Vincenzo and S. Sergio. The house of S. Severino grew on the island of Megaris next to the castellum of the Lombard dukes. Emperor Valentinian had fortified the villa of Lucullus on this island off Pizzofalcone; and during the Lombard period this "castrum" at S. Lucia began to take the shape of the present Castel dell'Ovo (Map III).

By the mid-ninth century, this tentative new culture was shaken by a series of civil wars among the Lombard princes[16] and by the growth of Frankish power under Charlemagne and his heirs, then allied with the popes against the Lombards. Equally important was the rise of the Arab threat from the south. Spreading from North Africa, by the 880s they had conquered almost all of Sicily and by the 840s were raiding the coasts of southern Italy itself. By 843 they had established a foothold in Bari at the invitation of Radelchi I of Benevento; and between 840 and 880 they held most of the southern heel and had a foothold at Garigliano on the east coast, from which they were dislodged only in 915. In 902 the Neapolitans, fearing immanent conquest by the Arabs, abandoned and totally destroyed the castrum on the

Megaride island. The monks of S. Severino took up new quarters in the walled city (pl. 11).

The ninth century also saw Naples lose whatever nominal grip it had over its new seaport rivals: Amalfi, Salerno, and Gaeta were quickly becoming major international trading centers and – with brief republican interludes – the capitals of their own Lombard dynasties that matched the creation of Naples' own dynasty under Sergio I in 840.[17] In the late tenth century the city enjoyed a period of cultural flourishing that saw the foundation of Duke Giovanni IV's library, the embellishment of churches and palaces; and the expansion of its overseas trade as Neapolitan merchants exchanged its famed manufactured cloths for oriental rugs and fabrics.

Despite the occasional presence of the Carolingian and later Salian German emperors in the south, the internecine wars among the Lombards continued into the tenth century. By the year 1000 these had combined with the continued incursions of Arabs and the sporadic Byzantine control of Apulia to create a nearly anarchic political vacuum in the Mezzogiorno.

The Normans (1137-1194)

In 965 the Byzantine Empire surrendered its last foothold on Sicily to the Arab Fatimid Caliphate; for the next fifty years Arabs, Greeks, and Lombards vied for control of southern Italy; often seeking the alliance and employment of their former enemies in constantly shifting balances. In 1016 a new element was added to this froth: at Monte Gargano, Meles, a Lombard warlord from Apulia in revolt against the Greeks, hired on as mercenaries some northmen returning from pilgrimage to Jerusalem. According to another source, their compatriots were also responsible for saving Salerno from Arab conquest that same year. These

"Normans"[18] as they had long been known in England and France, were the descendents of the Viking conquerors of much of England, Ireland, and the French region of Normandy, which still bears their name. Norman mercenaries were soon arriving in the south in substantial numbers.

Starved for lands in their own homeland, the Normans quickly established their first principality at Aversa, just north of Naples, in 1030. By that year the most famous of these Norman clans, the Hauteville, or "Altavilla" as their French name was Italicized, were already laying plans for their conquest of the South. By 1046 Drogo was named count of Apulia by the German Emperor Henry II; in 1057 a younger half-brother, Robert Guiscard (the "cautious"), had turned from cattle rustling and kidnapping in the hills of Calabria into duke of Apulia, the conquest of which he completed in 1071 with the capture of Bari. Meanwhile, Robert's younger brother, Roger, has begun the conquest of Calabria and already had his eyes on Arab Sicily.

More than Arab brows were raised by the Norman success. From their footholds in the toe and heel, the Normans gradually consolidated their territories from Byzantines, Lombards, and Italian coastal towns and began pushing northward and exerting considerable control over both Latin and Greek churches in their territories. In 1053, therefore, Pope Leo IX led a papal army against them only to be defeated and captured at Civitate. The price of his ransom was the eventual recognition of the Hauteville Guiscard as "duke" of Apulia and Calabria by Pope Nicholas II in 1059. In return the pope was recognized as feudal liege lord of the Hauteville lands; an event that would change the face of Neapolitan history again and again. By 1084, with their freeing Pope Gregory VII from German Emperor Henry IV's siege of the Vatican and their destruction of Rome (the worst damage that city ever suffered), the

Normans had become the recognized rulers of Italy as far north as the Tiber.

When Robert died in 1085, his real heir was not his son Roger Borsa, duke of Apulia, but his younger brother, Roger of Calabria. Once he had consolidated Calabria, Roger crossed to Messina in 1061 and by 1091 had conquered all of Sicily from the Arabs and began forming a state much like that other Norman conqueror, William, had done in England. With its capital at Palermo, Norman Sicily became an amalgam of Arabic, Greek, Latin, and Norman cultures and institutions. It also became a bridge linking the French, Norman and English worlds of the north with the cultures of the Mediterranean.

By 1128 Roger's son, Roger II (1130-1154), had forced the title "king" of Sicily from Pope Anacletus II. By 1130, Roger has taken his cousins' inheritances in Apulia and Calabria and had formed the Kingdom of Sicily on both sides of the Straits of Messina. In 1139 the city of Naples itself fell after a lengthy siege that left many dead of starvation and saw the overthrow of its count, Rainulf d'Alife, by a oligarchic republic. By 1154 the Norman Regno, as the kingdom would soon be called, controlled all the territory from Malta to Terracina, south of Rome; to the central mountain borders of Tivoli and Rieti; and to Ascoli on the Adriatic Coast.[19]

At the beginning of the twelfth century Naples itself was a second-rate maritime power, long eclipsed by Amalfi and Salerno. It could boast a circuit of walls of only about 4.5 km and a population of 25,000 to 30,000.[20] It was small by its former standards, and although about the same size as Florence, it was smaller than almost any other major Italian city.[21]

Ironically, Naples' absorption into the Norman state brought it unforeseen benefits. The Normans destroyed the independence of rivals Salerno and Amalfi, probably contributed to their commercial decline, and, given their international ties through Europe and their long-time ambitions – both in Byzantine territory and in the new Crusader states – they decided to strengthen Naples and restore its commercial status.

They refortified the old castrum of Lucullus, now the Castel dell'Ovo, which was to become a royal residence. After the uprising of 1156, they built the Castel Capuana (III:22) on the site of an old Byzantine castrum on the *campus Neapolis,* the plain at the city's eastern end. The Normans thus controlled access to the sea and to the hinterland, both to protect the city from external attack and to guarantee their rule of the city under their *compalazzo*, or "count of the city," and as a fief of the Principality of Capua. For the most part, however, they left the Neapolitans to their own affairs. In a way they were forced to; even at the height of their power the total number of Normans in the entire kingdom, from Marsala at Sicily's western tip to Terracina south of Rome, probably numbered no more than a few thousand: those feudal lords at the top of the political and social scale.[22] They left very little physical trace of their stay on the inhabitants of southern Italy.

With all of southern Italy united, the contentious wars between Lombard princes and city-states over, and trade once again flowing uninterrupted both from the interior and along the coast, Naples began to enjoy a period of steady growth. It became a nexus of trade between France, Spain, North Africa, and Sicily; and from the Byzantine and Crusader states. By the end of the twelfth century the royal claimant Tancred of Lecce recognized this preeminence by granting Naples' merchants the "liberty" of movement, without toll or tax, through all Norman lands and seas. With its regional hegemony it soon also attracted trade emporiums from Amalfi, Ravello, and Scala in the section called the

Scalesia (III:24). By the thirteenth century the Genoese had also established their own trade emporium there.

This internationalism was not confined to trade alone, however. The Norman kingdom became a leading cultural light of Europe.[23] With their centrally controlled state, stable political and economic life, and vast new-found resources, the Normans chose the wisest policy for governing a diverse and culturally rich kingdom: they assimilated themselves, accepted local rights, laws and privileges, tolerated local religions and practices – whether Latin, Greek, Moslem or Jewish – adapted Byzantine and Arabic administrative practices where long-established; brought the best and brightest of each culture to serve as their advisors and administrators, and issued laws simultaneously in Arabic, Greek and Latin. They transplanted much of their Norman feudal social structure to the south, creating fiefs as in the north, but governed their kingdom from a central royal court *(curia regis)* with chancellor, chamberlain, justiciar and later constable and seneschal, much as in England and Normandy. They added a grand admiral and a protonotary-logothete, or head of the secretariat, borrowing here from the Greeks. They also appointed provincial chamberlains, justiciars, and curias from among either the Norman feudal class or the native Arabs, Greeks, or Italians. Christians, Greeks, Saracens, and Black Africans alike all served in their royal armies. Norman financial administration converted the Arabic *diwan* into the Italian *duana,* a record that carefully tallied the extent and value of all holdings in the kingdom; a move parallel to the other Norman, William the Conqueror's, *Domesday Book.*

Culturally the Normans blended the Latin heritage of the South, based on Monte Cassino, which had long and strong ties directly to Naples, with the Greek learning of Apulia, Basilicata, and Calabria, and the Arab culture of Sicily, which had been tied to the Islamic and Greco-

Roman civilizations of Damascus, Baghdad, and Alexandria of the Abbasid Caliphate since the ninth century.

Beginning with the "Renaissance of the twelfth century,"[24] scholars from France and England seeking to recapture the wisdom of the East and of the Western classics flocked to their cousins in the South. At Palermo or Salerno one could meet and learn from people who could actually read the Greek and Arab philosophers and scientists in the original, who could provide manuscripts of works of Galen, Plato, Aristotle, or Ptolemy.

By 1050 the Normans had founded the first and oldest university in the Western world, the medical school of Salerno, less than a day's journey from Naples. Here students from all over Europe came to study the works of Galen and Hippocrates by scholars who knew them in the original Greek. By the twelfth century Naples and its region were active centers of European civilization.[25]

The Hohenstaufen (1194-1266)

The Hauteville dynasty ruled the kingdom of Sicily for the next two generations. They created a realm that was the envy, and at times the prey, of other emerging states. By the end of the twelfth century and the reign of William II (the Good, 1166-1189) the Normans had ties to the most illustrious royal families of Europe; and they took advantage of the system of marriage alliances to insure their status and position in Europe and the Mediterranean. William himself married the daughter of Henry II of England and married his aunt Constance, Roger II's daughter, to the German Emperor Henry VI, son of Frederick I Barbarosa, Hohenstaufen. It was a marriage born as much out of prestige as out of the desire to form an alliance that would benefit both against their real and potential enemy: the pope and his anti-imperial allies in the cities of central and northern Italy.

William was making plans to lead the Third Crusade when he died suddenly, and childless. His most direct heir was the son of Constance and the grandson of Roger II: Frederick II Hohenstaufen.[26] The Neapolitans joined many other southern Italians in siding with William's nephew, Tancred of Lecce, against the Hohenstaufen claim. In 1191 they fought off a three-month siege by Emperor Henry VI; but in 1194, with Tancred's death, the city fell to the Germans. In revenge, imperial troops entirely destroyed the walls of the city, which thereafter allied with Otto IV of Brunswick, the German Guelf opponent of Frederick Hohenstaufen.

"Stupor mundi," (the wonder of the world), the man who delivered Jerusalem back to the Christians without lifting a sword, the man excommunicated by the church and condemned as "Antichrist" by popes and prophets, who wrote some of the best medieval scientific work and turned his court at Palermo into the cultural center of Europe, Frederick II (1215-1250) was only a boy when he came to the Sicilian throne. His mother Constance therefore acted as his regent in the South and educated him in Sicily under the protection of the papacy, which since the first Norman investiture was the theoretical overlord of the kingdom.

As Holy Roman Emperor Frederick's realm encompassed both Germany and northern Italy, including their free republican city-states, the "communes." As king of Sicily, Frederick claimed the right of rule over all of southern Italy, except for the papal state. He therefore had many enemies: the papacy, the German princes, the northern Italian towns, the feudal barons of the kingdom of Sicily, and many within Naples itself. Frederick immediately made himself the enemy of the pope by refusing to abdicate the Regno once he had been crowned emperor and to pursue his grandiose plans for a new empire.

By 1223 Frederick had consolidated his control over all the Kingdom of Sicily. By 1231, despite papal condemnation and invasion, absences in Germany and on crusade and baronial revolt, he established peace and economic prosperity all over the kingdom. He encouraged agriculture and trade, lowered or eliminated trade duties, held annual trade fairs, built bridges, roads, and new towns, passed new and uniform laws and subordinated feudal rights to a central administration. In 1232 and 1240 he even summoned two representatives from each town to parliaments to solidify royal rule and to check the power of local barons. The kingdom had become the wealthiest and most civilized in Christendom. Frederick's court became a new center of philosophy, science, law, and art. The emperor also fostered the very first appearance of Italian literature: the Sicilian school of poets.

While Frederick retained his capital at Palermo, he preferred the climate of areas like Pozzuoli and the Bay's closeness to his northern borders with the papal state. Frederick thus came to favor Naples. He rebuilt its walls, expanded its commercial activity as a balance to the power of Pisa; and, in an attempt to seize the ideological and religious agenda from the papacy, in 1224 he issued the charter for the *"studium generale,"* the University, or *studio,* of Naples. Among the university's students was Thomas Aquinas, the most influential philosopher of the Middle Ages.

Frederick not only hoped to further the cultural life of the kingdom but also needed to cancel the influence of the University of Bologna and its pro-papal school of law and theology; he also wanted to break the papacy's monopoly on issuing university charters and to create a class of home-grown and trained bureaucrats for his kingdom. The emperor established the university as a public school, open to all, yet he also forbade his subjects from studying anywhere else for advanced degrees and placed it directly under his royal chancellor. While this brought great cultural activity and prosperity to the city, it also tied the school to the emperor's political fortunes. Given the Hohenstaufens' iron hand with the city, their efficient and heavy taxation spent on constant and fruitless wars, and their eventual revocation of many of the city's privileges, these fortunes were fragile within Naples' walls.

The Angevins (1266-1442)

In 1250 Frederick II died after a lingering illness. His enemies immediately regrouped all over Italy to undo his work and to seek revenge.[27] In 1251 Naples rose and, giving their ultimate fealty to the distant pope, formed a free commune. With Frederick's son, King Conrad IV, absent fighting his wars in Germany, his illegitimate son Manfred became *balio,* or regent, for both the Regno and the Hohenstaufen holdings in the north. Frederick's implacable enemy, Pope Innocent IV, now hoped to finally crush the Hohenstaufens in both Germany and Italy and raised up candidates among Europe's royal families to replace them. Conrad was able to reach the South in time, however, and consolidate his hold there.

The pope therefore looked for some candidate willing to depose the "heretics" by force of arms: Henry III of England backed an invasion force with cash; and with Conrad IV's death in 1254, shortly after his capturing Naples, Innocent entered the Regno with his young charge Conrad V (Conradin) as a figurehead for his plans to annex the South to the papal state. By the time the pope had entered Naples, however, Manfred was able to rally the Hohenstaufen forces; Conradin had defected to him; and in 1258 Manfred had himself crowned king of Sicily.

The Italian wars between Guelfs and "Ghibellines," as the imperial faction was called, and the papal "crusades" against the Hohenstaufen continued to embroil the entire peninsula. Finally, with the accession of King Louis IX's ex-chancellor as Pope Clement IV in 1265, the ambitions of one of the original papal candidates for Frederick II's throne rose to the fore again. Charles, duke of Anjou, Louis' younger – and ruthless – brother, had also been count of Provence since 1246. He now saw a means of uniting papal hostility, French resources, and his own ambitions to create an empire in the Mediterranean. He undertook a "crusade" against Manfred. On February 26, 1266 Charles' army crushed that of Manfred, who fell trying to rally his German forces after his Saracens and Italians had fled. Charles of Anjou entered Naples on March 7. All was not quite over, however. Conradin, now a youth of 15, rallied an invasion force of Germans and Ghibellines and entered the kingdom in August 1268. At Tagliacozzo Charles destroyed his army, mercilessly massacring the captives. Conradin was brought to Naples, where on the site of the present Piazza del Mercato (III:23) he was publicly beheaded, an act that shocked all of Europe and founded the Angevin dynasty.[28]

To efface the memory of the Hohenstaufen, Charles of Anjou, now King Charles I (1265-1285), immediately moved his capital from Palermo to Naples and began calling his realm the Kingdom of Naples. His change was prophetic, for on March 30, 1282, in a conspiracy designed to end Angevin ambitions throughout the Mediterranean and win revenge for Conradin and Manfred, the revolt ever since known as the Sicilian Vespers brought Byzantine emperor, king of Aragon (now married to the Hohenstaufen heiress), and former

Hohenstaufen officials together to wrest Sicily from the Angevins. The twenty-year "War of the Vespers" that followed saw the capture and imprisonment of the future Charles II (1285-1309) by the Aragonese and the eventual Aragonese control of Sicily. By the time of Charles I's death in 1285 his great Mediterranean empire was a shattered dream, and his kingdom had been reduced to the Italian Mezzogiorno. Yet the dynasty that he founded was to bring Naples into a new glorious age.

The Angevin period was one of international influence, prosperity, and cultural and religious brilliance for Naples.[29] The war and its aftermath, and the Angevins' possessions in Anjou, Provence, and Piedmont, created an immediate surge in the city's population and commercial activity. Merchants from Catalonia, Marseilles, and Florence founded trade emporiums next to the old Scalesia; bankers and investors soon filled the new section of the city to the southwest of the late Roman imperial walls; while to the east and south, along the waterfront, rose a new manufacturing district around the Piazza del Mercato. To expand the defenses of the city Charles added a "new castle," the Castel Nuovo (III:14), which soon became the royal residence, and dredged a new harbor and the tower on the Molo S. Vincenzo (III). Charles II built the castle of Belforte (III:3), later expanded to the Castel S. Elmo, next to the Certosa of S. Martino (III:4), which was begun in 1325 under his successor. Population estimates for the period range anywhere from 25,000 to 40,000.[30]

Charles II's son, Robert I, the Wise (1309-1334), and his second queen, Sancia of Majorca (1286-1345), brought Naples to the forefront of European culture and nurtured the earliest geniuses of the Italian Renaissance.[31] The court of Naples became a meeting place of poets and scholars from Sicily, of theologians from northern Italy, of dissident and heterodox

reformers, of great writers and artists.[32] The king had
a European-wide reputation for learning, and he was
immortalized by Dante for his deep, if prolix, sermo-
nizing. Petrarch recounts Robert's keen interest in the
city's classical remains and legends; while Boccaccio
paints a lively picture of the city's sophisticated culture,
social mores, and personalities.

During Robert's reign, the kingdom and city of
Naples became the focal point of Italian politics. Robert
tried five times to regain Sicily, now the "Kingdom of
Trinacria," with an immense war fleet based on the
Arsenal (III) built between 1301 and 1307 next to the
Castel Nuovo; he extended his influence over Rome and
was at times overlord or "protector" of Florence and
Tuscany and the upholder of Guelf interests in Italy for
the papacy. Yet his war efforts and his feudal "census"
payments to the papacy, the price for Charles I conquest, exerted tremendous pressures on the kingdom and
the city by way of taxes and in the concessions that
Robert was forced to grant the already independent-
minded barons. By the mid-fourteenth century there
were 3,455 fiefs of the lower nobility in the kingdom,
not including the great barons or the patricians of the
cities. Most of these nobles were so poor that their
desire for liveable holdings created a constant menace to
central authority, to their own impoverished peasant
populations, and to the maintenance of law and order.[33]

With the expansion of its residential quarters,
including those between the Castel Nuovo and the old
city walls and at Chiaia on the slopes of Pizzofalcone,
Naples' population reached new heights in this period
just before 1350, cresting to 100,000, along with
Venice, Milan, and Florence the largest cities of Europe.
Paris at the time numbered only 80,000, while
Constantinople, the largest city in the West, probably
totaled 200,000.[34]

Yet the city had reached its medieval limit. In a 1343 visit to Naples Petrarch had already witnessed the disastrous earthquake that destroyed much of the city and sank all its shipping in a bay turned to froth.[35] Then, in October 1347, the Black Death (bubonic plague) arrived from the Crimea aboard a ship to Messina. It reached Naples along the trade routes within a few weeks. Within two months, according to one estimate, it killed 63,000 in and around the city.[36] It returned in 1362, 1382, 1399, and 1411. By the end of the fourteenth century one estimate puts the population at 36,000.[37] Drastic population declines, in places of up to two-thirds, short-falls in agricultural output, famine, great inflation, and decreases in the tax base, all contributed to slow the pace of growth and exasperated the already growing economic failures, social disorder, and political confusion that characterize the early Renaissance.

While Robert and Sancia were able to stem the tide of disorder, there successors were not as lucky, or gifted. Robert's son, Charles, duke of Calabria, died while Robert lived; upon Robert's death in 1343, therefore, no direct male heir was available, though the Angevins' family ties with the throne of Hungary offered some possibilities. Queen Sancia became regent for Charles' daughter, who came to the throne as Giovanna I (1343-1381). History has not been kind to Naples' ruling Angevin queens, neither Sancia nor the two Giovannas. Giovanna I had a reputation for sexual adventure: she had four husbands and several lovers. The misogynist tradition seems to have gone back as far as Petrarch himself, who described her court as confused and superstitious, ruled by emotion and given over to the Rasputin-like machinations of the pro-Hungarian Franciscan Robert of Mileto.[38]

Giovanna I took the side of Clement VII and the French line of popes, based at Avignon, during the

Great Schism (1378-1417) against Urban VI, former archbishop of Bari and now Roman pope. Urban therefore excommunicated the queen and raised up as her rival Charles (III) of Durazzo, Robert the Wise's nephew, who seized the throne on 1381 and had her murdered in 1382. By that time, however, Giovanna had adopted Duke Louis I of Anjou as her son. He, however, died in 1384. Charles then went off to seize the Angevin claim to the crown of Hungary and died there in 1386. Louis II of Anjou then invaded the country; but Charles' young son, Ladislas, finally managed to retain the throne by allying with the Roman papacy in 1399.

The noble families of Naples exploited this royal weakness by seizing the government of the city and dividing it into five district councils or *seggi (sedie),* each controlled by its own faction.[39] By 1386 they felt strong enough to elect six nobles and two *popolani,* as the non-noble merchant class was called, as a city government and to force concessions from the young King Ladislas.

Upon Ladislas' death in 1414, his younger sister, Giovanna II (1414-1435), came to power. History has been even less kind to this Giovanna.[40] She attempted to stave off the growing power of the Neapolitan barons by forming marriage- and love-alliances with useful men. Her husbands were William, duke of Austria, and the brutal James de la Marche. Among her lovers were Grand Seneschal Giovanni Caracciolo and the condottiere captains Braccio di Fortibraccio Perugino, Filippo Maria Sforza, Francesco Sforza and Piccinino, whose "great companies" of mercenaries brought murder, rape, arson, and torture throughout the kingdom and peninsula. In 1421 she adopted Alfonso V, king of Aragon and Sicily since 1416, but quickly disowned him and drove him out in 1423, turning instead to her French cousin, Louis III of Anjou (d.1434), and then to his brother, the romantic, and ill-fated, René of Anjou.[41]

The Aragonese (1442-1495)

When Giovanna II died in 1435, claims to the kingdom were divided between the house of Anjou, through dynastic lineage and the adoptive clams of Duke René, and the house of Aragon, through Alfonso's adoption in 1421. Aragon had long been a major Mediterranean power since it had consolidated its own kingdom in the eleventh century and then conquered Catalonia with Barcelona, the Balearics, Sardinia, portions of Greece, and Sicily. René, held prisoner until 1438 by the duke of Burgundy, could not match Alfonso's initiative or resources.

In 1442, after Alfonso had been laying siege to Naples for weeks, a Neapolitan showed him the very same aqueduct used by Belisarius to enter Naples 900 years before. On June 6 Alfonso took the city; after years of war, René abandoned the kingdom. Despite Neapolitan loyalty to René and the Angevins and their disgust at his "barbaric" Catalans, Alfonso, the Magnanimous, followed up his conquest by showering mercy and favors upon the Neapolitans and began a reign that would make Naples a major center of high Renaissance.[42] As Alfonso I of Naples (1442-58), he built new piazzas and fountains, repaired walls and streets, palaces and religious institutions. The famed *Tavola Strozzi* (pl. 4), now at the Capodimonte Museum, accurately reflects the beauty and importance of the city in 1464.

Alfonso's reign saw the establishment of a Humanist center at the Aragonese court and at the revived *studio* of Naples.[43] Among the major Renaissance Humanists whom he patronized were Bartolomeo Fazio, Lorenzo Valla, Giannozzo Manetti, Panormita (Antonio Beccadelli), Giovanni Pontano, the noted Greek scholar

George of Trebizond, and many others. He refurbished the royal library, which had been moved from Castel Capuana to the Castel Nuovo after its renovation, vastly increased its size and importance, sponsored philosophical and literary discussions at the Academy there, and opened it up to selected students at the *studio*. Alfonso also turned Naples into one of the first capitals of a modern state: he established a permanent class of well-educated professionals and a bureaucracy drawn from the urban middle class, which he used to check the barons' power.

Despite foreign war and invasion, baronial revolt, and the devastating earthquake of 1450, Alfonso's heirs continued the beautification and enrichment of the city. Under Alfonso II (1494/95) Naples became the projected site of the most ambitious urban redevelopment plan of the Renaissance;[44] architect Giuliano de Maiano expanded the eastern walls north from Castel del Carmine (Sperone, III and IV:25), built by Charles II of Durazzo, to S. Giovanni a Carbonara (III:13). To the west a new expanse was added in the area now defined by Via Toledo (Roma), S. Brigida (V:13), and Castel Nuovo, which was strengthened and expanded and given a series of delightful gardens. In 1487 the palace at Poggio Reale (IV) was designed by Giuliano da Maiano. During this period the city became famed for its elegant villas capping the crests around the city.

By the beginning of the sixteenth century Naples was well on its way to being the largest city in Europe. By 1500 its population reached an estimated 150,000, larger than Venice or Milan, twice that of London. Fifty years later it had reached 210,000.[45] By contrast, the population of Constantinople, the largest city of the Mediterranean in the early modern period, numbered 80,000 in 1478 and 400,000 around 1530.[46]

The Aragonese sea-borne empire and Naples' predominance in southern Italy brought to it a vast network of commercial trade and manufacture. Administrators and nobility flocked to the city from all over the South and abroad; and the city was fast outstripping and absorbing its suburbs. The Aragonese regularized taxation and finance, granting Naples and other cities much autonomy in local administration. Under Alfonso's son, Ferrante I (1458-1494), silk manufacture was introduced to the kingdom, iron mines opened in Calabria, and the printing industry launched in Naples.[47]

Despite their largess to the city and its gains during the quattrocento, the Aragonese dynasty never rested secure on its throne. In 1459 Ferrante was faced with a serious revolt of the barons, in league with the aged René and Jean of Anjou, that was finally subdued in 1465; in the 1470s and 1480s Naples was a key player in the Italian balance of power and war; and in 1480 the Turks shocked Europe with the sack of Otronto. Perhaps even a worse enemy to Naples than the Turks was the Roman papacy, which under Innocent VIII was strongly allied with the house of Anjou and through it with the French crown, stirring another barons' revolt in 1485/86. The 1490s brought disaster to Naples, and to Italy as a whole. With Lorenzo de' Medici's death in 1492, the fragile balance of the peninsula crumbled. An alliance between Lodovico Sforza, duke-regent of Milan, and King Charles VIII of France finally tipped the balance.[48]

Charles lived on vain hopes of extending French rule over the old Angevin lands to the south; Lodovico's invitation into Italian politics gave him the opportunity when Ferrante died in January 1494. His son, Alfonso II (1494/95), quickly allied with the papacy, but their defensive strategy failed, and Charles turned south with a huge army (40,000), panicking Alfonso, who in 1495 abdicated in favor of his son Ferrante II (Ferrandino, 1495-1496). With barons in revolt and Naples itself in anarchy, Charles entered the city, almost without a fight, in February 1495. The Aragonese dynasty, and with it the political stability of Italy and the flowering of the Renaissance, lay dead.

The Spanish Hapsburgs and the Viceroyalty (1504-)

By May 1495 Charles' hold on Naples was tenuous, given long supply lines, an untrustworthy nobility, and the heavy toll of disease. By July Ferrante II had retaken the city and by 1496 most of the kingdom. All seemed on the mend when Ferrante fell ill and died in October. The throne passed to Ferrante's uncle Federico (1496-1501), but by then the papacy had allied with the French; and in 1500 the French in turn had signed the treaty of Granada to divide the Kingdom of Naples with a newly unified Spain under Ferdinand and Isabella. While Ferdinand of Spain had supported the Aragonese against both baronial revolt and the French, his lieutenant in Italy, Gonsalvo de Cordoba, *el Gran Capitán* who had taken Granada from the Moors, now worked to dismember the Aragonese inheritance as he fought a new French invasion, this time under Louis XII. By 1502 the French and Spanish were fighting one another; and by 1504 Gonsalvo had won the entire kingdom for Ferdinand "the Catholic." The last Aragonese claimant to the throne died a prisoner of Charles V in 1550.

With Ferdinand's conquest and visit in 1506 came the period of the Spanish viceroyalty over Naples, which was to last until 1734 under successive Hapsburg and Bourbon monarchies. In 1517 Charles I of Spain, the Hapsburg, inherited the throne of Naples and soon added it to his vast domain when he was elected Emperor Charles V. The most powerful monarch of his age, Charles ruled separately as king of Germany and as emperor over Germany, Austria and its eastern territories, the Low Countries, imperial Burgundy, Spain and all its overseas empire in the New World, and all its territories in the Mediterranean. He also inherited control over most of northern Italy from the Holy Roman Empire. Until the Reformation shattered German unity, only the Papal States, Venice, England, and France remained outside his European orbit.

Naples thus became one part of this great empire, ruled – as was Mexico or Peru – by a Spanish viceroy, who allied with the barons against the urban population. Under his authority sat a series of *audiencias,* or courts, with their *presidentes,* with local *alcades* (judges of minor crimes) and *corregidores* (appointed administrators). Local voices were heard in open councils, called *cabildos abiertos.* Firmly behind these colonial officials were the Spanish infantry, the dreaded *tercios,* so named after their unbeatable military formations. Nevertheless, Neapolitan feelings were respected; a parliament was reestablished to air the views and grievances of the baronage; and Neapolitans retained the privilege of appeal directly to the king in Spain, while the *seggi* kept much of their local powers.[49]

Spanish rule was not easy at first.[50] The wars of Hapsburg Charles V and Valois Francis I of France brought further havoc to Italy and saw the sack of Rome in 1527. A fresh French attack on Naples came in 1528 when Francis' lieutenant, Odet de Foix, viscount of Lautrec, besieged the city and cut it off with a naval blockade. Only his death along with most of his army from the plague and Charles V's winning the alliance of Genoa and its fleet under Andrea Doria saved the city and kingdom for the Hapsburgs. Naples continued to be a haven for religious dissidents and intellectuals of all types, despite the attempts of the ultra-Catholic Spanish to suppress them, to introduce the Inquisition, and to suppress the university. In 1547 Viceroy Pedro of Toledo (1532-53) had to put down a general revolt. Despite this, he would become a favorite of the

Neapolitans for his restoration of peace and economic
growth, his taxation of religious properties, his easing
intellectual restraints, his beautification of the city, and
his rebuilding of its infrastructure.

The city benefited from its membership in Charles
V's multinational empire. By the mid-sixteenth century
Naples' economy had come to center on its luxury
markets: "Naples had no equivalent in Christendom....
[It produced] lace, braids, frills, trimmings, silks, light
fabrics (taffetas), silken knots and cockades of all
colours, and fine linens. These goods travelled as far as
Cologne in large quantities.... Pieces of so-called Santa
Lucia silk were even resold at Florence."[51] The
countryside abounded with fresh produce, sheep for
wool and food, as well as livestock.[52] Florence and
Venice were major markets for Neapolitan goods and
raw materials; the trade within the Spanish empire
remained a continuous source of wealth. Even with the
gradual shift of maritime and commercial fortune to the
Atlantic seaboard states, by 1605 Naples' fleet had a
total tonnage of about 40,000, equal to that of Venice or
Marseilles; while all of England had about 100,000 tons
and Spain about 175,000.[53] The city and its wealth
played a key role in the defeat of the Turkish fleet at
Lepanto in 1572.

Wealth had its troubling side, however. The increasingly impoverished rural population continued to stream
into the city. By 1550 the population had reached
155,000.[54] Despite the 60,000 dead from the plague of
1529, and 20,000 in 1562, by 1595 the population had
risen to between 280,000 and 300,000, twice that of
Venice, and only second in Europe to Paris. The population of the kingdom as a whole, from which the city of
Naples drew its numbers, soared between 1505 and 1587
from 1 to 3 million.[55]

Under the viceroys the city entered its greatest
period of expansion. The first viceroy, Gonsalvo de

Córdoba, had the walls repaired. Pedro of Toledo extended the city westward, rebuilt the walls (V), paved most of the streets, and built the avenue that Neapolitans still call Via Toledo after him, even though it was officially named Via Roma in 1860. The Spanish also expanded the fortifications of Castel Nuovo and extended the ramparts up the slopes of the Monte S. Martino to Castel S. Elmo (V:3, pl. 19), which was modernized. The year 1562 saw the beginnings of new roads and a new aqueduct; the 1560s and 1570s expansion of the port and Arsenal, culminating in the 1596/97 projects on the Molo by Domenico Fontana. Further expansions would be undertaken in the 1660s and 1670s. The viceroys also commissioned Domenico Fontana to construct the Palazzo Reale (I,V:11) between 1600 and 1602. The nobility continued to build palaces both within and around the city; the seventeenth century, at which point Bacco's narrative concludes, began the great age of the baroque in Naples.

Cultural life continued to flourish. The university was refounded in 1610. Letters remained strong, producing such renowned poets as Jacopo Sannazaro (c.1458-1530), historians like Cesare Baronio (1538-1607) and the Neapolitan school of political economy in the seventeenth century. Naples had emerged as a major theatrical center by the time Bacco's text was written.[56] The age also saw the painters Domenichino (1630-1638), G. B. Caracciolo (1570-1637), and Salvator Rosa (1615-1673) and sculptors Pietro Bernini (1584-1629) and Cosimo Fanzango (1591-1678), among many others.

Yet cultural brilliance helped conceal deep-rooted problems. Urban growth escalated as never before. On the outskirts the *borghi,* or suburban boroughs, sprouted uncontrollably. The population continued to explode to a degree one historian has called "pathological."[57] By 1650 it had reached 450,000. Then, on December 16, 1631 Naples witnessed what has been called the "greatest natural catastrophe of the age"[58] as Vesuvius erupted, killing an estimated 17,000 around its slopes and burying village after village. In 1647 the people rose in bloody revolt under Masaniello (Tommaso Angelo Maya).[59] In 1656 came the "great plague" that claimed between 240,000 and 270,000 lives in Naples alone.[60]

A sprawling, and increasingly impoverished and crime-prone population, drawn from the overtaxed and landless rural poor, resulted in the creation of thousands of homeless, beggers, and countless bandit troops all around the South and the city itself.[61] The social crisis threatened both public health and political order. Yet the government continued to be obsessed with war, devoting over 55% of its annual budget in 1591/92 to military expenditures and less than a tenth of 1% for all health, education, and charitable expenses for the entire kingdom.[62] The people of Naples – and the church – therefore responded with the creation of huge, though inadequate, public assistance programs in the form of hospices, hospitals, orphanages, monastic and lay organizations devoted to social works.[63] Long before the Industrial Revolution and the modern state wrought the same situation in the north of Europe, Naples had quickly begun to take on the shape and character of the modern city.

BACCO'S *GUIDE* AS TRAVEL LITERATURE

We cannot, of course, go into exhaustive detail in our analysis of the *Guide* here. We can, however, outline many of its chief characteristics, fit it into its tradition, and show how it follows this tradition of urban guides and where it breaks new ground. At the same time, we can also suggest how the student of history might approach and use such a text, what he or she might derive from its general and unique qualities, and what it has to tell us both about the city it describes and about the time and place in which it was written. Finally, we can say a few words on how this specific book presents us with a valuable introductory tool for Neapolitan, and southern Italian, history.

Bacco's description of Naples finds its relatively late place in a long tradition of guide books going back to the Middle Ages, called the urban *descriptio*. These were relatively short texts, often appended to a larger work, that give a broad outline of the major urban features and amenities of the city in question, usually according to fairly regular rhetorical formulae.

Thus the *descriptio* would almost always survey what the medieval or early modern urban dweller would point to with great pride in his or her city: its pleasant situation, its healthy air, good agricultural surroundings, its proximity to rivers or oceans bringing trade and freshness, its walls, bridges, and gates – the public works of the time. It would then proceed to the population: its well mixed classes, its wealthy traders, happy artisans and working people, and its noble families. Often, then, such a guide would consider, if only briefly, the city's government, its unique and ancient constitution, its officers, its clergy, its councils and meetings. It might even include some notice of the popular pastimes of the inhabitants: songs, feasts, games, outings, and the like.

The *descriptio* differed in many important respects from the medieval *itinerarium,* or point-by-point guided tour. Such an "itinerary," more often than not written for the pious sightseer – the pilgrim – would carefully describe the chief holy sites of a country, region, city, or even shrine, making certain to carefully lay out the appropriate biblical texts, legends, and historical facts needed for the pilgrim's appreciation of what he or she was seeing. Examples of this genre include the *Mirabilia Urbis Romae* (Marvels of Rome,)[64] the various guides to Jerusalem and the Holy Land,[65] the detailed guide to the pilgrim route from France to Compostella found in the *Codex Callixtinus,*[66] and others.[67]

The *descriptio,* on the other hand, would generally only survey the chief buildings of the city: its fine churches, its formidable castles, its noble palaces, its fine residences of the chief citizens, its monastic and other clerical foundations, often offering only the chief examples and the numbers of each. Some "descriptions," as some "itineraries," might then offer the names of the chief saints buried at a site and the relics that make it an object of veneration. Finally a *descriptio* might, depending upon its context – whether in a larger work or as an independent text – briefly demonstrate the glory of the city by swiftly reviewing its history, often beginning with its foundations by Romans or Trojans, and then tying the present city to its chief historical periods. One need only glance through Bacco's text to see how well he fits into this tradition of history writing: neither medieval chronicle nor Renaissance moral history, nor indeed modern guide book, but a form of rhetorical praise for his city that is the product of the time and place.

Yet in many respects Bacco's work goes beyond either *descriptio* or *itinerarium,* for its reflects many of the new realities of early modern Europe and Naples' place within its burgeoning social and economic world. One is struck from the outset by Bacco's familiarity with, and constant use of, classical references. This is only natural, it would seem, for someone writing of a city smack in the center, and on top, of one of the chief centers of ancient civilization. This, of course, is true; but his book also reflects a new consciousness that separates seventeenth-century sensibility from the world of the medieval *descriptio.* This is the heavy reliance upon, and consciousness of, the classical heritage. This is not to say that medieval descriptions, as we already noted, were not full of references to the Romans and to ancient writers. Yet the early modern sensibility, shaped by the Italian Renaissance, saw all of cultural life through the eyes of its ancient sources that tied modern locations with ancient history with a clear possession of the appropriate ancient texts and an understanding of their historical meaning.

BACCO'S *GUIDE* AS A HISTORICAL SOURCE

Aside from this *Guide's* obvious descriptions of places, people and events in and around Naples, which have great historical value in themselves, a large part of the following book is taken up by apparently haphazardly strewn lists: of kings, princes, counts, bishops, of convents, hospitals and hostels, of garrisons and dowries. While such list-making might seem a particularly obsessive means of cutting down on the finer points of narrative and presenting "just the facts" in as unappealing a means as possible; their very presence in this book reflects another very new reality: the growing preeminence of the social and economic consciousness of early modern Europe: the quantification and categorization of reality.

Bacco includes lists because they seem the natural thing: they offer data in a concise way, whether for the Spanish ruling class[68] in a foreign city or for the sightseer; and data had begun, if only begun, to take on a new life of its own. But beyond this simple fact of a new way of describing a city: as a *compilation* of its assets and liabilities, as an urban balance sheet, we have a rich source both for the history of the city and for the play of our own historical imaginations.

Perhaps the greatest value of Bacco's lists for our present purposes are his genealogies of the royal, ducal, and other noble rulers of Naples and its kingdom, and again of its popes, cardinals, archbishops, and bishops.

Working from available documents, here he has created a valuable handbook of Neapolitan chronology. While often flawed (and corrections are marked in parentheses), these lists can be read as narrative and make this text of great use to the student of southern Italian history and art history who needs to place an event or a monument by a regnal year, dynasty or event.[69]

Let us take a few other examples. On pages 50-55 the author offers a lengthy list of Neapolitan religious houses and their populations, including houses for the poor, the destitute and the homeless.[70] In addition to offering a good locator index of these institutions, Bacco's list also offers the unanalyzed data of a tremendous population explosion and seventeenth-century economic decline. Elsewhere he has alluded to his method of compilation with proper statistics based on hearth-tax records, but here, prima facie, he points out for us a huge number of sick and homeless behind the lists, evidence apparently confronting the consciousness of even the highest levels of Neapolitan society in church and state.

Again, on pages 39-44 Bacco presents a list of lay charitable organizations that offer dowries, perhaps for impoverished nobility or, more likely, for the artisan middle classes too tightly pressed to provide the means of marriage for their daughters. The list indicates both a tremendous social support system and one of the chief problems of Renaissance and early modern Europe: the large numbers of young, marriageable men, probably from the trades, who could not afford to marry unless such dowries were provided.[71] The same list also gives us a very clear indication of the types of trades, guilds, and their various employments within the city.

Other statistics that warrant Bacco's attention are also worthy of our note: the very real and strong presence of the Spanish infantry garrisoned smack in the center of the city, the crews of galleys, and the fortresses (p. 10)

point to the importance of Naples as capital of a foreign
viceroyalty, the obsession with war already noted, and
the very recent – and bloody – revolt of the people
under Masaniello in 1647.

Another fascinating revelation that comes from
Bacco's lists is social: the vast number of titled nobility
(pp. 125-38), a characteristic of the kingdom of Naples
from its birth under the Normans and before them from
Lombard times, that only hints at the wide and profound
influence they bore on, and the troubles they presented
to, successive Neapolitan dynasties. These lists also
offer many opportunities to recognize the familiar
name, both from Italian and European history and from
current Italian culture. Here are the most influential
Neapolitan families occuring again and again: Caracciolo,
Brancaccio, Sanseverino, Pignatello. Here also are the
Orsini, the Colonna, the Palavicini, the Piccolomini, the
Carrafa; here also the Grimaldi of Monaco. Genealo-
gists might also take pleasure in many familiar
landmarks: the Barone, della Terza, Caputo, Santoro,
Caselli, Aiello, Corigliano, Moscone, Serra, Somma,
and many others long familiar in American cities.
These lists, of course, are not exhaustive: many ancient
families had long since died out without a trace by the
time of Bacco's edition; many modern noble titles,
created by successive Hapsburg and Bourbon monarchs
into the nineteenth century, had not yet been born.

The nobles listed here also reflect another Neapolitan
historical reality: the power of various foreign families.
We have already noted the Spanish Carrafa: here also,
especially among the lower nobility are the Suarez,
Ramirez, Enriquez, Sanchez, Torres, Zapata, Mendozza,
and Avalos, and the much-used Neapolitan title *"don,"*
all evidence of the growing influence of the Spanish
kingdom upon Neapolitan life. Here also an occasional
Slavic name, such as Radoivich or Scanderbeg.

Also take note of the long lists of ecclesiastics and of Neapolitan bishoprics (pp. 58-66); many of these from the earliest days of Latin Christianity. One can, ironically, also use the list of archbishoprics, of chief, and of suffragan bishoprics (pp. 67-70) as a gazetteer of southern Italy: few towns of any size were without a bishop. Find the archbishopric and you have found the chief city of a region; follow up the suffragans and you can locate each smaller city of any size. Southern Italy has, in fact, become so notorious for its many and small dioceses that one reformer at the Second Vatican Council in the 1960s was quoted as saying that if one southern Italian bishop dropped his beretta, it would fall in the diocese of his colleague!

Both these last two categories, of titled nobility and of clergy, present yet another reality of southern Italian life: the immense burden on the urban middle classes, and on the agricultural societies of the countryside, of direct taxation and local privilege that finally, by the end of the nineteenth century, had caused revolution at home and vast waves of immigration abroad.

NOTES

1.   For this modern act of "pointless vandalism" that destroyed up to 90% of the Neapolitan archives for these periods, see Riccardo Filangieri, "Report on the Destruction by the Germans, September 30, 1943, of the Depository of Priceless Historical Records of the Naples State Archives," *American Archivist* 7 (1944): 252-55; and E. M. Jamison, "Documents from the Angevin Registers of Naples: Charles I," *Papers of the British School at Rome* 17 (1949): 87-89. For a description of the life of the city in 1943 and 1944 see Norman Lewis, *Naples '44* (New York: Pantheon, 1978). Many Angevin records have, fortunately, been reconstructed from previously published or transcribed papers. See J. Mazzoleni, *Le fonti documentarie e bibliografiche dal secolo x al secolo xx conservate presso l'Archivio di Stato di Napoli* (Naples, 1974), pp. 31-52; and Riccardo Filangieri, *I registri della cancelleria angioina* (Naples, 1950-). Most of the Hohenstaufen records had already been published by German historians of the nineteenth century; and many Aragonese records were brought to Barcelona by mistake in the fifteenth century.
2.   *Storia di Napoli*, 10 vols. (Naples: Società editrice storia di Napoli, 1975-81).
3.   Alfonso De Franciscis, Daniela del Pesco Spirito et al., *Campania*, English trans. by Rudolf G. Carpanini et al. (Naples: Electa for Banco Nazionale del Lavoro, 1977).
4.   See Bartolomeo Capasso, *Napoli greco-romano* (Naples: Np, 1905); or his *Topografia della città di Napoli nel'XI secolo* (Naples: Società Napoletana di storia patria, 1895).
5.   His works are too numerous to list here. See the Bibliography, pp. 146-47.
6.   See the notes in Caroline Bruzelius' essay, below pp. lxxviii-lxxix.
7.   See, for example, Fernand Braudel, *The Mediterranean and the Mediterranean World in the Age of Philip II*, trans. by Siân Reynolds, 2 vols. (New York: Harper & Row, 1981).
8.   For ancient Naples, see *Storia di Napoli*, 1:1-212.
9.   In the thirteenth century AD the name of this river, gradually being buried by the city, was transferred to the Rubeolo, at the banks of Vesuvius. It appears on early modern maps as entering the sea to the east of the city.
10.   See John D'Arms, *Romans on the Bay of Naples. A Social & Cultural Study on the Villas and Their Owners from 150 BC to AD 400* (Cambridge, MA: Harvard University Press, 1970). For a more anecdotal approach, see Peter Gunn, *Naples: A Palimpsest* (London: Chapman & Hall, 1961), pp. 1-63.
11.   See Caroline's Bruzelius' introduction, pp. lxvi-lxvii.
12.   Ibid., pp. lxviii-lxx.
13.   For these events see the *Storia di Napoli*, 1:82-117; Eleanor Shipley Duckett, *Gateway to the Middle Ages: Italy* (Ann Arbor, MI: University of Michigan Press, 1961), pp. 1-57. For the early history of

southern Italy and Naples, see *Storia di Napoli,* 1:118-518; and Chris Wickham, *Early Medieval Italy: Central Power and Local Society 400-1000* (Ann Arbor, MI: University of Michigan Press, 1989), pp. 9-27.

14. See Wickham, pp. 74-79;

15. Ibid., p. 78.

16. For which see the chronologies below on pages 73-92.

17. See the list of dukes of Naples below pp. 82-85.

18. The best account in English remains Charles Homer Haskins, *The Normans in European History* (New York: W.W. Norton, 1966), pp. 192-217. For the Kingdom of Sicily, see Denis Mack Smith, *A History of Sicily,* 2 vols. (New York: Dorset Press, 1988), vol. 1, *Medieval Sicily, 800-1713,* pp. 1-48; and Benedetto Croce, *History of the Kingdom of Naples,* ed. H. Stuart Hughes, trans. Frances Frenaye (Chicago & London: University of Chicago Press, 1970), pp. 7-42; the *Storia di Napoli,* 1:521-51; and C. W. Previté-Orton, *The Shorter Cambridge Medieval History (SCMH),* 2 vols. (Cambridge: The University Press, 1966), 1:507-18.

19. See the excellent map, with text, of the Norman expansion in Donald Matthew, *Atlas of Medieval Europe* (New York: Facts on File, 1983), pp. 95-97.

20. Cesare De Seta, *Storia della città di Napoli: Dalle origini al settecento* (Rome and Bari: Laterza, 1973), p. 46.

21. For comparison, by 1250 Paris had a population of about 50,000; London, 25,000; Venice 100,000; Genoa and Milan 50,000 to 100,000; and Palermo, 50,000. Rome was little more than a small town, especially after the Norman sack. Medieval urban populations for this period are extremely difficult to determine. No exact census existed; figures, which vary widely from historian to historian, are based on such items as number of hearths, average estimated size of households, tax rolls, army and fleet sizes, building plots, extent of city walls, etc. For some estimates, see Daniel Waley, *The Italian City Republics* (New York: McGraw Hill, 1978), pp. 34-38; Joseph and Frances Gies, *Life in a Medieval City* (New York: Thomas Crowell, 1973), pp. 21-22; John H. Mundy and Peter Riesenberg, *The Medieval Town* (New York: Van Nostrand, 1958), p. 30; and Fritz Rörig, *The Medieval Town* (Berkeley and Los Angeles: University of California Press, 1967), pp. 111-21.

22. See Haskins, *Normans,* p. 224.

23. See Haskins, *Normans,* pp. 218-49; Mack Smith, *Sicily,* ibid.; Croce, ibid.

24. The term is Charles Homer Haskins'. See his *The Renaissance of the Twelfth Century* (Cleveland and New York: World Publishing, 1966), especially pp. 59-61; 238-40, 260-66; 291-95.

25. See Haskins, *Renaissance;* Nathan Schachner, *The Medieval Universities* (New York: A.S. Barnes, 1962), pp. 51-55. A typical product of the Salerno medical school is the *Regimen Sanitatis Salernitanum,* the "Salerno Health Diet Book," which appeared as early as 1100, rivalled the authority of Galen and Hippocrates, and established

Naples as the source for a vastly popular medical literature throughout Europe, the beautifully illustrated *Tacuinum Sanitatis,* or "Health Handbook." See *The Medieval Health Handbook,* Tacuinum Sanitatis, ed. Luisa Cogliati Arano (New York: George Braziller, 1976).

26. For the Hohenstaufen period, see *Storia di Napoli,* 1:552-603. For more specific works on Frederick II, see *SCMH* 2:682-95; John Larner, *Italy in the Age of Dante and Petrarch, 1216-1380,* Longman History of Italy 2 (London and New York: Longman, 1980), pp. 16-37; and David Abulafia, *Frederick II: A Medieval Emperor* (New York: Viking Punguin, 1988).

27. For the following narrative see Steven Runciman, *The Sicilian Vespers. A History of the Mediterranean World in the Thirteenth Century* (Cambridge: The University Press, 1958); Norman Housley, *The Italian Crusades. The Papal-Angevin Alliance and the Crusades Against Christian Lay Powers, 1254-1343* (New York: Oxford University Press, 1982); and *SCMH* 2:695-703; 768-69.

28. For a decription see Desmond Seward, ed., *Naples: A Traveller's Companion* (New York: Atheneum, 1986), pp. 80-81.

29. For this period see C. De Frede, "Da Carlo I d'Angio à Giovanna I (1263-1382)," in *Storia di Napoli,* 2:9-354; see Ronald G. Musto, "Queen Sancia of Naples (1286-1345) and the Spiritual Franciscans," in *Women of the Medieval World: Essays in Honor of John H. Mundy,* ed. by Julius Kirshner and Suzanne F. Wemple (Oxford and New York: Basil Blackwell, 1985), pp. 179-214 at 179-80 nn. 1-5, for additional bibliography. For first-hand sources translated into English see Seward, pp. 52-63.

30. See De Seta, p. 85.

31. See De Frede, "Da Carlo I;" Musto, "Sancia," pp. 179-80 nn. 2, 5 for bibliography; St. Claire Baddeley, *Robert the Wise and His Heirs 1278-1352* (London: W. Heinemann, 1897); and Gunn, *Palimpsest,* pp. 64-86.

32. For which see Caroline Bruzelius' introduction, below, pp. lxxi-lxxv.

33. See Larner, pp. 47-48.

34. See, for example, Harry A. Miskimin, *The Economy of Early Renaissance Europe, 1300-1460* (London and New York: Cambridge University Press, 1978), p. 73.

35. See Ernest Hatch Wilkins, *Life of Petrarch* (Chicago: University of Chicago Press, 1963), pp. 41-42; and Seward, pp. 101-4.

36. Philip Ziegler, *The Black Death* (Harmondsworth: Penguin Books, 1970), p. 52.

37. De Seta, p. 118.

38. *Familiares* V,3.9-15. For a translation see Seward, p. 60.

39. See Denys Hay and John Law, *Italy in the Age of the Renaissance, 1380-1530,* Longman History of Italy 3 (London and New York: Longman, 1989), pp. 30-31.

40.　*Storia di Napoli*, 2:184-278; and St. Clair Baddley, *Queen Joanna I* (London: W. Heinemann, 1893).

41.　For a recent treatment, with bibliography, see F. Unterkircher, *King René's Book of Love (Le Cueur d'Amours Espris)* (New York: George Braziller, 1975).

42.　For Alfonso's reign see Alan Ryder, *The Kingdom of Naples Under Alfonso the Magnanimous. The Making of a Modern State* (Oxford: Clarendon Press, 1976); idem, *Alfonso the Magnanimous, King of Aragon, Naples, and Sicily, 1396-1458* (New York: Oxford University Press, 1990); Hay and Law, pp. 169-72; and *Storia di Napoli*, 2:357-584. For source readings see Seward, pp. 66-73.

43.　For what follows see Jerry H. Bentley, *Politics and Culture in Renaissance Naples* (Princeton, NJ: Princeton University Press, 1987); and *Storia di Napoli*, 2:471-77. For the general history of the period, see Hay and Law, pp. 149-97.

44.　Giulio C. Argan has called Alfonso II's urban renewal plan "the most important document of Renaissance city planning, understood as an agent of government. It was clearly related to Alberti's concepts...." See Argan, *The Renaissance City* (New York: George Braziller, 1969), pp. 116-17.

45.　These figures can be disputed. See De Seta, p. 167; Carlo M. Cipolla, *Before the Industrial Revolution: European Society and Economy, 1000-1700* (New York: W.W. Norton, 1976), pp. 281-82.

46.　See Braudel, 1:345, 347.

47.　See, for example, Mariano Fava and Giovanni Bresciano, eds., *La stampa a Napoli nel XV secolo,* 3 vols. (Leipzig: Teubner, 1911-1913).

48.　For these events see *Storia di Napoli*, 2:585-672; Hay and Law, pp. 164-66; and *The New Cambridge Modern History*, vol. 1, *The Renaissance, 1493-1520,* ed. by Denys Hay (Cambridge: Cambridge University Press, 1975), pp. 343-67.

49.　See Eric Cochrane, with Julius Kirshner, *Italy 1530-1630*, Longman History of Italy 4 (London and New York: Longman, 1988); pp. 43-44, 170.

50.　For these events see *Storia di Napoli*, 3:1-84; F. C. Spooner, "The Hapsburg-Valois Struggle," in *The New Cambridge Modern History*, vol. 2: *The Reformation 1520-1559,* ed. G. R. Elton (Cambridge: Cambridge University Press, 1975), pp. 334-58; for a general history, see Cochrane, pp. 33-54; for source readings see Seward, p. 74.

51.　Braudel, 1:345.

52.　See Cochrane, p. 183.

53.　Braudel, 1:446.

54.　De Seta, p. 210.

55.　Braudel, 1:408, 523 n. 355.

56.　See Cochrane, pp. 245-49.

57.　De Seta, p. 196.

58.　Cohrane, p. 281.

59.　See *Storia di Napoli*, 3:200-245; and Seward, pp. 82-90.

60. Ibid., p. 306.
61. See De Seta, pp. 237-41; and Cochrane, pp. 170-71, 275-76.
62. Cipolla, p. 53.
63. See Bacco's own lists, pp. 39-44, 50-55.
64. Most recently edited by Eileen Gardiner (New York: Italica Press, 1986).
65. See the many texts published by the Palestine Pilgrims' Text Society; and Theoderich, *Guide to the Holy Land* (New York: Italica Press, 1986).
66. The *Liber Sancti Jacobi,* from the Cathedral Library, Santiago de Compostella. An English edition of this text by William Melczer is forthcoming from Italica Press.
67. See, for example, John Kirtland Wright, *The Geographical Lore of the Time of the Crusades* (New York: Dover, 1965); or Mary B. Campbell, *The Witness and the Other World: Exotic European Travel Writing, 400-1600* (Ithaca and London: Cornell University Press, 1988).
68. For this trend see Cochrane, p. 167.
69. Such handbooks, of course, exist quite apart from these. The most commonly used for Italian history is probably A. Cappelli, *Cronologia, cronografia e calendario perpetuo* (Milan: Hoepli, 1978). See also, for example, John E. Morby, ed., *Dynasties of the World: A Chronological and Geneaological Handbook* (Oxford and New York: Oxford University Press, 1989).
70. For the widespread popularity and influence of these institutions in post-Tridentine Italy see Cochrane, pp. 111-18.
71   See, for example, David Herlihy, "The Medieval Marriage Market," *Medieval and Renaissance Studies* 6 (1976): 19.

7. Castel Capuana (center) and Harbor.
Detail from *Tavola Strozzi* (Plate 4).

8. S. Chiara (top, center) to the Arsenal.
Detail from *Tavola Strozzi* (Plate 4).
The campanile of S. Maria Nova is at extreme left.

ART, ARCHITECTURE AND
URBANISM IN NAPLES

CAROLINE BRUZELIUS

Not the lone and level sands, but earthquakes, war, fire, and above all, dense and constant human habitation have obliterated the vestiges of ancient and medieval Naples. For unlike Rome, the circumference of the ancient city of Naples was small: no part of the center was abandoned or left empty by a dwindling population in the early Middle Ages.[1] The ancient forum and market remained at the center of urban life from antiquity until the late thirteenth century.[2] Indeed, the extreme scarcity of ancient and early medieval remains in Naples prompts the ironic reflection that few things may be worse for buildings and urban environments than the people they were designed to serve.[3]

Yet if the dense and concentrated life of the city has meant the destruction of its ancient buildings, one fundamental characteristic of central Naples has been less vulnerable to change and testifies to the city's ancient Greek origins. The grid plan of the center, established by the city's Greek founders, still dominates the character of the old city. The grid consists of long rectangular blocks running roughly north-south that average about 185 by 37 meters; it is still perceptible to the modern pedestrian, who will note that in the old city the three streets running east-west, the *decumani* (corresponding to Via Tribunali, Via S. Biagio dei Librai, and Via Anticaglia), are wider than those running north-south, along the long axis of the rectangular city blocks (such as Vico dei Maiorani), which are much narrower. The latter correspond to the ancient *cardines*. In the early Middle Ages the siting of churches and monasteries usually conformed to the ancient grid, so that many of the churches were established on a north-south, rather than the more conventional east-west, orientation. Such deviations from traditional orientations can still be seen at the churches of S. Restituta, S. Paolo Maggiore, S. Domenico, S. Nicola a Nilo, and S. Maria Donnaregina, for example. Only in the late thirteenth century did the expansion and reconstruction of some of the more important Neapolitan churches and cloisters on an east-west axis, often under the domineering hand of royal or aristocratic patrons, tend to entail the closing or blocking of one or more of the ancient *cardines*. This is visible in the reconstruction of the cathedral complex under Charles II of Anjou.[4]

Some traces of the Greek city wall were excavated and are exposed at Piazza Bellini on the west side of the city and at Piazza Calenda on the east. Of the center of civic activity, the Greek *agora,* and then its Roman successor, the forum (II:4), both at the site of S. Paolo Maggiore (Temple of the Dioscuri, II:3) and S. Lorenzo Maggiore (Roman Basilica, II:5), nothing but a few vestiges reincorporated into later buildings remain. The forum was intersected by the main *decumanus* (Via Tribunali, II:9), which led directly to the Porta Capuana on the east side of the city. The baths and the commercial quarter (II:6) were located on the lower *decumanus* (Via S. Biagio dei Librai, II:10), while the ancient stadium and hippodrome (II:12, 13) were on the southeastern corner of the city, beneath or intersecting with what is now Corso Umberto I. The lay-out and successive expansions of the old city can be seen in Map II.[5]

In the late Roman period, in response to the increasing importance of shipping and trade, the city was expanded southwest of the original walls towards the harbor. This area (II:E) is now marked by the churches of S. Giovanni Maggiore (II:11) and S. Maria la Nova (III:2). To enclose the first of a series of expansions of the town towards the waterfront and the western periphery, the ancient walls were enlarged and reinforced under Valentinian III (450-55), enclosing the zones now occupied by the churches of the Gesù and part of the convent of S. Chiara (I, III:16).

During the ducal period, the walls were enlarged again in 902 to contain the area occupied from the church of S. Maria la Nova along the south side of Corso Umberto as far as S. Pietro Martire (III:5), and on the north side to contain the area as far as the north side of Via Depretis until its intersection with Rua Catalana. Under the Normans the extension of the margins of the city was continued with the enlargement of the Castel dell'Ovo (pl. 14) and the construction of the Castel Capuana on the east (III:22, pl. 7); both anticipated the further expansion of Naples southwest and northeast.

The primary phase of urban development of Naples during the Middle Ages came under the first three generations of the Angevin rulers (1266-1343), who made Naples capital of the kingdom. The circumference of the walls was enlarged to include S. Eligio (III:18) and S. Maria Egiziaca (III:17). The civic works of Charles I of Anjou and his successors included canals to empty the insalubrious swamps to the northeast of the city, repairs to the old aqueducts, and moving the market center from the ancient forum (by S. Lorenzo Maggiore) to the area near the harbor that still functions today as the Piazza del Mercato (III:23).[6] These public works were enlarged in 1279 by the beginning of construction of a new royal palace, the Castel Nuovo (III:14, pl. 6), which made the area to the southwest of the ancient city not only the primary royal residence, but also increasingly the center of administration. Under Charles II, the land around the Castel Nuovo became a palatial neighborhood occupied by the residences of members of the large royal family and their aristocratic retainers. Charles II also paved the streets of the city.

The remains of ancient monuments – temples, basilicas, houses, fora – are virtually nonexistent. Throughout the Middle Ages churches were erected directly over or adjacent to the remains of ancient temples. The new religion literally supplanted the old. Fragments of ancient pagan monuments were reutilized in the walls of subsequent buildings in the city and are particularly obvious in churches and their attendant structures. The lower story of the Romanesque campanile adjacent to S. Maria Maggiore (III:10) is constructed from chaotically arranged architectural fragments, *spolia,* attesting to the ubiquitous pillaging of ancient monuments. More coherent and systematic approaches to the reuse of ancient remains, sometimes even the entire sequence of columns from an the original temple, can be seen in the monoliths utilized as various forms of support in a number of the medieval churches, a practice especially common in the Angevin period.[7] Striking examples of such *spolia* are visible in the columns applied to the nave walls of S. Lorenzo Maggiore (III:11), the marble columns embedded in the piers of the Duomo (III:20), and above all the splendid fluted columns and other fragmental remains from the Temple of the Dioscuri applied to the facade of the baroque church of S. Paolo Maggiore (V:17).

Few monuments erected in early medieval and Byzantine Naples survive intact, but fragments and partial remains of early Christian monuments permit some conclusions about what must have been a rich and eclectic period of Neapolitan architectural history.[8] The most significant remains are the catacombs, especially that of S. Gennaro, located to the northeast of the city (II:14, III:8). These contain a number of important early Christian wall paintings and mosaics. By the end of the third century, especially after the death of S. Agrippino,

the catacombs had become important religious centers of
the city, though the suggestion of some Neapolitan
authors that these presented the first places of worship
seems most improbable. The sites were marked by
several churches, the most important of which was a
funerary basilica dedicated first to S. Agrippino and
later to S. Gennaro, the patron saint of Naples martyred
during the persecutions of Diocletian. This church
maintains some of its original masonry, in spite of
successive reconstructions and additions. Known as S.
Gennaro extra Moenia, the church was a single-naved
cemetery basilica of c.400; it became an important
pilgrimage site and burial place, later receiving the
remains of other bishops and rulers. The site went into
a decline only when the relics of S. Gennaro were stolen
by the prince of Benevento (831); by the middle of the
ninth century the other relics of the saints were
translated from the catacombs and nearby funerary
churches to the protection of the cathedral of Naples
within the walls.[9]

Wall paintings and later burials dating to the tenth
and possibly the eleventh century attest to the continued
use of the catacombs as a place of pilgrimage and
entombment, activities no doubt promoted by the
Benedictine abbey established at the site. Within the city
there were four primary basilicas: S. Giovanni
Maggiore, SS. Apostoli (V:21), S. Maria Maggiore, and
S. Giorgio Maggiore (V:18), as well as the numerous
smaller parish churches and the cathedral. The huge
church of S. Giorgio Maggiore, erected around 400,
seems to have had a tripartite apse, which now serves as
the entrance to the building. Although most of the the
church was heavily redecorated by Cosimo Fanzago
(1593-1678) after a fire in 1640, the fifth-century
remains are noteworthy for the three arched openings in
the curve of the apse, which gave access to a truncated
ambulatory behind. This feature is also found at S.

Gennaro extra Moenia. Above the reused Corinthian capitals, the high square imposts, marked with a cross, are related to those of fifth-century monuments in the Aegean and in Ravenna.

At the cathedral (III:20, pls. 16-17), the basilica of S. Restituta, originally dedicated to the Savior and renamed for the saint whose remains were translated to the site at the end of the eighth century, now exists in largely rebuilt form. It was truncated by the construction of the adjacent Duomo under Charles II c.1300 and has a number of structural features related to North African monuments.[10] The nave is wide, the apse is raised on steps that project into the nave, and a prominent triumphal arch constricts the area in front of the apse. The location of the square baptistery adjacent to S. Restituta, S. Giovanni in Fonte, placed at the end of the right-hand aisle, may reflect North African prototypes. The cathedral complex as it evolved by the sixth century seems to have consisted of two parallel basilicas, a disposition recalling the double cathedrals commonly found in early Christian episcopal complexes. Under early medieval episcopal rulers the cathedral(s) and their attendant buildings functioned as the center of public and political activity in the city.

Although replaced beginning in the late thirteenth century by the Gothic church at S. Lorenzo Maggiore (III:11, pl. 12), it is worth noting that the older basilica at S. Lorenzo was another important early Christian monument in Naples.[11] Founded between 534 and 554 by Bishop Giovanni II, the plan of the first church reflects eastern influences, particularly in the presence of a *prothesis* and *diakonikon* flanking either side of the apse. The entire eastern end of the church is enclosed by a straight wall on the exterior, a feature most commonly found in Syria.[12]

Little remains of other medieval monuments prior to the Angevin conquest of the kingdom. While there are indications of active religious life and many new monasteries in the Byzantine period, little more than the names of the abbeys of the foundations survive to attest to this important phase of Neapolitan history. A rare example of Romanesque construction of the eleventh-twelfth centuries can be found in the tower beside the Renaissance church of S. Maria Maggiore (III:10). Two further striking testaments to a rich Romanesque-early Gothic sculptural tradition, which is now otherwise completely lost, are the marble reliefs representing scenes from the Old Testament and the Passion in the Principio chapel on the left side of S. Restituta.[13]

With the advent of Naples as capital of the kingdom under Charles of Anjou and his successors, the city began to take on the attributes of a major royal center. Aside from the public works mentioned above, and the construction or refurbishment of numerous castles, there is also a shift in the character of monumental building and patronage in the city, which from then onwards tended to reflect the tastes and aspirations of the ruler and his court. For example, under the Angevins, particularly during the reigns of Charles II and Robert the Wise, religious patronage became almost exclusively mendicant, and Naples became one of the strongholds of the new religious orders. While Charles II favored the Dominicans – S. Domenico Maggiore (III:9, pl. 11), S. Pietro Martire (III:5, pl. 11) – his son Robert and his wife Sancia of Majorca founded a number of Franciscan houses, especially establishments for women.

The most important medieval monuments of Naples thus date to the Angevin rule of Naples between 1266 and 1343. Of the large numbers of churches founded by these kings and their retinues in Naples, only S. Lorenzo Maggiore, S. Domenico Maggiore, S. Chiara (III:16, pls. 8, 11), S. Eligio, S. Maria Donnaregina (III:12, pl. 12), and the Duomo survive. In spite of their altered and restored states, the churches as a group constitute an impressive testament to the extent and importance of royal patronage during the Angevin period. Yet as all of these monuments had been encrusted with heavy baroque decoration in the seventeenth and eighteenth centuries, only since the restorations undertaken at the end of World War II has it has been possible to consider the character and design of most of these churches as originally conceived, for in almost every case the original wall structures had been entirely concealed.[14] This group of churches present important evidence of the importation of French culture in Naples, but it is important to recognize that they do not present a uniform approach: to the contrary, there are significant shifts in aesthetic and religious sensibility between the reigns of Charles I, Charles II, and Robert. Even within three generations the religious foundations of the Angevins attest to the personal character of royal and aristocratic patronage from the late thirteenth century onwards.

The Angevin period brought to Naples close and repeated contacts with the French Gothic style, a style that in the thirteenth century carried with it great glamour and prestige.[15] This concern with French culture was especially strong during the reign of Charles of Anjou; the documents from his reign attest to the king's deliberate and consistent utilization of the French Gothic style as a symbol of the new political regime. The most frequently cited example of this phenomenon is the Gothic choir of S. Lorenzo Maggiore, rebuilt probably beginning c.1284, and certainly the most handsome extant example of Gothic architecture in Naples (pl. 15). The reconstruction of the choir has been attributed to Charles of Anjou himself. Yet the king's direct involvement seems unlikely in view of the complete absence of any substantial documentation for his role.[16] His son, the more conspicuously pious Charles II, founded a number of important Dominican abbeys: S. Pietro Martire, S. Pietro a Castello, and S. Domenico Maggiore. Charles II also rebuilt the cathedral of S. Gennaro in Naples beginning about 1296 (pl. 15). His wife, Queen Mary of Hungary, reconstructed the Franciscan convent church of S. Maria Donnaregina, an ancient Basilian foundation of the eighth century damaged by the earthquake of 1293. Although a new church was built for the convent in the early seventeenth century, the Gothic structure was preserved. It contains the handsome tomb of Mary of Hungary (d. 1323) by Tino di Camaino (1285-c.1337) and Gagliardo Primario (?-1340).

The reign of Robert the Wise and Sancia of Majorca presents one of the most interesting periods of royal patronage in Naples, not only for art and architecture, but also for literature and learning. The architectural and artistic projects ranged from the lavish redecoration and remodeling of castles and fortifications, such as the Castel Nuovo, the palace at Quisisana, and the Castel Belforte (S. Elmo III:3, pl. 19), to a series of ascetic religious foundations that reflected the particular piety of Queen Sancia: S. Chiara (III:16), S. Croce, S. Maria Egiziaca and S. Trinità (III:15) and of her family. Charles of Calabria founded the abbey of S. Martino (III:4, pl. 19), completed by Sancia after his death.

The only monument that survives of the many established by Sancia is her enormous church and double monastery of S. Chiara, founded in 1310 (pl. 8). The double convent is one of the largest and most imposing Gothic churches in Naples. It may also have been the single largest monastic foundation for women ever erected in Europe.[17] Partly decorated by Giotto (1266?-1337), its original cycle of painted decoration, which probably strongly reflected the queen's own pious concerns, was completely covered with baroque incrustations in the eighteenth century. This church was also restored to an approximation of its original medieval

appearance after World War II: the grand, severe
interior volumes reflect on the one hand a dedication to
the spirit of poverty espoused by St. Francis but on the
other the need for a vast interior in which state occa-
sions (funerals, coronations, etc.) could take place. As
protectors of the radical Franciscans known as the
Spirituals,[18] Queen Sancia and King Robert the Wise
seem to have made the double convent of S. Chiara the
center of religious dissent in Naples. Within the church,
the double tomb of King Robert by Giovanni and Pacio
Bertini (mid-fourteenth century) presides over the nave,
while a single effigy of the king appears on the reverse
of the same wall in the nun's choir. The public monument, severely damaged in the bombardment and fire of
1943, presents at the top the king majestically en-
throned; below is a recumbent barefoot effigy of Robert
dressed in Franciscan habit. In this complex sepulchral
monument the king's role as a patron of the arts and
learning is suggested by personifications of the Virtues,
which support the sarcophagus, and the Seven Liberal
Arts, which stand behind the effigy. The tomb of Robert
is flanked to the right by that of his heir, Charles of
Calabria, (d. 1328) whose wife, Mary of Valois (d.
1331), is buried adjacent to the entrance to the sacristy,
and to the left by the tomb of Maria di Durazzo (d.
1366).

The royal tombs of the early fourteenth century
represent one of the most important periods for the
flowering of sculpture in Naples. Although the tomb of
Charles I of Anjou (d. 1285) no longer survives, those
of his descendants attest to the frequent presence of
Tuscan sculptors (especially Tino di Camaino and his
shop) in Naples. There is frequent evidence for the importation of ancient marbles from Rome for the
construction and carving of the tombs, one of the most
splendid and well-preserved of which is that of
Catherine of Hungary (d. 1323) to the right of the altar

of S. Lorenzo Maggiore.[19]   Other important royal and aristocratic tombs, primarily of the fifteenth century, are in the churches of S. Giovanni a Carbonara (III:13) and S. Angelo a Nilo (III:7). The most important of these are the tombs of Cardinal Rinaldo Brancaccio (d. 1423) in S. Angelo by Donatello (1386?-1466) and Michelozzo di Bartolomeo (1396-1472)[20] and the tomb of King Ladislas (d.1414) in S. Giovanni.

After the death of Robert the Wise in 1343, the city degenerated into a state of decadence, violence, and disorder. It was to witness a new period of revitalization, reconstruction, and expansion only a century later with the conquest of Naples by Alfonso of Aragon in 1442. The new king showered money on Naples, repairing streets, walls, and houses and constructing new piazzas and fountains. Talented and educated bourgeois bureaucrats provided an alternative to the violent and domineering baronial control, although significant artistic patronage tended to remain the province of the ruler.[21] The intellectual and artistic sophistication of the new king and his retainers is reflected in the reconstruction of the Castel Nuovo (IV:14, pl. 6), whose new monumental and richly sculpted entrance commemorates Alfonso's triumphal entrance to Naples in February 1443. The reconstruction of the castle gave new vitality to the port, while the construction of numerous palatial residences in the old city and near the Castel Capuana revitalized the old center.

Fifteenth-century Neapolitan architecture presents an interesting mixture of imported Catalan Gothic forms with the new Renaissance architectural vocabulary. Unfortunately, the most beautiful Renaissance church in Naples, S. Anna dei Lombardi (Monteoliveto, IV:7), begun in 1411, was severely damaged in the bombardment of 1943. A number of its sculptural monuments were also affected, including the tomb of Domenico Fontana (d. 1607) located to the right of the entrance.

In the interior there is an important terracotta Pietà of 1492 by Guido Mazzoni (1450-1518). Among other Renaissance monuments, S. Giovanni dei Pappacoda (IV:21), founded in 1415 by a family of wealthy sea merchants, still maintains certain Gothic features (the entrance portal), whereas the Capella Pontana, founded in 1492, is firmly modeled on classical prototypes, such as the temple of Fortuna Virilis in Rome. The crypt of the cathedral (IV:20), the Succorpo (also known as the Cappella Carafa), is one of the most elegant and best-preserved Renaissance monuments in Naples. Designed by Tommaso Malvito between 1497 and 1506, the rectangular room, subdivided into three vessels by columns, is especially noteworthy for the elegance and subtlety of its low relief decoration of garlands, putti, and classically inspired motifs.

Naples is also endowed with a number of splendid Renaissance palazzi, built by the nobility of the kingdom who increasingly found it useful to have a residence in the capital in order to fully participate in the advantages of urban life and culture and to take part in the political life at court. Though most have suffered acutely from either severe remodelings or neglect and abuse, they nonetheless attest to the vitality of civic life in the court under Aragonese rule. Most noteworthy are the Del Balzo-Petrucci palace (IV:8), to the left of the apse of S. Domenico (in deplorable condition), the Penna (IV:9) (begun in 1406 in a late Gothic style), the Panormita, the Carafa di Maddaloni (IV:6), and Cuomo (IV:10) palaces. The facade of the Sanseverino palace, begun in 1470, was transformed to become the entrance to the church of the Gesù Nuovo (V:15).

In several successive phases the dimensions of the city were expanded to accommodate the rapidly growing urban population. By the mid-sixteenth century new city walls came to include the Castel S. Elmo (IV, V:3, pl. 19), thus greatly enlarging the residential areas. The zone to the west of Via Toledo, Montecalvario (V:5, pl. 19), was developed for military housing, and this part of the city still retains its character as a popular residential area. Between 1532 and 1553 the urban projects of Don Pedro Alvarez de Toledo, who created a series of new, large avenues, such as the Via Toledo, decorated the old center with fountains and monuments, and enlarged the harbor, dramatically improved the character of the city.[22] By the seventeenth century Naples was undergoing another major expansion. But the needs of the urban environment were largely ignored in favor of private aristocratic projects: a new palace, the Palazzo Reale (V:11), constructed under the direction of Domenico Fontana (1543-1607), and the Palazzo degli Studi (now the Museo Nazionale, V:9). New baroque churches by Fanzago and Francesco Grimaldi (1545-c.1630) – S. Paolo Maggiore, S. Giorgio Maggiore, SS. Apostoli, S. Maria degli Angeli (V:7), S. Ferdinando (V:12) among others – provided Naples with important monuments in the new style.

A brief sketch of Naples can only hint at the richness and diversity of the artistic heritage of this city. And a sketch that ends with the seventeenth century also leaves aside one of the richest and most spectacular periods of Neapolitan art, the baroque. Yet more than any other city in Italy, Naples prior to 1600 was subjected to a multitude of extraneous influences brought to the city by its foreign kings. As the capital of a kingdom, the city was repeatedly reconceived in terms of the political vision and ambitions of its rulers. The private tastes of the reigning monarchs affect Naples in a way that is unmatched in any other Italian city. Yet the story is also a tragic one, filled with loss and destruction; even the most dedicated of visitors will be frustrated by the number of major monuments that are either in ruinous condition, never opened, or simply in an eternal process of *restauro*.

Caroline Bruzelius

NOTES

1.   In this sense, urban development for long stretches of Neapolitan history was strictly centripetal. Ancient *Neapolis* comprised the area roughly between Piazza Cavour to Via S. Giovanni a Carbonara on the north, towards the Castel Capuana on the east, and was bordered on the west by Via S. Maria di Constantinopoli. See Map II. The continuation of dense habitation in the center was enforced by repeated decrees promulgated between 1566 and 1718 that no building could take place outside the walls.

2.   Although there had been various phases of expansion of the city towards the harbor and the southwest, the decisive shifts of mercantile and political action towards the south came only with the creation of a new market and royal palace by Charles of Anjou (1266-85) and his successors.

3.   Yet few cities have a more long and venerable tradition of scholarly study. See, for example, the excellent and thorough bibliography in Gennaro Aspreno Galante, *Guida Sacra della città di Napoli,* ed. Nicola Spinosa, (Naples: Società editrice napoletana, 1985). The most useful, though also at times unreliable and superficial, study on the history and art of Naples is the multi-volumed *Storia di Napoli,* under the direction of Ernesto Pontieri, Roberto Pane, et al. (Naples: Società editrice storia di Napoli, 1975-81).

4.   See Roberto di Stefano, *La Cattedrale di Napoli: storia, restauro, scoperte, ritrovamenti* (Naples: Editoriale Scientifica, 1974).

5.   See also the general and still very useful studies by Bartolommeo Capasso, *Napoli greco-romana* (Naples: s.n., 1905); *Topografia della città di Napoli nell'XI secolo* (Naples: Società Napoletana di storia patria, 1895).

6.   It is interesting to note that the urban activities of Charles I in some ways parallel those of his illustrious grandfather, Philip Augustus, in Paris. This is especially noteworthy in the moving of the market from the densely congested city center to the periphery.

7.   It may be that the frequent use of *spolia,* especially in the Angevin period, may reflect an attitude of alliance towards Rome, or towards the Roman church. In any event, it seems to reflect the tastes of the time, as can also be seen, for example, in the nave of S. Maria Aracoeli in Rome.

8.   The most complete study to date of the phenomenon is Arnaldo Venditti, "Problemi di lettura e di interpretazione dell'architectura paleochristiana di Napoli," *Napoli nobilissima* 12 (1973): 177-88.

9.   The relics of S. Gennaro were moved from Benevento to Montevergine in the twelfth century, and thence back to Naples during the fifteenth.

10.   Richard Krautheimer, *Early Christian and Byzantine Architecture,* The Pelican History of Art (Harmondsworth, England and New York: Penguin, 1986); see also Roberto di Stefano, *La Cattedrale di Napoli,* passim; Venditti, "Problemi," passim.

11. Antonio Rusconi, "La basilica paleochristiana di S. Lorenzo Maggiore di Napoli," *Atti del VI congresso internazionale di archeologia cristiana, 1962* (Città del Vaticano: Vatican Press, 1965), 709-31.

12. See, for a summary of the early Christian material at S. Lorenzo, Jürgen Krüger, *S. Lorenzo Maggiore in Neapel: eine Franziskanerkirche zwischen Ordenideal und Herrschaftsarchitektur,* Franziskanische Forschungen 31 (Werl/Westfalen: Dietrich-Coelde, 1986); and more recently Cornelia Berger-Dittscheid, "S. Lorenzo Maggiore in Neapel, Das gotische 'Ideal' Projekt Karls I. und seine 'franziskanischen' Modificationem," *Festschrift für Hartmet Biermann* (Weinheim, 1990), pp. 41-64.

13. These may have formed part of an early altar or choir screen. See the discussion of these reliefs in Dorothy Glass, *Romanesque Sculpture in Campania: Patrons, Programs, and Style* (University Park, PA and London: Pennsylvania State University Press, forthcoming).

14. In the process of restoring the buildings it was decided not to attempt to reproduce the baroque ornament, but to return the churches to an approximation of their medieval appearance.

15. See, for example, Robert Branner, *St. Louis and the Court Style in Gothic Architecture* (London: Zwemmer, 1965), pp. 112-37.

16. The absence of evidence for significant royal patronage is especially striking in view of the hundreds of documents that survive concerning the king's two Cistercian abbeys, Realvalle and Vittoria. It is likely that what we have here is primarily an example of court patronage, similar to that of the foundation of the church and hospital S. Eligio in 1270 by three of Charles' knights for the soldiers wounded in his battles.

17. The problems of women's monastic architecture remain largely unstudied. A disproportionately large number of convents have been destroyed. It is evident, however, that women's communities tended to be small and that their churches were often simple, even primitive, structures.

18. See Ronald G. Musto, "Queen Sancia of Naples (1286-1345) and the Spiritual Franciscans," in *Women in the Medieval World,* ed. by Julius Kirshner and Suzanne F. Wemple (Oxford and New York: Basil Blackwell, 1985), pp. 179-214.

19. A recent study with a full bibliography can be found in Julian Gardner, "A Princess among Prelates: a Fourteenth-Century Neapolitan Tomb and Some Northern Relations," *Römisches Jahrbuch für Kunstgeschichte* 23 (1988): 30-60; see also in general Stanislao Fraschetti, "I Sarcofagi dei reali angioini in Santa Chiara di Napoli," *L'Arte* 1 (1898): 385-438.

20. See James Beck, "Donatello and the Brancacci Tomb in Naples," in *Florilegium Columbianum: Essays in Honor of Paul Oskar Kristeller* (New York: Italica Press, 1987), pp. 125-45.

21. See on this subject in general Jerry H. Bentley, *Politics and Culture in Renaissance Naples* (Princeton: Princeton University Press, 1987), pp. 48 ff.

22. See in general Giulio Pane, "Pietro di Toledo, Vicerè Urbanista," *Napoli nobilissima* 14 (1975): 81-95, 161-82.

9. PALAZZO REALE AND THE HARBOR. Drawing by Lieven Cruyl, 1673.
Palace (L), Darsena and Arsenal (R), Jupiter Terminus and Elevated Street (C).

AUTHOR'S PREFACE

The number of marvelous things in this city and kingdom of Naples is so vast that it dismays foreigners to remember so much of what they see and hear told of them. Therefore, both from distant countries and from those who come to nourish their curiosity in these parts, comes continuous demand for some book that might describe all the wonderful things below, or at least that the most notable, major ones receive notice and recognition.

So many repeated requests have been finally satisfied today by the present *Description of the Kingdom of Naples,* told primarily through the erudition of Cesare d'Engenio, then gathered together from various authors at different times and finally, after many printings, edited together and published, with other additions, by Ottavio Beltrano, by whom it was often edited for publication. Since this book has been out of stock for many years, because of continuous sales, I have reprinted it again to meet a welcome public demand.

I ought to advise the readers of some things that at first might seem to be errors, but they truly are not. At least they are not mine, nor are they the errors of those who have the task of making corrections. These had to be made in many places, and they were made. So, the book was cleansed of any errors that appeared obvious.

This edition adds the present King Charles II, our lord, God protect him, who has ultimately succeeded King Philip IV, his father of glorious memory. It also adds the present cardinal archbishop, Don Iñigo Caracciolo, our most vigilant pastor, who succeeds to the former Cardinal Ascanio Filomarino, and some others of the same type, to bring us up to date.

I thus accepted my task, which no one else wished to do, except for reprinting Beltrano's edition already mentioned. Therefore, to do this more accurately, I have chosen as my exemplar and original Beltrano's last printing, since that was printed not only once, as I mentioned, and to which were made not a few additions and subtractions. Therefore errors ought not to appear.

In making a catalog of monasteries, convents and other pious places of the city of Naples, with the number of monks and religious, both men and women, and which habit they wore, the precise number of their inhabitants was changed accordingly, in some cases diminished and in others increased. Clearly increased by a great number is the Spanish infantry, who protect this city, to which have also been joined again many companies of Burgundian cavalry, who were not here when Beltrano's edition was printed. This edition adds another fortress named the Torrione del Carmine sul Mare, with a garrison of 500 souls, Spanish infantry-men; while all the other companies of this said nation remain in their great new barracks, which is able to lodge an army on the delightful point of Pizzofalcone. It also adds the cavalry barracks in the Borgo of Chiaia.

To the monasteries and pious places this edition adds so many others, built in the modern style after the first printing of this book, among which two ought not to be left out. The first is the monastery of Santissima Concezione of the Eremite monks on Monte S. Elmo, under the care of the Theatine Fathers. Near there they have taken another place for themselves, besides the six that they have in the city. The other is the hospital of SS. Pietro and Gennaro in the Borgo dei Virgini, in which, through the pious providence of the excellent lord Don Pedro of Aragon, most vigilant viceroy, are gathered nearly a thousand poor men and women, who used to go through the city begging. Others are the great monastery of the nuns named S. Maria della Providence alla Montagnola, not yet finished completely; that of the Order of Divine Love also of nuns, already completed in the middle of the city; and so many other monasteries, convents, conservatories, churches, chapels and pious places newly erected or better reconstructed, in so copious a number that they have almost redoubled, as is seen on page 50 and following.

Among the new and beautiful chapels mention was not made of that most sumptuous one called the Treasury inside the Duomo, built as its own chapel by the most faithful city, also opened only after Beltrano's printing. Placed there are the most precious relics of the head and blood of the glorious S. Gennaro and of all the other holy protectors of this city and kingdom.

While I find myself in the Duomo (pls. 16-17), before leaving I ought to advise foreigners that, when they go to see it, they remember to observe the most beautiful inscription recently placed in the ancient Chapel of the Santissimo, on the right of the main altar belonging to the Galeota family, where the holy body of S. Attanagio, bishop of Naples, is. For those who are not able to come here, I wish to show it to the eye, registering it here below, so that they have some notice of the most worthy works of the lord regent Giacomo Galeota, chief hereditary minister of the civil administration to his master in this kingdom, and the most clear light and ornament of this city. The inscriptions are three, the first of which has been there since the end of 1414 and which follows here:

> Hic iacet corpus Magnifici, & strenui Viri
> Rubini Galeotæ Regni Sicilæ Marescalli.
> Anno Domini MCCCCXIV die VIII mensis Maii
> VIII Inditionis.

The other two, placed recently, are the following:

D.O.M.
Quisquis ades,
Aram Eucharistico Deo dicatam.
Sacris inauguratam cæremoniis,
D. Athanasii Neapol. Episc. cinere augustam.
Venerare. Veneratus abis? mane,
Et eandem, quod lautè ornatam,
Quòd antiquissimo, liberoque iure renouato,
In Familiæ ornamentum conductam vides,
Iacobum Capycium Galeotam Sancti Angeli Ducem,
Iacobææ militie Equitem, & Regentem à latere,
Fratrisque Filium, Ducem Reginæ, D. Fabium,
Ordinis Calatrauæ Equitem,
Aræ, & Sacelli totius Reparatores, Possessoresque:
Honestis laudibus cumula: mox, si lubet, abi.
Anno reparatæ salutis humanæ MDCLXVIII.

D.O.M.
Fabius Capycius Galeota
Auorum Nobilitate clarus,
Clarissimus sua:
Quippe in forensibus causis
Iudex, Regius Consiliarius, Advocatus pro Fisco, Regiæ
Cameræ Præsidens,
Madritis primùm,
Mòx Neapoli summi à latere Consiliarii Regens
In tanto honorum concursu
Illud vnum debuit fortunæ,
Quod hæc semper aduersa
Id effecit, vt nihil ipsi deberet.
Doctissimis literarum monumentis
Æternitati nomine commendato,
Quo Tempore
Ad Regium in Apulia Patrimonium reficiendum incumbit
Extrà Patriam, non extrà gloriam obijt
Anno ætatis suæ LXXIII.
Iacobus filius
Benemerentissimo Parente vsque ab Apulia elato;
Allectis vltrà cineribus Camilli fratris de Collaterali Consilio:
Fortissimi Viri,
Ad Capitanatæ Provinciæ legationem
Vita non laude functi;
Allecturus quoque Aloysii, item fratris, Hierosolymitani Equitis,
Nisi is apud Colibrem pro Rege decertans,

Multò maluisset cæsis hostibus Marte suo,
Quàm à cæsis lapidibus aliena pietate, excitatum tumulum.
Collata D. Fabii ex Camillo filii
Ergà tam caros cineres obseruantia
Anno à Virginis Partu MDCLXVIII.
Doloris, amorisque ergò monumentum.
P.

After detouring to discuss the chapels of the Duomo, I now return to the holy places and the churches of Naples. Their growth has been so well redoubled and increased that if I wished to mention them all, I would have to publish another book. But I ought not to neglect them by pointing out only those two sumptuous productions, namely that of Monte della Misericordia and the Monte dei Poveri Vergognosi (pl. 10). They have been recently raised with a noble structure, the work of the most wise design of Signor Francesco Antonio Picchiatti (1619-1694), royal engineer and architect in this kingdom. His name has become celebrated for the designs and models formed by him for the major part of these new edifices, holy as well as profane.

One of these is the new and graceful elevated street that leads from the Royal Palace to the likewise new and marvelous Darsena (pl. 9), which is not mentioned on page 8, where the Molo is treated. The other is the Arsenal for the galleys, which are now transferred to the Darsena together with the hospital for the sick to be newly constructed by the same Viceroy Don Pedro of Aragon, by whom all these truly admirable works are done for the benefit of this city and kingdom.

This may be read of by foreigners in the following inscription placed under the gigantic statue of Jove Terminus erected at the beginning of this elevated street in front of the Palazzo Reale. I have considered it necessary, for the glory of this most excellent viceroy and for the satisfaction of those that are not able to come to see it, to record it here:

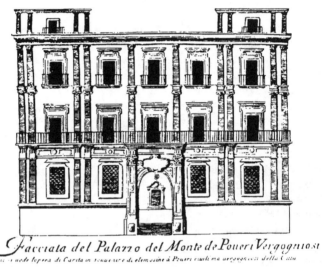

Facciata del Palazzo del Monte de Poueri Vergognosi

Questo vede lo pera di Carita in soua e suo di elemosine à Poueri ciuili ma vergognosi della Citta

10. PALAZZO DE POVERI VERGOGNOSI. LATE 17TH CENTURY.

Siste Viator:
Et Vetustum
Iouis terminalis bustum
Contemplare,
Quod cœnoso loco eductum,
Petrus Antonius Aragon
Segorbiæ, & Cardonæ Dux,
Huius Regni Prorex
Post aucta Iudicibus stipendia,
Pauperes hospitio coercitos,
Armamentarium instructum,
Prætoriana castra ædificata,
Baianos fontes repurgatos,
Nauibus stationem effossam,
Templa asciteria excitata,
Subiectamque viam pensili tramite
Leniter productam,
Fontibusque fœcundam,
Huc pro tantorum operum coronide
Transferri iussit.
I nunc, & perenne iuuandi
Stadium
A fabuloso Numine
In optimi principis Genium
Æquiùs, veriusque transferto.
Anno MDCLXX.

For the same reason that they were not in Beltrano's edition, I have not added here the infinite number of dowries that are dispensed today, larger than what one may read on pages 39-45, or the redoubled number of saint's bodies and remarkable relics that have appeared in Naples, other than those that appear on pages 45-49. The same was done in drawing from the rolls of the noble families, both of this most noble city of Naples and of each other province of the kingdom, of the families newly extinct, and of those moved within the *Catalog (of the Barons),* or even of those added who in the past few years have been appended or reintegrated. The same ought to be said of the titled nobility. Although these have only doubled, they are not included here, except for those that are enrolled in that last printing by Beltrano. There are so many more because the titled nobility do not stop multiplying continually every day, on account of the continuous concessions that are made to them; of whom it would be fruitless to make additions day by day.

Dealing next with the *borghi* and *casali* of Naples: where it speaks of the Grotta delli Sportiglioni on page 25, a few years ago a church was built by the name of S. Maria del Pianto, above the grotto, to bury a great part of those who died of that terrible plague of 1656. Then, on page 28, be advised that the garden of Giunnazzi has passed into the dominion of the Tocco family; and that the delightful garden of the former marquis of Vico appears so empty and destroyed today that it seems surely to be and to have become much like its ancient name of Guasto (wasteland). But among the many other delightful gardens aside from this, the most beautiful and charming is recently constructed and succeeds it. It is truly worthy to be seen and admired both by citizens and foreigners. This enchanted garden that, through its similarity to the enchanted and fabulous garden of Armida, is so-called by its patron, the prince of Monte Miletto, Don Carlo di Tocco, knight of the *Toson* of Gold. He also enjoys living in a spacious palace in the middle, or center, of this location, a short distance from the church of Gesù e Maria in the borgo of that name.

At the outset of a discussion of the provinces of the kingdom it must be noted that I have used the last two listings of hearths (census) made by royal command and taken from books printed under royal patronage. In the first of these is the old listing entitled *Nuova Situatione de Pagamenti Fiscali,* made by order of the lord count of Oñate, viceroy, and printed in 1652. The other, recently printed in 1670, is entitled *Nuova Situatione de Pagamenti Fiscali from January 1, 1669,* made in the time of the present viceroy, Lord Don Pedro of Aragon.

Furthermore, several cities and regions, those that were royal or, as is said, of state demense, have been removed from royal taxation and have passed under the dominion of various barons and titled nobility. Among these are the casali of Aversa and S. Germano in Terra di Lavoro; Marsico Nuovo and La Sala of Principato Citra; Rossano, Policastro, and Seminara in Calabria; Ostuni and Squinzano in Terra d'Otranto, and perhaps still some others.

It ought to be added that in the province of Principato Citra the Royal Audiencia with its president resides in the city of Salerno and that of Basilicata resides in the city of Matera, recently added to this province. Also, that of Abruzzi Ultra – to be distinguished from Abruzzi Citra – resides in the city of Aquila. In addition, it ought to be known that the use of the halberdiers is already given up by all the presidents of the provinces, by having doubled the number of squadrons of soldiers that are called Campagnan. In all the audiencias today three royal judges with a prosecutor administer justice equally, along with those other officials who will be discussed in their places. It has also recently been initiated in every audiencia to add a fourth judge with the title of judge of the grand court of the viceroyalty of Naples and head of the rota (tribunal) in the audiencia.

I have considered it necessary to advise the reader this much, not leaving for last to provide information on what has not yet been written by any other author. Anyone's curiosity for whatever pertains to the kingdom will be satisfied totally by the volume – divided into several parts – of the *Intiera Historia e Descrittione del Regno di Napoli,* compiled and gathered by Lord Andrea Giuseppe Gittio, which he will publish after his Latin orations, or *Allegationi Historiche e Giuridische e le Italiane sue Relationi Historiche de varie cose curiosissime,* which are actually now at the printer's.

11. S. Chiara (99) to SS. Severino e Sossio (44). Detail from Baratta Plan. L to R: S. Maria Nova (88), S. Domenico (58), S. Pietro Martire (foreground 50).

DESCRIPTION OF NAPLES

The most noble and delightful Kingdom of Naples, which takes its name from the great city of Naples, also called the Kingdom of Sicily on this side of Punta del Faro, is surrounded by three seas, the Adriatic, the Ionian, and the Tyrrhenian, all around its outline, except for its border with the Ecclesiastical State. The boundaries begin at Terracina at the Uffente River, which empties into the Tyrrhenian Sea through part of the Mezzogiorno. They make their way through Gaeta, Naples, Salerno, Tropea and through the straits of the lighthouse of Messina of Sicily finally to the Cape of Spartivento, which is at the end of Calabria. They follow their way from the Ionian Sea toward the east, through Geraci, Stilo, Squillace, Catanzaro, Crotone, Rossano, Taranto, up to the Cape of Otranto, and from there take the route of the Adriatic into the northern parts up to the river Tronto, which empties into the Adriatic.

The kingdom has the shape of a peninsula; its boundaries within the land from the Tronto River along the course of the Uffente River mentioned above are more apparent in the west, all subject to the state of the Holy Church: the whole circuit is 1468 miles, its length is 450 miles, and the width is 140 miles, according to the best opinion.

In ancient times this region was divided into seven major provinces: Terra di Lavoro, the Contado di Molise, Basilicata, Capitanata, Abruzzi, Terra d'Otranto, and Calabria, which in our time are divided into twelve; and they are as follows. The first province is Terra di Lavoro, called Campania Felice in ancient times. The second is

1

Principato Citra, formerly called the Picentini with part of Lucania. The third is Principato Ultra, where Samnium and Irpino were. The fourth is Basilicata, anciently called Lucania, which is situated in the center, or the umbilical, of the kingdom. The fifth is Calabria Citra, called de'Brutii. The sixth is Calabria Ultra, a part of Magna Graecia. The seventh is Terra d'Otranto, formerly called Iapigia, Hidrunto, Messapia, and Salentina. The eighth is Terra di Bari, formerly called Puglia Peucetia. The ninth is Abruzzi Citra. The tenth is Abruzzi Ultra, which is beyond the Pescara River. These two provinces were generally counted by the ancients in Samnium, and more recently called Abrutium. The eleventh is the Contado di Molise, or of the Samnite people. The twelfth and last province of the kingdom is Capitanata, where the (Castle of) Daunia was, and the Iapigia (Peninsula) with Monte Gargano, now called Monte S. Angelo.

For its coat of arms or insignia the kingdom has a number of gold lilies on a field of blue, given to them by King Charles I of Anjou, when he came to take over the kingdom, and by handsome Manfred, retaining from him the same arms with a portcullis of four red bars.

Nor does the kingdom have other arms, although others have said that it has used the horse as arms, even though we do not want to say that the horse, the coat of arms of Naples, the head of the kingdom, could still be assigned to the whole kingdom. It is true that in front of the main church (Duomo, pl. 16) was seen a horse of bronze, which the *Chronicle of Naples* says was made by Virgil, which cured all the diseases of horses, and which was afterwards destroyed by the order of archbishop of Naples in 1322 to remove the cause of this superstition. But whether Virgil might have made it or whether he might have had such power, I leave the truth to others.

But that the horse was the true and ancient arms of Naples is verified by the silver coins made until the time when Naples was a republic, where on one side there is a cross with a circle and letters around it that say CIVITAS, and on the other side a horse with the inscription NEAPOLIS, which together say CIVITAS NEAPOLIS. This coin was shown to me years ago by Signor Colantonio Dentice from among the memorabilia of Signor Sebastiano, his father, then lent to Giulio Cesare Capaccio, who today retains it.

That the horse was the arms of Naples is confirmed, besides what has been said, because before becoming Christians the Neapolitans had Castor and Pollux for their titular gods and protectors; under their protection were the horses. Then later it happened that the king of Naples struck small copper coins, impressing the horse on each, which was called the "Cavallo" (or horse). Further, the *seggi* (district councils) of (Porta) Capuana and of Nido, which represent the nobility of Naples, have made, and make, the horse their arms (see pp. 132-33). Besides, it is not many years ago that in making the foundations to reinforce the walls of the cortile of the palace of the Vicaria that a marble horse was found.

That the horse was the arms of Naples is clearly seen, because the Emperor Conrad, after having subjected the city of Naples (in 1253), went toward the Metropolitan Church (S. Restituta) and, seeing the above-mentioned horse of bronze, made them put the bridle and the following verses on it:

Hactenus effaenis, domini nunc paret habenis
Rex domat hunc equum. Parthenopensis equus.

If this figure of the horse did not represent the city, then the bridle and the motto that the emperor, mentioned above, made them put on it did not signify his intention, which was to say that not the horse but the city, which had refused to obey, had put on the bridle and been broken.

In this region, among the cities, lands and castles, there are 1981, of which part there are none of demense, and which the king has conceded in fief to the barons of the kingdom in reward for their merits. These nobles derive their ultimate origins from different nations, most of them as soldiers under different kings of the kingdom who came here to make a home. These lords of vassals total one thousand, namely 67 princes, 107 dukes, 148 marquises, 67 counts; and the remaining barons, all obligated to the defense of the kingdom.

The people are a bold and valorous nation, both on land and on sea, and in all the most suitable sciences and arts most qualified, and of the greatest excellence, but more than in all other faculties inclined to the law.

It is usual for the king to concede to some titled people and barons one or more "reserved rooms," that is, to make some of their lands frank and free from the duty of billeting, conceding the place free for their lodging and for that of their families; and these places thus frank and free from the duty of billeting are called "reserved rooms," which are signified with this sign: +.

*

The ancient and true city of Naples, capital of the kingdom, which takes its name from it, sits in the middle of Italy in the region or province that was called the Campania Felice by ancient writers, and today Terra di Lavoro, from the Leborini Fields that are here. It is laid out in the shape of a beautiful theater, which beautiful and pleasant hills enclose from the Tramontana (north wind). In the middle of it is an inlet of the beautiful and calm sea, which gracefully forms a gulf; on the west Monte S. Erasmo overhangs it, and to the east are the green and flowered fields. Lengthwise they reach up to the Acerrani plains, and in width they stretch up to Monte di Somma. In the area of the marina the city is a plain, and clearly it appears that a great part of it has been stolen by the sea.

In ancient times it was called Parthenope, after Parthenope its founder, not the Siren, as some have fabulated, but the very wise and generous daughter of Eumelo, king of Fera, city of Thessaly, who brought the first colony there. It was rebuilt afterwards by the Cumaeans and the Chalcedonians, who (according to Strabo) left the island of Euboea, now called Negropont, and came and built the city of Cumae. Then they left and, considering the beauty of the place of Parthenope, they rebuilt it, calling it Naples, which in the Greek language means "New City."

According to all the writers, the city was extremely ancient and was already famous before the Roman Empire, flourishing among the most famous Greek cities in Italy, according to the philosopher Pithagoras, in such a way that when the Roman Empire was in flower and was subjugating Campania, Naples was welcomed among the number of free cities in the Roman Confederation (328 BC). Afterwards as the affairs of the republic were in a poor way because of the Carthaginian Wars, not only did it remain constantly in friendship with the Romans, as Livy (*History of Rome* 22.32) wrote; but also, in an act of generosity, it commanded forty weighty platters of gold to be presented to the Roman Senate – for which great thanks were offered to the Neapolitans – and they (the Romans) retained the one of smallest weight as a sign of their gratitude.

Because of its continued faithfulness Naples was always honored and considered among the free cities, and a confederate of Italy in the time of the consuls as well as in the time of the emperors. But since it missed the power of the Roman Empire, it was subjugated by the Goths and then recovered by Belisarius, captain of Emperor Justinian (as Procopius wrote). But once the Lombards had occupied Italy at the request of Narses, they occupied the major part of the provinces that today are called the Kingdom of Naples, parts held by the Greeks, such as Naples. These were governed by John Campsino (John I Lemigio, 611-616), the Constantinopolitan, the duke of that province, who after occupying the exarchate, made

5

himself king. But Eleuterius, the new exarch (616-619), came against him in 619 and killed him.

Naples remained under the dukes, although often harassed by the Saracens, who had come into the kingdom from Africa and had taken all the way from Gaeta to Reggio Calabria, which they held for the space of thirty years up to the time of Pope John X. With the help of Alberico, marquis of Tuscany, he chased them from the borders of Rome, and following them finally to the Garigliano, had a great battle with them (in 915) and conquered them, in a way that left the Saracens reduced to activities at Monte Gargano, in which they fortified themselves, as Biondo, Platina (Bartolomeo de'Sacchi, 1421-1481), Sabellico and Colennuccio write.

Afterwards they remained troubled by the Greeks and by the Saracens until the arrival of the Normans, by whom these were defeated and conquered, after whom the kingdom passed to the house of Swabia through the only heir, Empress Constance. When Charles of Anjou conquered and killed Manfred (1266), and then Conradin (in 1268), it came under the French. After 180 years, the kingdom came to the Aragonese (1442) and then to the Spanish (1503).

THE CITY OF NAPLES

Naples has always been as well attended by the agreeableness of its site, as by the studies and fine arts that flourished in it, as has been made so clear by many writers who lived there to devote themselves to the study of letters; and by Virgil particularly, who lived in Naples a long time, and who there composed many works. Dying in Brindisi, he wished that his body would be buried in Naples, as is stated on his tomb; and today it is adorned by the Academy where all the sciences flourish. The rich and regal courts of princes, dukes, marquises, counts and other lords, and the beautiful and numerous breeds of strong and noble steeds celebrated by all – which the majority of the barons keeps almost entirely for themselves – give much ornament to the city.

In Naples one sees a flourishing and brilliant nobility, no less ancient than famous through the dominion of vassals, titles, offices, and dignities from every part not only of Italy but of the world. It is divided into two orders, one of these enjoys the government of the city through their *seggi* (district councils), the other does not either enjoy these *seggi* or involve themselves in the city's public affairs. The resident nobility live here in splendor, in every act of chivalry, watching the youths and bigger boys every day at the riding school where the knights from different parts of the world come together to learn riding skills and to manage horses with great mastery. These excellent ones then succeed in peace and in war.

It has its population, numerous and civilized of choice people, who live the equal to any nobility in splendor. It has the richest merchants and artisans in great supply, who come here from everywhere. Its wide and spacious streets are adorned by the most noble and magnificent palaces and temples, with fountains of the clearest and freshest water, which bring great ornament and dignity to the city.

Not to be left out are the beautiful and delightful gardens that are inside the city, ornamented by various architecture, excellently composed for the recreation and relaxation of its inhabitants: in truth, a marvellous thing. For without leaving the city, one can enjoy a continuous greenness and springtime, the same in winter as in summer, besides the other things that are outside the city, of which mention will be made in the appropriate place.

Returning to Naples, that most famous city: it is aggrandized by the most beautiful structures, and most marvelously ornamented with new walls, towers, castles, and bulwarks, which have rendered it little less than impregnable. Now we will speak of the port called the

Molo (pl. 9) by the Neapolitans where numberless galleys, galleons, ships, and other vessels great and small are frequently seen. The port was built by King Charles II in 1303. It was afterward enlarged at great expense by King Alfonso I of Aragon.

Near the port is the great Castel Nuovo (pl. 6) of Charles I, both expanded and adorned by the above-mentioned Alfonso, and by el Gran Capitán brought to the form in which it is seen today, situated on the shores of the sea, built above the water that flows below it and on every side in order that it could not be damaged by sappers, which are the most important reason for every ruin. Inside appears a dwelling that exactly resembles a city. Here previously was the monastery or convent of S. Maria della Nova of the Observantine Friars of St. Francis and called the Torre Maestta. It was then moved by the said Charles to where it is seen today, giving in exchange this place where the said castle first stood. It was also fortified to such a degree by the Emperor Charles V that today it is considered one of the strongest fortresses in Italy.

Foreigners are astounded by so many war machines, so much artillery and such a great amount of balls of iron, helmets of gold and silver, shields, lances, swords and all the rest of the apparatus of war, tapestries of silk, and brocade of gold, magnificent sculpture, statues and paintings, and the rest of all their treasures of a pleasantness and beauty little less than regal. King Charles also built a tower in the sea to watch and defend the moats of the castle, inside of which ran the harbor. In ancient times it was called S. Vincenzo (pl. 5), because within it stood a small church dedicated to that holy martyr, as ancient tradition holds.

Quite nearby is the Royal Arsenal (pl. 9), where the galleys and other ships are made, where more than a hundred artisans of all the arts that pertain to the afore-mentioned manufacture continually work. A little further is the Castel dell'Ovo (pl. 14) and that of S. Erasmo, which we will discuss in their appropriate places.

Predating these is the Castel Capuana (pl. 7), so named for the gate that leads to Capua (pl. 18), which was nearby, built by the previously mentioned King Charles I, before having begun the above-mentioned Castel Nuovo, although some are accustomed to say it was the work of the Normans. Later this castle was converted by the Viceroy Don Pedro of Toledo into a wide and most marvellous court to accommodate the merchants, as it is seen today divided into four parts, namely civil and criminal vicaria, the council, and the summaria, besides the other courts of the mint and of the bailiff.

The city is also very celebrated for so many beautiful and sumptuous churches of priests, monks, friars, nuns, and homes for women, children, and the aged, with their beautiful and spacious monasteries and convents, which will be discussed in their appropriate places.

Naples renders itself no less remarkable and beautiful than marvelous also for the great remains of the ancient buildings, of so many statues, columns, inscriptions, which are seen as much in the palaces of the lords as scattered throughout the city. Among others are the ruins of the Temple of Castor and Pollux (II:3, V:17, pl. 12). This temple was built to Castor and Pollux before the coming of our Lord Jesus Christ by Tiberius Julius Tarsus, a freedman of Augustus and procurator of the fleet, which the emperor kept on these shores. Today there can be seen the front of the portico of this temple, with six fronting columns of marble, and above them a great Corinthian architectural cornice, amazing for its size and skill, with the most beautiful capitals and baskets, from which hang flowers and folded acanthus leaves. In the embellishment of the marble architrave supported by these columns is carved an inscription to the aforementioned Tiberius and many gods. When this city was made Christian and Catholic, thanks to the majesty of God, the temple was appropriately dedicated to the truly heavenly lights, the apostles Saints Peter and Paul, as the inscription of the new church (S. Paolo Maggiore) makes note.

Already, in a calculation made in 1614, the number of souls was found to exceed 167,972. But today it is found to have grown so much more, and the number of hearths to sixty thousand, so that to give five to a hearth more or less, and no more, there are 500,000 people. Add to them the monasteries and ecclesiastics and the foreigners, and those who visit the city at every hour, besides those who come and go and do not make an ordinary residence, who increase in great numbers, so that every day in the city and in the borghi they eat more than six thousand *tomoli* (27.5-55.5 liters) of grain. This does not include those who make bread at home, which is a large part, or the different clerics, religious, or nuns who are numerous.

INSTITUTIONS IN THE CITY OF NAPLES

Location	Population
FORTRESSES	
Castel Nuovo	250
Castel dell'Ovo	128
Castel S. Elmo	250
Torre di S. Vincenzo	60
Spanish Infantry	1500
Galleys	4500
PRISONS	
Vicaria	1000
Admiralty	80
The Archbishopric	30
The Nuncio	30
Silk Guild	70
Wool Guild	40
Justiciar	40
Moccia, or Portolan	25
Spanish	100
Bailiff	50
Mint	50

12. S. Paolo Maggiore (147) to the Duomo (with Cupola). From Baratta Plan. L to R: S. Lorenzo Maggiore (80), Girolomini (156), S. Maria Donnaregina (102).

THE BORGHI AND CONTADO
OF THE CITY OF NAPLES

Now that we have dealt with the site and origin of the city of Naples as briefly as one might, we will discuss the environs and districts, for they are no less interesting and delightful. Therefore I note that although this very noble city does not have a great circuit, no more than five and one-half miles, it has, nevertheless, seven borghi that seem so many great towns, as we will talk of directly. No one city, however, surpasses its delights, the numbers of its inhabitants, its good and handsome horses, since it exceeds all the others by far. But above every other thing, its site is beyond all the well-located major cities in whatever part of the world, even though some might opine that the city of Constantinople, positioned on the Aegean Sea, exceeds it.

The greater part of the city is washed by the sea and contains seven major borghi, in which are seen the most beautiful palaces with pretty and charming gardens so full of all kinds of fruits and herbs throughout the year, with fountains of lively and artful water. They are also completely full of inhabitants, both lords and barons, as well as every sort of people, so that each borgo (suburb outside the city walls) seems a populous and very ornate city. And the majority of them would see themselves far larger if building in them had not been prohibited.

Almost all these borghi have taken the name of the churches that are in them. The first, beginning with the one that the sea washes, is called S. Maria di Loretto, the second S. Antonio, the third S. Maria dei Vergini, the fourth is S. Maria della Stella, the fifth is Gesù e Maria, the sixth is S. Maria del Monte, the seventh, which is the most delightful, on the shore of S. Leonardo, which is called Chiaia in the uneducated dialect because of the shore bathed by the sea.

The countrysides of these borghi are wide and flat, partly covered with shrubs and partly rural, and all very fertile. The hills are all cultivated, delightful, and charming.

Posillipo and Nisida

But leaving the borghi, we now come to the *contado* (countryside) and the places adjoining the city. What in the world more pleasing could be desired than the happy coast of Posillipo? Hills so well cared for and of such beauty that one could not find better in the whole world, for being a pleasant place, adorned with superb palaces washed by the sea, full of delights that mitigate every sorrow that afflicts the heart.

For this reason this place of quiet and repose was the habitation of those ancient Romans who were free from the burdens of every care, who retreated there from the serious business of the Senate and of other occupations, of which the ancient buildings, which became rocks in the sea and give shelter to the shellfish and sea urchins, make full testimony. Here are some of the most beautiful palaces, with charming and delightful gardens, that are seen along the whole coast, built by the Neapolitans for comfort and the pleasures of summer and for the good and beneficial climate of the air.

Pliny wrote in chapter fifty-one of book nine (of his *Natural Histories)* that at Posillipo was a villa not far from Naples, at which were the fisheries of Caesar in which Vedius Pollio threw a fish that died after sixty years. In Dio Cassius we read that as this Pollio was nearing death he left a great part of his inheritance to Augustus, which included Posillipo, a villa situated between Naples and Pozzuoli.

This mountain called Posillipo was dug and bored out in three places: first by Lucullus in the Via del Mare, to the center of Posillipo, connected with Nisida to this day;

the second by Cocceius from the land side to make a level way to go to Pozzuoli, as we will discuss in the appropriate place; the third by the Emperor Nero, which is still visible today, to make a passage for the aqueduct that came from Serino and goes toward Pozzuoli.

With its two peaks this mountain encircles most of the city, taking on different names from pass to pass, as we will discuss. It spreads its arm toward Mezzodi, through which it extends to embrace its beautiful Nisida, a delightful islet greatly acclaimed by Pontano (Giovanni, 1426-1503) and Sannazaro (Jacopo, 1458-1530), who portray it in the person of a nymph who was changed into a mountain. Many other authors also mention it.

In the area between Nisida and Posillipo are seen certain places that have come to be called the Gaiola from the similarity they have with jail cells. Similarly, below this hill there is a plain of villas and gardens full of many delights, and at the top of the hill was the Temple of Fortuna at the time of the pagan empire. Now it is called S. Maria a Fortuna.

Here also – besides the parish church of S. Strato – there are other churches and monasteries of religious orders, such as the Fathers of S. Girolamo, who were founded by B. Pietro di Pisa; the Carmelites in S. Maria del Paradiso, first called a Pergola; the Dominicans in S. Brigida; the Eremites of the Congregation of Carbonara in S. Maria della Consolatione, with the church of S. Maria del Faro and the church of S. Basilio. These do such honor to the entire mountain of Posillipo that those from Naples make visits most solemnly all year long.

Mergellina and the Grotto

From the other side toward the east is the beautiful and lovely Mergellina (so called for the charming underwater world of fish) celebrated by Sannazaro in his *Fisherman Eclogues,* for he owned it through the generosity and gift made to him by King Federico. Here he composed his most beautiful and learned works; he likewise built around 1510 a beautiful monastery with a church in honor of the glorious Virgin under the title of S. Maria del Parto, and here are also the friars named Servants of the Blessed Virgin, where he lies in a sepulcher of whitest marble.

This pleasant place of Mergellina is so lively and delightful that, in the immeasurable heat of summer, it alone is a continuous delight to noble men and women, since the inlet of its most graceful sea is so tranquil that the rocks, the vegetation, the buildings, and the sky itself gleam in these crystalline waves. And it is appropriate that the winds joined together there in all their fury should subside, and that the waves also stirred up by the rage of Neptune rest themselves there together in continuous peace.

From this side of the mountain is seen the most devout church and monastery dedicated to the Mother of God, served by the Canons Regular of the Lateran, which is situated near the grotto, in the entrance to it. It is called S. Maria di Piedigrotta and was built through a miracle of this same Blessed Virgin who, on the night before September 8, 1353 appeared to a Neapolitan devoted to her, to a nun of the royal blood called Maria di Durazzo, and to a hermit called B. Pietro, who were all in different places. In the same hour they were exhorted to build the church in her honor; and in memory of the vision the celebration of her feast on September 8 was established.

In this church there are many marble tombs of knights and valorous captains with their epitaphs. Inside the sacristy of this church there are four tombs of four knights of the most illustrious house of Cardona. These tombs are made of wood covered with black velvet and gold brocade.

Since we are discussing the venerable church dedicated to the glorious Virgin Mary, Mother of God, it

15

is convenient for me to mention the marvelous work of the Grotto (which forms the road from Naples to Pozzuoli), from which the aforementioned holy image takes its name, and also the tomb of Virgil, which is described by so many famous and illustrious authors, and which I will describe later.

Lucius Lucullus, a Roman gentleman, cut out the mountain of Posillipo towards Naples with the greatest expense in order to make a channel of the sea come in. For this reason Pompey the Great called him Xerxes Togato (Xerxes in a Toga, Vellerius Patercerius II.33.4). On this authority many have been caught in an error, believing that Lucullus had made the grotto of which we speak. But it was not so, because the grotto that he had dug was on the shores of the sea at the Cape of Posillipo, which is now joined with Nisida. He made this – so wrote Falco (Benedetto di, late 15th-early 16th century) – to go more conveniently and with a shorter sail to the baths. Because it would be a long voyage leaving from Castello Lucullano, his home (now called dell'Ovo) and circling Nisida, being all continuous and solid land. Because the length of time ruins all buildings, the grotto was ruined, so Nisida is divided from the mountains and remains an islet, as we have already seen. In this part of the sea the ruins of the ancient grotto are visible up to the present. Today this place is called the Gaiola by the sailors. And now the royal court has built the Casa del Purgatorio for the people infected by the plague.

Plutarch speaks of this grotto in the life of Lucullus (39.3), saying that he dug out the mountain of Posillipo near Naples in a long and wide arch, in order that he might be able to go sailing under the carved-out vault to Bagnoli. Marcus Varro (Rust. III.17.9) speaks of the same Lucullus and of his works, but he doesn't discuss the Grotto from the land, as some have believed, but of the same near the sea. Strabo (V.4.5), who was from Augustus' time, discussing the grotto that went underground from Averno to Cumae, reports that Cocceius had made this cave, and another likewise from Pozzuoli to Naples. Further along, wishing to give the story of this grotto, he says that it is carved in the mountain that is between Pozzuoli and Naples, made like the one in Cumae, which he says was large enough to allow two carts to pass easily, and that for quite a lot of its length light penetrated inside through the windows that were cut in many places in the upper part.

Therefore it becomes clear that the grotto we are speaking of on the land side was the work of Cocceius. But Giovanni Villani (1280?-1348) in the *Chronicle of Naples* reports that this grotto was the work of Virgil. Stirred up by this, the foolish common herd believes – because of the incredible things that are discussed in that book about him – that Virgil made such excellent works through the magical arts. According to the authority of Francesco Petrarch, he is thoroughly useless. Petrarch found himself in the company of King Robert; and passing through the already mentioned grotto, Robert asked him if it were true that Virgil had carved out this mountain through a work of magic. Petrarch answered that he did not remember that he had ever read that Virgil had been a magician, and with the calmest face he answered that what appeared all around was the remains of iron, not of a magician.

Lorenzo Scradero, in his book entitled the *Monumenta Italia,* said that this grotto was made in fifteen days on the order of Cocceius by 100,000 men. Pietro Razana Panormitano affirms that this is the work of Cocceius. Paolo Giovio (1483-1552) in his life of Cardinal Pompeo Colonna agrees. Leandro Alberti (1479-1553), in his *Description of Italy,* discusses it at great length and concludes the same. Francesco Lombardo in his work on the *Miracles of Pozzuoli* affirms the same. But now, who this Cocceius was, and in what time, none of these authors say. But I do not know whether he was M. (L.)

Cocceius Auctus of the Emperor Nerva, who was an excellent architect, who gained the greatest praise for bringing water to Rome, or if it was another Cocceius. But it is enough to say that that one who did this very worthy work was a famous and rich man.

At present this grotto appears luminous, spacious and pleasing, a mile long and so wide that it can comfortably contain two carriages. It was widened by King Alfonso I of Aragon. Then its windows were enlarged and the floor was paved by Don Pedro of Toledo, viceroy of the kingdom for the Emperor Charles V.

Near the entrance to this grotto Virgil, whose body was brought from Brindisi, was buried in a little square temple made of brick, placed under a piece of marble with his epitaph.

The following is such a most worthy and marvelous thing. A great laurel tree, which was born naturally many years ago at the summit of the cupola of this temple, was broken by a poplar tree that fell over on it on account of the wind in the year 1615. Nevertheless, out of its old roots another sprouted. Therefore it seems that Mother Nature had had it born in the beginning, just as later, to give a sign that there lay the ashes of this great poet, wonder of the world. In addition to this the whole temple appears covered with myrtle and ivy, which create a most beautiful sight. It brings a wonder to each one who looks at this place, seeing that nature might have produced it as much to show its greatness as to decorate the roof for such a great man.

To facilitate the ascent needed to see the place of the tomb one should enter the cloister of the monastery of S. Maria di Piedigrotta, near there, or go along the road that goes to Posillipo, which one cannot go to from the other place.

Fuorigrotta

After coming outside this grotto, one sees an ancient chapel with the name S. Maria dell'Hidriae.

One then discovers the villa outside the Grotto, as well as a part of Naples brought together in the S. Spirito quarter that – not many years ago – had the worst air, since the sun was blocked for a part of the day by Monte di Posillipo. Such places, because of this effect, are marshy, and the vapors are not so quickly dispersed. But in these most recent days, because of greater expenditures and more careful cultivation, the inhabitants have improved greatly the mildness of the atmosphere, but one still cannot live satisfactorily here. All the surrounding area is very fertile, full of fruit, planted with shrubs, which in many areas produce excellent wines. Nevertheless, because of a soil that is too damp, the greatest part of them do not manage to become alcoholic.

The Church of S. Martino and the Castel S. Elmo

Returning to this mountain, I should mention to you that, in spreading out farther toward the east, it takes on other names. This is because on the height of the hills is situated the church of S. Martino, built by Charles, the illustrious son of King Robert, in 1325 and given to the Carthusian Fathers with a most beautiful monastery. Near this church is seen the very strong Castel S. Ermo (Elmo), named because of an ancient church that was dedicated there to S. Erasmo. Therefore sometimes the mountain became called S. Martino because of the church, and at other times S. Ermo because of the castle, which was built by Charles II in order to defend Naples on every side. It was not considered much by his successors.

Afterwards it was greatly fortified by Charles V who had demolished and devastated many old streets that surrounded it. He almost rebuilt it completely and turned it into a very strong fortress, as is noted in a marble inscription that is seen above its door.

At the top of this mountain there is a place called Olympus, where in ancient times they held the games in honor of Olympic Jove. Now it is a possession of the monks of S. Severino.

Further outside, at the base, is situated the noble church and monastery of the Ascensione, of the Celestine monks, built by Nicolò Alumno d'Alise, chancellor of the kingdom, as the inscription on his tomb notes.

Chiaia and the Church of S. Maria a Cappella

From the side that looks toward Posillipo is the most delightful slope of most temperate air, called Chiaia in the uneducated dialect. Because of that, when anyone wishes to recover from some indisposition, he tries to stay there for some time; and with its view of most charming gardens and with its delight, in a brief time he becomes almost resuscitated from death to life from the variety of flowers, fruit and boughs of the fragrant trees of cedar and orange, which flourish at all times, clothed with great majesty and artifice.

In truth this is the place that has the most famous coast in Europe. Besides that, the magnificent palaces with their ornamental gardens on this slope cause all the people who might live there longed-for peace, putting an end to the upheaval of human desires.

Near the slope on the shore of the sea, under the little mountain of Echia, one sees a temple or cave that was dedicated by the Neapolitans to Serapis, goddess of the Egyptians in the time of the pagans, under which name they honored the Sun in this place. After this city was made Catholic and Christian – thanks to God through the work of Saint Peter the Apostle – to its merit it was willing to honor and adore there the one Sun, Christ, with the temple built to the honor of the Most Holy Virgin, Mother of God, now called S. Maria a Capella, who is seen with her most holy son in her arms, and at present is served by the Canons Regular of the Congregation of the Holy Savior of Bologna.

Platamone, Today Called Chiatamone

Near here is a place that the ancients called Platamone, of which Galen wrote that it was of stones, among which the waves go spreading lightly. Up to our time the grottos in this place gushed forth the freshest waters, which people therefore frequented to cool off from the enormous heat of the summer, making sumptuous banquets there. Now, as one sees, it is gone into ruins because of the new building that encloses this mountain.

In this place it is believed that there may also have been hot baths. As Strabo wrote, there were baths in Naples no less healthful than those of Baia. Here is built a church (S. Maria degli Angeli a Pizzofalcone) served by the Theatine Fathers, and a little farther the church of the Concezione of the Ministers of the Infirm.

Echia, Castel dell'Ovo, Called in Ancient Times Castello Lucullano, and the City of Megara

Above the Platamone sits the most lovely little mountain, called Echia by Hercules, who dwelt there. Having overcome Caccus, the most powerful man in the Roman Campania, he placed this land in liberty and came to Naples, and there left a great memorial to himself, which Pontano mentions in the book, *Bello Neapolitano*. In this place in ancient times there were the fisheries of Lucullus, as Falco mentions, which therefore was called Lucullano, as Pontano, Cicero (Att. I. 18.6, 19.6, 20.3),

21

and others affirm. His palace was at the Cape of Echia, which on account of its age or earthquakes was separated from the mainland, and remaining isolated in the sea was made a fortress called Castello Lucullano, so named in the *Life of S. Severino, Abbot.* St. Gregory the pope also made mention of it in his register in several places.

It was also called Island and Castle of the Savior, as can be read in the office of S. Attanagio, bishop of Naples. Finally it was called Castel dell'Ovo. And although the site of this castle at present does not appear very spacious, nevertheless on account of the rocks that outline it, its ancient greatness is made clear and also from what Falco mentions, saying that in this place the ancient Greeks built the city of Megara, which Pliny (*Nat. Hist.* III.62) also mentions, saying that the city of Megara was between Posillipo and Naples.

This castle, first founded by Lucullus as a palace, was then established as a fortress and guardian of the city by the Norman king (Roger). Later destroyed, it was fortified by Don Juan di Zuñiga, viceroy (1579-1582), who had the stone bridge built from the land up to its gate.

Pizzofalcone

At the point of Echia opposite the castle is also called Pizzofalcone (pl. 5), which, according to Falco, means a high place. Therefore every high building is so called, after the highest flight of the falcon, in which place Andrea Carrafa della Spina built this magnificent place that is seen today and by the populace is called Pizzofalcone.

This place, commonly called Echia, in very recent years was completely overgrown, almost like a den of thieves. In our time it has become such that it might, in a certain way, be compared with the earthly paradise. This is as much because of the healthy and cheerful air, as because of the number of beautiful and devout churches and monasteries, and also because of its sumptuous palaces and the pleasant and cheerful gardens at all times full of fruit, and its population of great lords and officials.

Antignano, Nazareth, Conocchia, Prospetto, Camaldoli, S. Maria della Sanità, S. Maria della Vita, S. Severo

Returning again to the above-mentioned mountain, I note that after S. Elmo comes the hill of Antignano, so-called because it was opposite the lake, or Nymphaeum Antiniana, praised by some poets, or by the Emperor Antonius, as Tarcagnota says. This place is famous for its healthy air, and for its abundant and well-adorned villas, where Pontano had his. Above Antignano at the summit of the mountain is a place situated there called Il Salvatore, which because of the height and the beautiful view is called the Prospetto, a name that is not inappropriate, since from there one sees the whole Tyrrhenian Sea with all its shores that extend from east to west, with many islands. To the north one sees the fertile Terra di Lavoro, on the right bountiful Gaeta and on the left the great city of Naples.

Near there is the church of S. Maria di Nazaret, rebuilt by Giovanni Battista Crespi (1557-1633), a Neapolitan, which is situated in his beautiful possessions, which look like a well-protected fortress. He desired to bring back to this place the Camaldoli monks, as much for the service of God as for the benefit of the neighboring villas, around the year 1585 under the title of S. Maria Scalaceli. Although it may be a solitary place and far from the city of Naples, their exemplary life causes them to be visited every day not only by laypeople of every condition, but also by religious and prelates.

After Antignano comes Conocchia, where four ancient catacombs are seen, in which the bodies of dead Christians were buried, according to Panvino in his treatment of the catacombs. In our era these were converted into churches.

The first catacomb is that of the Reformed Dominican Friars, who with the alms of the Neapolitans have dedicated it to the Glorious Virgin, Mother of God, because of a very ancient figure of her found there painted on the wall, giving it the name of S. Maria della Sanità. Here up to today one sees the ancient sepulcher where the body of S. Gaudioso, bishop of Bithynia, was buried. There was engraved a beautiful epitaph of mosaic work, although it is partially broken. The second catacomb is of the Carmelite Friars, who similarly with alms have dedicated it to the mother of God under the title of S. Maria della Vita. The third is that great catacomb that is behind the church of S. Gennaro, where plague victims are usually brought. The fourth and last is that of the Franciscan Friars, which they dedicated to S. Severo because there the body of S. Severo, bishop of Naples, is buried.

Capodimonte, Montagnola, S. Maria degli Angeli and S. Antonio

Returning to our discussion, after Conocchia follows Capodimonte, where the most beautiful possessions and gardens of the Neapolitans are. Near Capodimonte, comes Montagnola where the church of S. Maria degli Angeli of the Zoccolanti Friars is located. From there a little farther one sees the church of S. Antonio Abbate, in which there is a beautiful garden with a palace where there is also a hospital for those who suffer from *male di fuoco* (leprosy).

Cupa di S. Antonio

There is a street that in ancient times was called the Cupa di S. Antonio, which before was very difficult and broken and almost a shelter for thieves. After, by order of Don Pedro Girón, viceroy of the kingdom at the time (1616-1620), it was relaid, and the name was changed. Girón ordered it no longer Cupa but Strada Cueva. The inscription in marble that is seen in this street makes note of all this.

S. Eusebio, Generally Called S. Eufemio, S. Maria delli Monti, Capo di Chino, S. Giuliano

From the other side of Montagnola in a somewhat low position is the ancient church dedicated to S. Eufemio, one of the masters of the City of Naples. The Franciscan Capuchin Friars are there. Not far from this place of the Capuchin Friars one finds another devout church dedicated to the Mother of God, which is called S. Maria delli Monti, since it is situated between the mountains. It was built by Don Carlo Carrafa; here there is a devout congregation of priests. In this place near the summit of Chino, where the first slope of the mountain begins, is the ancient church of S. Giuliano.

Lautrecco, Grotta delli Sportiglioni

Toward the middle of the next slope is the pleasant and delightful mountain of Lautrecco, where there are very beautiful vineyards and gardens with comfortable houses of different citizens. This place took the name of Monsieur Lautrec (Odet de Foix), captain general of the French army, who, while he held the city of Naples under siege for four months (in 1528), was camped there with his whole army, particularly under this mountain. Here there is a great cave that is still visible today, called the Grotta delli Sportiglioni, although in part made by the bandits who operate there.

13. Poggio Reale and District. From Baratta Plan.
The gardens and fountains of Lautrecco and Monte Oliveto.

Poggio Reale, Dogliolo

On the side that looks back at that mountain of Lautrecco, there are the fountains of the charming and delightful Poggio Reale (pl. 13), which are many and very full of water. Although the place is not public, but belongs to the king of Naples; nonetheless, with the permission of his guards, it is enjoyed happily and easily by everyone. But behind it and in public there is the aqueduct with many fountains made for the use of everyone, as we will discuss. This place, then, is a mile from the city of Naples on the Via dell'Acerra, called the Dogliolo further on, very celebrated by poets and most of all by Pontano.

Alfonso, the son of King Ferrante I (1458-1494), there built the most beautiful buildings with large rooms in which he had painted the conspiracy and war of the barons of the kingdom against the same king (1459-1465) with other worthy successes that are seen up to our day. It has delightful gardens, fountains, and incredible plays of water, decorated with marble and statues. Giorgio Vasari (1511-1574) writes in the second part of the *Lives of the Most Excellent Painters, Sculptors and Architects* that Giuliano da Maiano (1432-1490), famous sculptor and architect, built Poggio Reale in Naples at the insistence of King Alfonso II, at that time duke of Calabria (1448-1494). The architecture of this magnificent palace he had entirely painted by Pietro del Donzello and by Polito, his brother. There, at times, past kings used to go for their amusement in the summertime to enjoy that delight and those clear and fresh waters that are there to refresh their souls, just as in a calm port secure from the fortunes of the sea.

Besides the many fountains that are inside the palace and garden, there are also some on the public streets – very pleasant and delightful, decorated with marble and sea shells that scatter water in abundance and great supply. These were made for the leisure and recreation

of the citizens by Don Juan Alfonso Pimentel at the time
he was viceroy of the kingdom (1603-1610), as is seen in
an inscription on one of the fountains.

The Garden and Monastery of
Monteoliveto

Opposite Poggio Reale is a beautiful garden with charming
and delightful fountains and playing waters, often visited
in the summer, which belongs to the Olivetan Fathers.

The Garden of Giunnazzi

Quite near is seen another garden no less beautiful and
delightful, called the Giunnazzello, since it belongs to the
Giunnazzi family. In this garden is a great spring of
water that is very good to drink because of its lightness.

Canal of Poggio Reale

At the exit of this place is the canal called Poggio Reale.
Here under its vaults is painted the image of the Mother
of God, with the name of S. Maria dell'Orto.

The Water of Bufala

Walking a little distance from there, one arrives at
another place where there is another spring of fresh and
good water called the Acqua della Bufala. Here there is a
holy chapel dedicated to the Mother of God, under the
title of S. Maria di Constantinopoli del Ponte Picciolo.

Fountains of the
Garden of the Marquis di Vico

Most graceful are also the fountains of the garden of the Marquis di Vico, a place anciently called the Guasto. In addition are statues of marble, the fountains and aviaries with well arrayed plays of waters, which come suddenly from underground to bathe those standing around on every side, as so many enemies in a battle. One can see the water gush with incredible artifice from a trunk of a fruitful tree of white mulberry, which gives wonder to whoever looks at it.

The Guasto

There is also the district called the Guasto, "the ruin," from which the whole area has taken its name – a most delightful place with great and beautiful buildings with large rooms, fountains, fish ponds and other comforts.

S. Maria delle Fratte e alle Paludi

Passing that garden and the palace of the Marquis di Vico, on the left hand one sees the holy church dedicated to the great Mother of God, which because it was situated in the *paludi,* or marshes, of the city is called S. Maria delle Grazie alle Paludi. In this church, Alfonso I heard mass every day while he held Naples under siege.

The River Sebeto,
the Mills of the Marshes of the City

Walking not far from this church, one arrives at the pleasant and delightful Sebeto River, which Sannazaro called the Neapolitan Tiber in his *Arcadia*. It runs through its bed in various channels through the grassy fields around to the marshes of the city; and increasing in course from hand to hand, it gains greater force. After making some tortuous tracks and turnings, it gathers all together, passing softly under a beautiful bridge, and there it joins the sea two hundred feet from the city. The river is very famous, because authors, both ancient and modern, have recorded it. Then, this river brings the city two greatly useful things: the first is its turning around to the marshes, and the convenience it allows itself in replenishing itself often, and in irrigating the gardens. For this reason the lands of the marshes of Naples are so fertile that it is a great wonder; for at all times of the year they are most abundant with every kind of vegetation necessary for human life. The other usefulness is that eleven mills grind there with the convenience of the water.

Ponte di Guizzardo and Ponte della Maddalena

In ancient times the villas of Naples used this water to treat flax. Because near the bridge, called Guizzardo, 300 feet from the city, there grew the fusari (fungus) that caused malaria, King Charles II had them clear out to a place near the city. As it joins the sea the river, as it is called, passes under the great bridge called the Maddalena, after a small church that is there above this bridge dedicated to that saint. It was rebuilt in 1555 by order of Don Bernardino di Mendozza, at that time viceroy of the kingdom of Naples.

Pietra Bianca

To complete the districts of the city let us proceed to the shore that is at the foot of the fertile and delightful Vesuvius, where for the amenities of the site many have built pleasant buildings with very beautiful gardens. Among the others there is a beautiful villa, commonly called Squazzatorio di Pietra Bianca, with a beautiful palace and large rooms. Among all the other worthy things there is a grotto of marvelous artifice all of sea shells and made and composed with great skill. Its pavement is of various and beautiful vermiculite marbles, with such an abundance of playing waters, which is why it is called Squazzatorio.

It is truly a place that each one desires not only to enjoy but also just to see. Emperor Charles V did not disdain to lodge there before he entered Naples in 1535, when he returned from the enterprise in Tunisia, as we read in a marble inscription above the gate of this same place. Inside this Squazzatorio is also a fountain made of those seas shells, in which reclines a most beautiful nude Aretusa of white marble.

Monte Vesuvio

Above this villa rises the great Monte Vesuvio, most famous for the fertility of its shrubs and vines, which produce the best Greco grapes and a *Lacrima (Christi,* wine) very pleasant to the taste. This mountain has thrown up flames of fire, ash, and balls of sulfurous minerals from its summit many times, with burning stones, great ruin, and notable damage to the city and neighboring villas, as many different authors write. Among the places that it destroyed were Pompeii and Herculaneum, ancient cities. We – to our great sorrow – saw the strange madness that this mountain made in the eruption of 1631, which destroyed so many places. There an infinite number of souls died; an event that gave material to more than 150 writers to recount these fatal events.

From the great number of stones that this mountain has thrown out many times and because of these eruptions, besides having ruined the two cities, it also destroyed many streets and, among other things, the public way to Torre del Greco, which was later restored by Don Fernando Afan de Ribera, viceroy of the kingdom (1629-1631), as his inscription notes. Ruined in this last eruption, that street was partially rebuilt. Nevertheless, it still needs resurfacing. On the same slope there are many and different palaces and villas built by different people drawn there by the pleasantness of the place.

This is as sufficient as it has seemed to me to discuss borghi and ancient places around the circuit of the most pleasant district of the city of Naples.

CASALI OF NAPLES

The *casali* (hamlets) of Naples number thirty-seven. These form one body with the city, also enjoying its immunities, privileges, and prerogatives. The Neapolitan customs compiled by order of Charles II also have the force of law in these villages.

Now, of these villages many are large, and the number of their inhabitants are enrolled as citizens. They are located in four regions: nine of them are almost on the seashore, ten in the interior, ten on the mountain of Capo di Chino, and eight in the area of Monte di Posillipo. Here they are.

Torre del Greco,
the Villa of Alfonso II of Aragon

Torre del Greco, which is well within the territory of Naples, is otherwise not a village but a well fortified castle, inhabited by civilians. This castle is located near the bank of the sea on a high place and on the rocks that rise above the seashore at the foot of Mount Vesuvius.

It was the villa of Alfonso II, most pleasant for the view that it had towards Naples, Sorrento, the Isle of Capri and the Promontory of Miseno, along with the other maritime places. Below the villa at the shore there is a beautiful fountain of clear and fresh water where this king was frequently accustomed to amuse himself in the summer.

The others include: Torre dell'Annunciata, Resina, Portici, S. Sebastiano, S. Giorgio a Cremano, Porticello, Varra di Serino, and S. Giovanni a Teduccio.

Fragola, Casal Nuovo, Casoria, S. Pietro a Paterno, Fratta Maggiore, Arzano, Casavatora, Grummo, Casandrino, and Melito.

Marano, Mognano, Panecuocolo, Secondigliano, Chiaiano, Carvizzano, Polveca, Piscinola, Marianella, and Miano.

Artignano, Arenella, Vomero, Torrichio, Chianura, S. Strato, Arcarano, and Villa di Posillipo.

The City of Herculaneum

The names and locations of some of these villages, according to Summonte (Pietro, 1453-1526), are these. The first, which is Torre del Greco, is eight miles from Naples. This place is not only delightful, but is very helpful to the sick because of its temperate air. Therefore the kings of Naples frequently stayed there. Near there was the ancient city named Herculaneum, built by Hercules as many wrote, which was destroyed, as we said above, leaving only the castle.

The City of Pompeii

Torre dell'Annunciata, as San Felice writes, was in ancient times the famous city of Pompeii, founded also by Hercules when he brought back the victorious pomps of the cattle from Spain (Cattle of Geryon), as many worthy authors refer to. This city similarly became a casale because of the fire of the eruption of Vesuvius. On May 8, 1544 it was declared to be in the territory of Naples and to enjoy the Neapolitan immunity and

33

privilege and is called Torre dell'Annunciata by the decree of the Royal Chamber, because of the ancient church by that name located there.

Resina

Resina became famous because of the memory of St. Peter the Apostle who there celebrated Mass and converted so many of its citizens to the Christian faith. It is called this because of that bituminous material that Vesuvius threw out.

Portici

Falco refers to Portici as being the villa of Quintus Pontius Aquila, Roman citizen, who was named by Cicero when he wrote to Pomponius Atticus.

S. Giovanni a Teduccio

Concerning S. Giovanni a Teduccio, one sees that it has the name of its church, dedicated to the precursor of Christ, combined with the name of the ancient Roman family, Teduccia, who lived in this beautiful area. Falco mentions this, quoting from an ancient stone found in a field near Poggio Reale with an inscription of the pagan Romans.

Fragola was mentioned in the Register of Charles I in 1269.

Grummo

Grummo was mentioned in the translation of S. Attanagio, bishop of Naples, in 881, and in the Registers of Charles II in 1305 and 1306.

Casandrino

Memory of Casandrino is made in the Register of Charles I in 1269 and the Register of Charles the Illustrious (of Calabria) in 1319.

Marano

Marano is mentioned in the Registers of Charles II in 1294 and 1295.

Concerning the other *casali*, there is not found any verifiable account in any ancient writers, and therefore they will be left out.

These *casali* are full of fruits of every kind and quality, and they can be enjoyed all year around. They are also very fertile in precious and delicate wines, wheat, the finest linen, and hemp in great supply, provisions of all kinds, woods, nut trees, poultry, birds, and four-footed animals, some for working, as for example in harvesting. The inhabitants of these *casali* go to Naples almost every day to sell their products, truly the greatest convenience for the Neapolitans.

14. CASTEL DELL'OVO.
FROM C. PERRIELLO. *Veduta della spiaggia di Chiaja e di Posilipo.* NAPLES, SECOND HALF OF 17TH C.

15. S. Lorenzo Maggiore, the Duomo, and S. Agostino della Zecca. Detail from *Tavola Strozzi* (Plate 4).

THE CHURCH IN NAPLES

PARISH CHURCHES

The archbishop's palace (pl. 16) was built by Charles II, king of Naples, which appears in the register of the Royal Mint for the year 1298, even if others speak of Charles I. There are thirty canons, including the First Deacon, the *primicerius*, and the *cimiliarca*. There are also the *edomadarii*, who together with eighteen priests, or chaplains, make forty. There are two sacristans, twelve deacons, and about a hundred young clerics of the college, called the Seminary, founded in 1586. There are, in all, 184 besides the other chaplains of different families, who are of great number.

Inside the Duomo is the church of S. Restituta (pl. 15-17), cared for by the above-mentioned canons, whose congregation has become called the Chapter. There are also four principal parishes with thirty-six other minor parishes, all subject to a major church. They are S. Maria in Cosmedin, called Portanova, S. Gregorio Maggiore, S. Giovanni Maggiore, and S. Maria Maggiore. These are served by their *edomadarii* priests and ordinary deacons. Every time the archbishop or his vicar general comes outside they exit in procession with a silver cross and accompany him.

The other, minor, parishes are S. Maria a Segno, S. Maria Ritonda, S. Maria a Piazza, S. Tomaso Apostolo (a Capuana) near the Palazzo della Vicaria, S. Sofia, S. Giovanni a Porta, S. Gennarello called *ad diaconiam*, S. Maria a Cancello, S. Maria di Scala, S. Caterina al Mercato, S. Eligio, S. Agnello Maggiore served by the Regular Canons of the Holy Savior, S. Arcangelo at

Piazza delli Armieri, S. Giovanni in Corte, S. Giacomo degli Italiani, S. Bartolomeo, S. Giuseppe, S. Maria della Carità, S. Marco, S. Maria della Catena at S. Lucia a Mare, S. Anna di Palazzo, S. Marteo, S. Maria Ognibene, S. Maria della Neve at Chiaia, S. Strato at Posillipo, S. Maria dell'Avvocata outside Porta Reale, S. Maria del Soccorso all'Arenella, S. Maria della Misericordia at Borgo dei Vergini, S. Maria della Grazie at Capodimonte, S. Maria di Tutti i Santi outside the Borgo di S. Antonio, SS. Giovanni e Paolo in the same place, S. Angelo dell'Arena outside the Porta del Carmine, S. Maria dell'Annunciata a Fonseca.

The priests of these churches are called *confrati*, and the *edomadarii* of the four major parishes exit with their crosses to accompany the dead of their order, without which burial could be given to no one. But when the cross of the great church is present in the funerals, with the canons or the *edomadarii*, that of the parish is quickly removed at its appearance. The archbishop, as head, and the above-mentioned thirty-six parishes in ancient times took the role of administering the sacraments and burying the dead throughout the city and districts. Today this is divided into twenty-seven *ottine* (administrative districts). After the year 1536, the city having grown and added two other *ottine*, many churches were added to the parishes, which were called *grancie* (granges), to take part in the administration of so many sacraments.

Besides the parishes, there are seventy churches and chapels served and officiated at by secular priests, with thirty other chapels located in different churches, and more than one hundred others built by the citizens near their houses, similarly served by secular priests. Among these are twelve under the direction of different communities of foreigners, including the Spanish, Catalonians, Genoese, Florentines, Lucchesi, Lombards, Germans, Greeks, and those from Gaeta, Agérola, Cetara, and Massa Lubrense, with another thirty-two under the direction of communities of artisans, such as the silk makers, the weavers of linen, tailors, gipon (men's over-vest) makers, hosiers, embroidery workers, shoemakers, leather workers, saddlers, retailers, barbers, pharmacists, bakers, bottle makers, tripe-sellers, fish vendors, fishermen, innkeepers, wine storers, bottlers, pasta makers, chicken vendors, greengrocers, candle makers, boatmen, carpenters, ironworkers, painters, musicians, artillerymen, well keepers, sewer cleaners and policemen. All these, as well as the majority mentioned before, are governed by the master of the laity.

Now, both in the aforementioned churches and the houses of monks there total more than one hundred congregations, or companies, of lay persons who are governed by the best institutes and rules, and who attend frequently the most holy sacraments. On feast days they gather in the oratories, practicing prayers, meditations, and disciplines. The greater part of these go in procession dressed in linen, disguised, accompanying the poor dead in burial. There are others who take care of visiting the poor in prison, paying their debts. There are also those who comfort the impoverished sick in the hospitals, making them gifts of sugared food and delightful fruit. Others visit the embarrassed poor in their own houses with generous alms. Others practice comforting those who are condemned to death by the courts, truly an angelic duty. Finally, others practice the office of hospitality with other holy works, which for the sake of not going on too long, I will leave out.

LAY CHARITABLE ORGANIZATIONS IN NAPLES

Today, through the charity of the citizens, these congregations marry every year a great number of poor unmarried women, which totals 665. The dowries, which are listed here alphabetically, amount to 33,679 ducats (silver coins first issued in 1140).

A

The Casa dell'Annunciata weds 100 of its abandoned girls with a dowry of 90 ducats.

The same house through different bequests weds 160 with a dowry of 60 ducats.

The same house for the poor of the city and others weds 160 with a dowry of 24 ducats.

The church of S. Agnello Maggiore, through the bequest of the notary Tiseo Graffo, every two years weds one with a dowry of 300 ducats.

The *carnegraffa* chapel of S. Agnello weds two with a dowry of 24 ducats.

The chapel of S. Antonio di Padova in S. Lorenzo weds six with a dowry of 36 ducats.

The chapel of S. Agrippino through the bequest of Pietro Sommonte weds five with a dowry of 50 ducats.

The tailors' chapel of S. Angelo weds four with a dowry of 24 ducats.

The gipon makers' chapel of S. Angelo dell'Arena weds two with a dowry of 36 ducats.

The hosiers' chapel of S. Andrea weds four with a dowry of 60 ducats.

The musicians' chapel of S. Angelo in S. Nicola weds two with a dowry of 36 ducats.

The church of S. Anna dei Lombardi weds three with a dowry of 36 ducats.

The chapel of S. Antonio Abbate in S. Agostino degli Agérolani weds four with a dowry of 30 ducats.

The pasta-makers' chapel of Ascensione at the Carmine weds one with a dowry of 24 ducats.

B

The artillerymen's chapel of S. Barbara in Castel Nuovo weds one with a dowry of 24 ducats.

The chapel of S. Biase dell'Olmo of S. Lorenzo weds two with a dowry of 24 ducats.

The chapel of S. Bonifacio near the Egiziaca weds one with a dowry of 24 ducats.

C

The greengrocers' chapel of S. Croce in S. Maria della Scala weds four with a dowry of 36 ducats.

The chapel of S. Croce dei Lucchesi in S. Eligio weds one with a dowry of 24 ducats.

The barbers' chapel of SS. Cosmo e Damiano weds two with a dowry of 24 ducats.

The bottle-makers' chapel of S. Ciriaco in S. Eligio weds four with a dowry of 36 ducats.

The church of S. Crispino dei Calzolari weds five with a dowry of 60 ducats.

D

The chapel of Nome di Dio in S. Pietro Martire weds one with a dowry of 24 ducats.

E

The church of S. Eligio weds ten of its orphans with a dowry of 60 ducats.

The chapel of S. Eligio dei Ferrari in S. Eligio weds ten with a dowry of 24 ducats.

F

The church of SS. Filippo e Giacomo dell'Arte della Seta weds four with a dowry of 24 ducats.

G

The church of S. Gennaro extra Moenia weds two with a dowry of 25 ducats.

The chapel of Gesù in S. Giovanni a Mare weds one with a dowry of 24 ducats.

The wood-cutters' church of S. Giuseppe weds four with a dowry of 60 ducats.

The *staurita* of S. Giorgio Maggiore weds five with a dowry of 12 ducats.

The discipline of S. Giovanni Battista in S. Giovanni a Mare weds one with a dowry of 30 ducats.

The church of S. Giovanni Battista dei Fiorentini weds two with a dowry of 36 ducats.

The retailers' chapel in S. Giovanni in Corte weds three with a dowry of 36 ducats.

The church or hospital of S. Giacomo degli Spagnoli weds six with a dowry of 30 ducats.

The church of S. Giacomo dei Pisani, now called degli Italiani, weds two with a dowry of 24 ducats.

The church of S. Giacomo della Sellaria weds two with a dowry of 24 ducats.

The chapel of SS. Giacomo e Cristoforo d'Albina weds one with a dowry of 14 ducats.

The bakers' chapel of S. Giacomo weds two with a dowry of 24 ducats.

The church of S. Giorgio dei Genovesi weds three with a dowry of 30 ducats.

H

The hospital of the Santissima Trinità dei Pellegrini weds eight with a dowry of (?) ducats.

L

The painters' chapel of S. Luca weds one with a dowry of 24 ducats.

The embroidery-makers' chapel of S. Luca in S. Marta weds one with a dowry of 24 ducats.

The church of S. Luigi dei Minimi, through the bequest of Giovanna Martiale, weds three with a dowry of 50 ducats.

M

The conservatory of S. Maria dei Vergini dell'Arte della Seta weds six with a dowry of 50 ducats.

The hospital of S. Maria del Popolo, through the bequest of Giovanni Coscia, every three years weds one with a dowry of 120 ducats.

The same hospital through the bequest of Donna Dianora Sanseverino weds two with a dowry of 25 ducats.

The church of S. Maria della Carità through the bequest of Giulia Gallo weds six with a dowry of 60 ducats.

The congregation of the Bianchi of S. Maria Succurre Miseris weds two with a dowry of 24 ducats.

The chapel of S. Maria della Misericordia in S. Eligio weds five with a dowry of 24 ducats.

The chapel of S. Maria della Grazie in S. Eligio weds two with a dowry of 24 ducats.

The chapel of S. Maria della Grazie in S. Giorgio Maggiore weds two with a dowry of 24 ducats.

The chapel of S. Maria della Grazie at Orto del Conte weds one with a dowry of 24 ducats.

The chapel of S. Maria della Grazie delli Paludi weds four with a dowry of 24 ducats.

The chapel of S. Maria della Grazie in the wheat customs house weds two with a dowry of 24 ducats.

The chapel of S. Maria della Grazie at the leather tannery weds 1 with a dowry of 25 ducats.

The fish vendors' chapel of S. Maria della Grazie weds four with a dowry of 24 ducats.

The chapel of S. Maria della Bisogna in S. Giovanni a Mare weds two with a dowry of 24 ducats.

The chapel of S. Maria del Soccorso in S. Agostino weds two with a dowry of 30 ducats.

The chapel of S. Maria del Soccorso in S. Nicola weds two with a dowry of 24 ducats.

The church of S. Maria di Constantinopoli near the wall of the city weds seven with a dowry of 36 ducats.

The leather makers' chapel of S. Maria di Constantinopoli in S. Caterina del Carmine weds three with a dowry of 24 ducats.

The chapel of S. Maria dell'Avocata in S. Giovanni a Mare weds one with a dowry of 24 ducats.

The innkeepers' chapel of S. Maria della Catena at S. Nicola weds two with a dowry of 36 ducats.

The candle makers' chapel of S. Maria della Candelora at the Pietà weds three with a dowry of 50 ducats.

The fishermen's chapel of S. Maria della Neve weds one with a dowry of 24 ducats.

The chapel of S. Maria Incoronata in S. Pietro Martire weds three with a dowry of 24 ducats.

The chapel of S. Maria del Rosario in S. Pietro Martire weds two with a dowry of 24 ducats.

The oratorio of the Bianchi of the Holy Spirit, called S. Maria Regina di Tutti i Santi, weds one with a dowry of 72 ducats.

The church of S. Maria di Portosalvo of Barcaroli weds one with a dowry of 24 ducats.

The well-keepers' chapel of S. Maria a Forte in S. Maria a Piazza weds one with a dowry of 24 ducats.

The pedlars' chapel of S. Maria di Monte Vergine at the Pietà weds four with a dowry of 30 ducats.

The church of Monteoliveto, through the bequest of Don Filippo di Lano, weds six with a dowry of 36 ducats.

Sacro Monte della Pietà weds six with a dowry of 50 ducats.

The chapel of Monte of the city of Massa (Lubrense) in S. Pietro in Vincoli weds four with a dowry of 24 ducats.

The chapel of Monte di Cetara in S. Pietro Martire weds six with a dowry of 24 ducats.

The Regiment of the Street of the Goldsmiths weds four with a dowry of 80 ducats.

The church of S. Marta weds two with a dowry of 18 ducats for each.

The *staurita* of S. Maria Maddalena in S. Agnello Maggiore weds four with a dowry of 24 ducats.

The linen weavers' chapel of S. Marco weds 4 with a dowry of 24 ducats.

The wine warehousemen's chapel of S. Marco in S. Andrea weds six with a dowry of 20 ducats.

The chapel of S. Marco in S. Eligio weds one with a dowry of 24 ducats.

The chapel of S. Margarita dei Tedeschi weds two with a dowry of 24 ducats.

N

The *staurita* of S. Nicolò di Pistasi weds four with a dowry of 24 ducats.

P

The *staurita* of SS. Pietro e Paolo in S. Paolo Maggiore weds two with a dowry of 36 ducats.

The church of SS. Pietro e Paolo dei Greci weds two with a dowry of 36 ducats.

The church of S. Pietro in Vincoli de' Spetiali weds three with a dowry of 36 ducats.

The Regiment of the Piazza del Popolo of Naples weds 14 with a dowry of 36 ducats.

S

The church of Spirito Santo weds ten of its girls with a dowry of 60 ducats.

The same church, through the bequest of Rodrigo Diaz, weds one with a dowry of 50 ducats.

The chapel of Santissimo Sacramento in S. Maria Maggiore weds one with a dowry of 24 ducats.

The chapel of Santissimo Sacramento in S. Giovanni Maggiore weds six with a dowry of 24 ducats.

The chapel of Santissimo Sacramento of S. Angelo weds seven with a dowry of 24 ducats.

The chapel of the Sacrament of S. Eligio weds three with a dowry of 24 ducats.

The chapel of Santissimo Sacramento of S. Caterina del Carmelo weds three with a dowry of 24 ducats.

The *staurita* of S. Severo Maggiore weds seven with a dowry of 24 ducats.

The chapel of S. Salvatore a Piazza Larga weds one with a dowry of 24 ducats.

U

The leather-tanners' chapel of S. Ursola in S. Maria del Carmelo weds ten with a dowry of 30 ducats.

But in the midst of all the other works of charity and holiness that take place in this most faithful city of Naples, no less than the others, and also of great benefit, is the Pio Monte of the Gentlemen of the Court erected within SS. Giovanni e Paolo, at the base of the mountain, and it is called the Chapel of S. Maria della Sanità, whose founder is Giovanni Battista Crisci (b. c.1593), a Neapolitan gentleman graced by great wisdom and belles lettres, just as his writings fully testify. These are the *Orintia,* the *Defense of Rome,* the *Lamp of the Courtiers,* the *Light of Princes,* and finally he has in press the *Forest of Various Hieroglyphic Undertakings,* a very curious work. This Monte was dedicated under the protection of the Most Serene Philip IV. Here there are noted and inscribed 400 courtier gentlemen. It occupies itself with all the works of mercy, spiritual as well as corporal, as their constitution clearly shows. They make other marriages of private persons, who are numerous. The others marriages of the Monti arranged by the nobility, which are many, with great dowries, I will omit so as not to drag on.

SAINTS' BODIES IN THE CHURCHES OF NAPLES

There are preserved in the mentioned churches a good number of bodies of saints and beati, and most worthy relics. First, in the archbishop's church, there is the body of the most glorious martyr S. Gennaro, with saints Euticeto, Acutio, and Massimo; the martyr saints Aspreno, Agrippino, Attanagio, Lorenzo, Giuliano and Giovanni, bishops of Naples; S. Restituta, virgin and martyr; Blessed Tiberio, bishop with Blessed Nicolò Romito. In S. Maria Maggiore, S. Pomponio, bishop. In S. Giorgio Maggiore, S. Severo, bishop. In S. Maria Cosmedin, S. Eustasio, confessor and bishop of Naples. In S. Giorgio Maggiore, Friar Luca of Genoa, a man of the most holy life who, as may be read on his sepulcher, after he persevered in penance for 40 years, went to a better life in 1375. In the church of S. Eufemio, saints Eufemio, Fortunato and Massimo, bishops of Naples. In the church of the monks of Cassino, S. Severino, confessor and S. Sofio Levita, martyr. In the church of S. Agnello, S. Agnello, abbot. In the church of S.

45

Gennarello, the body of S. Nostriano, bishop of Naples.
In the church of S. Gaudioso, saints Gaudioso and
Quodvultdeus, bishop; S. Gaudioso, bishop of Salerno; S.
Fortunato, bishop and martyr, with three brother martyrs
Carponio, Euachristo, and Prisciano. In the church
behind the monastery there are the bodies of 33 martyrs.
In the church of S. Maria Donnarómita, S. Giuliana,
virgin and martyr. In the church of S. Peregrino, S.
Peregrino, confessor. In the church of the Annunziata
two little bodies of the Holy Innocents. In April 29, 1590
the relics of saints Primiano, Firmiano, Alessandro and
Tellurio, martyr; with those of saints Savino and
Eunomio, bishop, Pascasio, abbot; and Ursola, virgin and
martyr, were transferred. In the church of S. Patrizia, S.
Patrizio, bishop. In S. Pietro ad Aram, S. Candida
widow, with seven other holy bodies. In S. Andrea a
Nido, S. Candida the younger. In S. Domenico, Blessed
Guido, Neapolitan, of the Marramalda family. In S.
Chiara, Blessed Filippo Aquerio. In S. Francesco della
Limosina, Blessed Maddalena of the Costanza family. In
S. Maria la Nova, Blessed Giacomo della Marca; and in
the church of S. Giovanni a Carbonara, Blessed
Christiano Francese. In S. Paolo Maggiore, Blessed
Gaetano Tiene, founder of the fathers regular clerics; of
Blessed Giovanni Marinonio and of Blessed Andrea
Avellino of the same order, the ninth protector of the city,
besides the fifty-two bodies of the holy martyrs who are
preserved in a particular chapel. In S. Lorenzo, the body
of Blessed Donato, disciple of St. Francis.

RELICS OF SAINTS IN THE CHURCHES OF NAPLES

Among the notable relics that are kept in the above-
mentioned churches, besides the bodies of saints already
mentioned, in the chapel of the treasury of the archbishop
there are seven heads of the bishop martyrs, such as the

head of the glorious S. Gennaro, martyr, his blood; that of S. Aspreno, first bishop of Naples; those of saints Agrippino, Eufemio, Severo, Attanagio, bishops of Naples. There are also the relics of S. Agnello, abbot; of St. Thomas Aquinas, of Blessed Andrea Avellino, and of S. Francesco di Paola, and all those relics of the protectors of the city are preserved in images of silver.

There is the head of S. Massimo Cumano, martyr, the arm of St. Jude, apostle. A part of the face of St. John the Baptist; a side of the apostle, St. Paul; a piece of the cross of Christ, Our Lord; the staff of St. Peter the apostle which cured S. Aspreno, with the small biretta of this saint. In S. Maria Donnaregina, the head of St. Bartholomew, apostle. In S. Giovanni Maggiore, a good part of the head of St. Matthew, apostle. In S. Liguoro, the head of St. Stephen, protomartyr; with that of S. Biaggio, bishop and martyr, and the head of St. Gregory, commonly said to be brought to Naples from Armenia by S. Liguoro. In the church of the Annunziata, the head of S. Cordula, martyr. In S. Maria della Concezione of the Jesuits, the head of S. Cornelius, the pope and martyr, with two others of the eleven thousand virgins and one of the eleven thousand in S. Maria del Rosario and one other in S. Caterina a Formello, and other relics in other churches.

In the church of S. Agostino are preserved an infinite number of relics of many saints, and among others, the head of St. Luke the Evangelist, which at first was placed inside the said church, in a magnificent theater of marble, worked in the spot where the chapel of Rinaldo Squarcella, counselor of King Ferrante I, was. Afterwards it was presented to that of the Anna family, in which are sculpted the following words, which can be read today:

> THE HEAD OF LUKE THE EVANGELIST
> HAS BEEN PLACED HERE TO VENERATE.

The relics were placed by the fathers in the same church in another chapel called the treasury, with other relics. Here is also the head of St. Clement, and the blood of S. Nicolò da Tolentino, which is not a small wonder. They preserve in this church a large piece of the wood of the cross of Christ Our Lord, which has been delivered for the greatest honor and veneration into the custody of these fathers by the brothers of the most ancient Oratorio of the Discipline of the Cross, next to the said church, where the head of Pope St. Clement was also preserved.

In this church also resides the Tribunal of the Piazza of the most faithful people, in which they choose their elected officials.

In addition, this church is decorated with many sepulchres and memorials of noble people and families of the city, and in particular by the nobility of the *seggio* of Capua, such as the surviving families of Caracciolo, Somma, Galeota, and the Pisacella, and by the extinct families in the same *seggio*, of Squarcella, of Rinaldo already named, and of Barone, whose insignias are seen sculpted there. These are, in the ceiling of the small aisle of the church near the marble theater mentioned above, that of the Squarcella consisting of three towers, or haystacks, with a border of silver on a blue field. On a pilaster in the chapel of the Villarosa family there is painted in a corner the arms of the Barone family, consisting of a cross with four roses. Therefore the great church can be named among the greatest that are held in esteem in this city.

Under the altar of the Rosary in the church of S. Caterina a Formello are preserved forever the bones of those who suffered death by the most cruel Turks in the city of Otranto in 1480, because they did not wish to deny their faith in our Lord Jesus Christ. These were brought here from Otranto by Alfonso, duke of Calabria.

In the church of S. Gaudioso is the blood of St. Stephen, protomartyr. In the churches of S. Giovanni a Carbonara, of S. Liguoro, of S. Maria Donnarómita, of the Fathers of the Oratorio is the blood of St. John the Baptist; in the church of S. Patrizia, the blood of this same saint with the blood of St. Bartholomew the apostle; and in the church of S. Agostino, the blood of S. Nicolò da Tolentino; and in S. Paolo that of Blessed Andrea.

There are five noteworthy pieces of the cross of Our Lord Jesus Christ: in the Archbishop's Palace, in S. Giovanni a Carbonara, in S. Maria del (Monte di) Carmelo, at the Fathers of the Oratorio, and in S. Paolo Maggiore, a most beautiful cross.

In other churches are the thorns of the Crown from the head of Our Lord Jesus Christ; as in S. Martino of the Carthusians, in S. Maria Incoronata, in S. Maria Maggiore there are five; in S. Maria Donnarómita, in S. Maria Annunziata, in S. Giovanni Maggiore, in S. Patrizia, in S. Pietro Martire, in S. Paolo Maggiore. There are two of them at the Fathers of the Oratorio, and at Spirito Santo; and finally in the church of S. Patrizia is preserved one of the nails with which our Lord and Redeemer Jesus Christ was crucified.

There are many other relics in different churches, which I will omit for the sake of brevity, as in the Treasury of the Archbishop's Palace, a finger of S. Lucia, virgin and martyr, and in S. Giovanni Maggiore the eye of the same saint; and in the church of S. Lorenzo a little of the *graffo*, of the blood, and part of the rib of this saint. Besides so many bodies of saints and worthy relics are preserved in the Treasury of the great church of the Annunziata and in other churches, and in particular in a most beautiful reliquary in S. Paolo Maggiore.

RELIGIOUS INSTITUTIONS
IN THE CITY OF NAPLES

Location   Population

DOMINICANS
S. Domenico (Maggiore)	150
S. Pietro Martire	128
Monte di Dio	15
S. Tomaso d'Aquino	28
Rosario (di Palazzo)	25
S. Rocco	4
S. Lucia a Mare	4
S. Leonardo (ad Insulam)	4
S. Brigida a Posillipo	8
Maddalena al Ponte (S. Maria)	2
S. Caterina a Formello	80

REFORMED DOMINICANS
Spirito Santo	85
S. Maria della Sanità	110
Gesù e Maria	40
S. Severo	60
S. Maria della Libera	10
S. Maria della Salute	12

NUNS OF THE DOMINICAN ORDER
S. Sebastiano	100
Sapientia (S. Maria della Sapienza)	88
S. Giovanni Battista (delle Monache)	50
S. Caterina da Siena	80
Divino Amore	–

FRANCISCANS IN SANDALS
S. Maria la Nova	250
S. Gioacchino (a Portonuovo?), commonly called Lo Spedaletto	60
Montecalvario	60
S. Maria degli Angioli	35

REFORMED FRANCISCANS IN SANDALS
Croce	45
Trinità	28
S. Maria della Salute	20

CAPUCHINS

Concezione	120
S. Efremo Vecchio (Eufemio)	70

FRANCISCANS IN SHOES

S. Lorenzo	120
S. Anna	30
S. Caterina	20
S. Maria del Monte	25
S. Francesco di Capodimonte	10
S. Severo ai Vergini	20
Spirito Santo a Limpiano	10

REFORMED FRANCISCAN IN SHOES

S. Lucia al Monte	90
S. Maria dei Miracoli	30

FRANCISCAN NUNS

S. Francesco (delle Monache)	100
S. Girolamo (delle Monache)	100
Cappuccinelle	30
S. Francesco della Limosina	30
S. Chiara	350
S. Antonio di Padova	85
Il Gesù (delle Monache)	90
Gerusalemme (S. Maria di)	54
Consolazione (S. Maria della)	52
Donnaregina (S. Maria)	100
Trinità (delle Monache)	50

AUGUSTINIANS

S. Agostino	150
S. Giovanni a Carbonara	120
Consolazione a Posillipo (S. Maria della)	18
S. Maria del Soccorso	20
S. Maria dell'Oliva	11
S. Maria della Speranza fuori Porta Capuana	10

REFORMED AUGUSTINIANS

S. Maria della Verità	70
S. Nicola da Tolentino	30

AUGUSTINIAN NUNS

Maddalena	176
Egiziaca	100
S. Andrea	70
S. Giuseppe dei Ruffi	50

CARMELITES

S. Maria del Carmine	150
Speranza	25
Paradiso a Posillipo (S. Maria del)	15
Concordia	17
S. Maria del Carmine a Capo di Chino	20
S. Maria del Carmine a Chiaia	16
S. Maria della Vita	50

CARMELITE NUNS

Croce di Lucca	100

CARMELITES IN SHOES

Madre di Dio	70
S. Teresa a Chiaia	30

CARMELITE NUNS IN SHOES

S. Teresa a Pontecorvo	40

CARTHUSIANS

S. Martino	100

CELESTINES

S. Pietro a Maiella	70
Ascensione a Chiaia	20

REGULAR CANONS OF THE HOLY SAVIOR

S. Agnello	15
S. Maria a Cappella	12

CRUCIFERS

S. Maria dei Vergini	38

CANONS REGULAR OF THE LATERAN

S. Pietro ad Aram	90
S. Maria di Piedigrotta	60
Regina Coeli Montalto	100

BENEDICTINES

S. Severino	150

BENEDICTINE NUNS

S. Marcellino	100
Donnarómita	100
S. Gaudioso	100
S. Potito	80
S. Patrizia	120
S. Liguoro	130
Donnalbina	80

OLIVETANS

Monteoliveto	120

MINIMS OF S. FRANCESCO DI PAOLA

S. Luigi di Palazzo	100
S. Maria della Stella	60
S. Francesco fuori Porta Capuana	26

SERVITES (DEL PARTO)

S. Maria del Parto a Mergellina	30
Mater Dei	10
S. Maria Ognibene	16

EREMITES

S. Maria delle Grazie	80

CAMALDOLITES

Il Salvatore a Nazareth	60

MONTEVERGINES (WILLIAMITES)

S. Maria di Montevergine	36

BASILIANS

S. Agrippino	16

SPANISH MONKS

Trinità	25
S. Ursola, or la Mercede	30
Monserrato (S. Maria di)	61

SPANISH NUNS

Concezione a S. Giacomo	80
Soledad Conservatorio	80
Frati Benfratelli del B. Giovanni di Dio, called La Pace	80

JESUITS

House of the Professed	130
College	230
Novitiate, called Annunciata	80
College of St. Francis Xavier a Palazzo	15
College of S. Ignatio, called Carminello	20
College of S. Giuseppe a Chiaia	12

PAULINES OR THEATINES

S. Paolo	120
Santi Apostoli	100
S. Maria degli Angeli	65
S. Maria di Loreto a Toleto	10
S. Maria dell'Avvocata at Borgo di S. Antonio	10
S. Maria della Vittoria in the Borgo di Chiaia, at Chiatamone	20

MINOR REGULAR CLERICS

S. Maria Maggiore	80
S. Giuseppe	20
S. Margarita a Porto	6

SECULAR CLERICS

Congregation of the Oratorio of the Girolamites	129

MINISTERS OF THE SICK

S. Maria Porta Coeli	80
Concezione al Chiatamone	20
S. Aspreno ai Vergini	60

BARNABITES

S. Maria di Portanova	50
S. Carlo	10

HOLY WORKERS OF CHRISTIAN DOCTRINE

S. Giorgio Maggiore	60
S. Maria delli Monti	20
Carità	10

FATHERS OF THE PIOUS SCHOOLS

S. Maria delle Scuole Pie alla Duchesca	30
S. Felice	10
Fathers of Maria of Lucca at Chiaia	15

BOYS' CONSERVATORIES

Seminary of the Archbishop	100
S. Maria di Loreto dei Bianchi	360
S. Maria della Pietà dei Turchini	200
S. Maria della Colonna di S. Francesco	120
Boys of S. Honofrio at the Vicaria	50
Old Men of S. Honofrio a Porto	50

CONSERVATORIES OF WOMEN

Tempio delle Scortiate	80
Tempio delle Paparelle	60
Sisters of Suor Orsola	50
Refugio	120
Convertite (reformed prostitutes) at Incurabili	186
Spanish *Convertite*	120
Illuminate	80
Conservatory of Women of S. Honofrio at the Vicaria	60
S. Maria Succurre Miseris	80
Conservatory of Widows in S. Margarita	30

GIRLS' CONSERVATORIES

Carità	60
Concezione di Montecalvario	120
Annunciata	70
S. Eligio	400
Spirito Santo	400
SS. Filippo e Giacomo	350
S. Crispino	100
Splendore	80
S. Maria di Constantinopoli	10
S. Maria della Grazie dell'Arte della Lana	25
Convertite of S. Giorgio	50

HOSPITALS

Annunciata	1000
Incurabili	1300
S. Angelo a Nido	50
S. Giacomo degli Spagnoli	150
Vittoria	10
Pace del B. Giovanni di Dio	50
S. Eligio di Donne	200
Misericordia dei Sacerdoti	20
Pellegrini	30
S. Nicola de Marinari	20
S. Maria della Pazienza Cesarea	30

16. MEDIEVAL DUOMO.
FROM B. SERSALE, *Discorso istorico della
Cappella...dentro il Duomo Napoletano.* NAPLES, 1745.
Showing S. Restituta (2), SS. Salvatore (6), the bronze horse
(13), and the bishop's palace (11), on street at right.

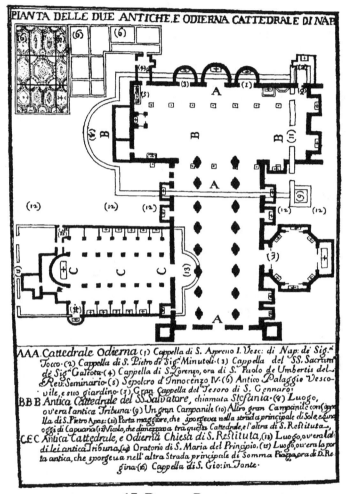

PIANTA DELLE DUE ANTICHE, E ODIERNA CATTEDRALE DI NAP

AAA. Cattedrale Odierna (1) Cappella di S. Aspreno I. Vesc: di Nap: de' Sig.ri
Tocco. (2) Cappella di S. Pietro de' Sig.ri Minutoli. (3) Cappella del SS. Sacrum.
de' Sig.ri Galeota. (4) Cappella di S. Lorenzo, ora di S. Paolo de Umbertis del
Rev. Seminario. (5) Sepolcro d'Innocenzo IV. (6) Antico Palaggio Vesco-
vile, e suo giardino. (7) Gran Cappella del Tesoro di S. Gennaro:
BBB Antica Cattedrale del SS. Salvatore, chiamata Stefania. (8) Luogo,
ov'era l'antica Tribuna. (9) Un gran Campanile (10) Altro gran Campanile con Cappel-
lla di S. Pietro Apos: (11) Porta maggiore, che sporgeva nella strada principale di Sole, e una
oggi di Capuana (12) Vicolo, che dimezzava tra questa Cattedrale, e l'altra di S. Restituta,
CCC Antica Cattedrale, e Odierna Chiesa di S. Restituta, (13) Luogo, ov'era la
di lei antica Tribuna, (14) Oratorio di S. Maria del Principio, (15) Luogo, ov'era la por
ta antica, che sporgeva nell'altra Strada principale di Somma Piazza, ora di D. Re
gina. (16) Cappella di S. Gio: in Fonte.

17. DUOMO, PLAN.
FROM B. SERSALE, *Discorso istorico della
Cappella...dentro il Duomo Napoletano.* NAPLES, 1745.
S. Gennaro (A-B), S. Restituta (C), the Treasury (3), with
the Bishop's Palace (6).

THE BISHOPS OF NAPLES

St. Peter, the prince of the Apostles, coming from Antioch to Rome, passed through Naples in 44 AD and preached the faith and instituted the first bishop who was

S. Aspreno, who lived until 79. His body is entombed in the Maggiore church (Duomo) in the chapel built in his name.

S. Patrobo, disciple of St. Paul the Apostle, whose body lies in the church of S. Maria Maggiore in Rome.

Epitamito.

Marone.

Probo.

Paolo I

S. Agrippino, ancient father, and defender of the city of Naples, as may be read in his life; his body is buried in the high altar of the cathedral of Naples.

S. Eustasio, whose body lies in the parish church of S. Maria di Portanova.

S. Eufemio, whose body is buried in the church dedicated to his name outside Naples where the Capuchin priests live, and so it is called the Old Capuchins.

Cosmas flourished at the time of St. Silvester I (pope, 314-335) and the Emperor Constantine.

Calepodio flourished at the time of Julius I (337-352).

S. Fortunato, whose body was buried in the church of the Old Capuchins together with S. Eufemio.

S. Massimo, whose body lies in the aforementioned church together with the holy bishops mentioned.

Zosimo was an intruder after he ordered into exile the above-mentioned Massimo who, as Baronio says, was stained by the Arian heresy.

S. Severo, whose body was buried in the church outside Naples dedicated to his name, then he was transferred from there inside Naples and was buried in the parish church of S. Giorgio Maggiore.

Orso, nephew of S. Severo, flourished in the time of Pope Damasus (366-384).

Giovanni I flourished under Pope Siricius the Great (384-399).

S. Nostriano, whose body was transferred to the church of S. Gennarello all'Olmo.

Timasio flourished under Pope Caelestinus (422-432).

Felice flourished in the time of St. Leo, the pope (440-461).

Sotero lived under Pope Hilarius (461-468).

Vittore established his church in the time of Pope Gelasius I (492-496).

Stefano I who lived under Pope Anastasius II (496-498) and built the church called the Stefania in Naples.

S. Pomponio whose body lies in the church of S. Maria Maggiore, founded by him and from whose bones a liquor sprung that became called *manna*.

Giovanni II flourished at the time of Pope John II (533-535).

Vincenzo lived at the time of Pope Pelagius I (555-561).

Renduce established his church under the pontificate of Benedict I (575-579).

Demetrio was bishop in the time of Pope Pelagius II (579-590).

Paul II lived at the time of St. Gregory the Great (590-604).

Florentio was elected at the time of St. Gregory.

Fortunato II under the same pontificate.

Pascasio at the time of the same St. Gregory.

Giovanni III was in the pontificate of Deusdedit I (615-618).

Cesario lived at the time of Pope Honorius I (625-638).

Gratioso established his church under Pope John IV (640-642).

Eusebio under Pope Martin I (649-655).

Leontio lived at the time of Pope Eugenius I (654-657).

Adeodato flourished under Pope Vitalian I (657-672).

Agnello lived at the time of Pope Deusdedit (II, 672-676) and during his time in 685 was the fire of Monte di Somma (Vesuvius), where S. Gennaro showed his protection in freeing Naples, his country, from the ruin that this fire threatened. To give thanks they dedicated to him the church of S. Gennaro ad Diaconiam, which today is called S. Gennarello all'Olmo.

S. Giuliano whose body was buried in the Chiesa Maggiore.

S. Lorenzo whose body was buried in the chapel of the Santissimo Sacramento in the Duomo together with the body of S. Attanagio.

Sergio lived under Pope Gregory II (715-731).

Cosmo II established his church under Pope Zacharias (741-752).

Paul III lived under Pope Paul I (757-767).

Stephen III, once the leader of the city of Naples, left the pomp of the secular world and became a cleric and then was elected bishop of Naples under Pope Stephen IV (816-817).

Paul IV of this name.

Blessed Tiberio was a man of most holy life and lived under Pope Paschal I (817-824).

S. Giovanni, called Acquarulo, whose body lies under the high altar of the church of S. Restituta on the Capitol of Naples.

S. Attanagio, the son of Sergio (I), duke of Naples, whose body lies together with the body of St. Lawrence, as we said above.

Attanagio II was the nephew of the above, holy son of Gregorio, duke of Naples, and after he was driven out of the city of Naples, his brother Sergio (II) was elected duke to govern the city.

Attanagio III.

THE ARCHBISHOPS OF NAPLES

Niceta, made the first archbishop around 668.

N., the second archbishop.

Sergio I, who was present at the Beneventan Synod called by Pope Nicholas II (1059-1061).

Gentile, a monk from Monte Cassino.

L. to whom St. Gregory VII (1073-1085) wrote that he excommunicated the duke of Naples.

Giovanni I who attended the consecration of the church of Monte Cassino by Alexander II (1061-1073).

Marino solemnly received Roger (II), the first king of Naples (1139-1154) and gave him hospitality in his archiepiscopal palace.

Anselmo I.

Pietro Bellense, archdeacon of the *Chiesa Battoniense* in England, elected archbishop and renounced this dignity.

Sergio II.

Tomaso di Capua.

Anselmo II, to whom Pope Innocent III (1179-1180) wrote many letters.

Bonifacio Nauclerio.

Peter of Sorrento.

Berardino Caracciolo, master of King Manfred (1258-1266).

St. Thomas Aquinas was elected to, and renounced, the archbishopric under Clement IV (1265-1268).

Ayglerio of Burgundy, monk of Monte Cassino and man of very holy life, who received the mother of Conradin when she came to Naples after the death of her son, who was decapitated by the order of Charles I (1265-1285).

Filippo Minutolo, in whose time the new buildings of the archbishopric, which are seen today, were begun by Charles II in 1298.

Giacomo da Viterbo of the order of St. Augustine who was confirmed by Charles II of all the privileges conceded to the great church of Naples.

Humbert of Monte Auro of Burgundy, who was made treasurer of the church of S. Nicolò of Bari by Charles II.

Matteo Filamarino elected archbishop.

Anibaldo da Caccano was made cardinal by John XXII (1316-1334) in 1327.

Bertoldo.

Pietro.

Giovanni II Ursino, attended at the coronation of Queen Giovanna I (1343-1382).

Bertrand di Meyshonesio.

Giovanni III from Capua.

Bernardo I, the French Bosquet, was made cardinal by Urban V (1362-1370) in 1368.

Bernard II of Monte Auro, who in the time of the schism of Urban VI (1378-1389) went from the side of Clement VII, antipope (1378-1394), and was deposed from the church of Naples.

Giovanni IV Bozzuto, noble Neapolitan, made archbishop by Urban VI; he suffered many injuries on account of the Great Schism from Queen Giovanna I and was expelled from his church.

Tomaso de Manatis of Pistoia, who was imposed on the church of Naples by Antipope Clement VII after the above-mentioned Giovanni was expelled.

Ludovico Bozzuto, noble Neapolitan.

N. Guindazzo, noble Neapolitan.

Guillelmo Zanzio, otherwise called Pagano.

Arrigo Minutolo, noble Neapolitan, who was made cardinal by Boniface IX (1389-1404) in 1389.

Giordano Ursino was chosen to be a cardinal by Innocent VII (1404-1406).

Giacomo de'Rossi of the lords of Parma.

Nicola di Diano, noble Neapolitan.

Gaspas de Diano, being archbishop, was made president of the Sacred Council by Alfonso I (the Magnanimous, 1442-1458).

Rinaldo Piscicello, noble Neapolitan, was chosen to be a cardinal by Calixtus III (1455-1458) in 1456.

Timoteo Maffeo.

Juan V Fernandez, Spaniard.

Oliviero Carrafa, noble Neapolitan, being archbishop, was made president of the Sacred Council and in 1464 was made cardinal by Paul II (1464-1471).

Alessandro Carrafa, noble Neapolitan, brother of the above-mentioned Oliviero.

Giovanni Vincenzo Carrafa, made cardinal by Clement VII (1523-1534) in 1527.

Francesco Carrafa.

Ranuccio Farnese, nephew of Pope Paul III (1534-1549) and made a cardinal by him in 1546.

Giovanni Pietro Carrafa, made cardinal by Paul III in 1536, then ascended to the papacy as Paul IV (1555-1559) after the death of Julius III.

Giovanni Marinonio of the order of the Theatine Fathers renounced the archbishopric offered to him by Paul IV in 1555.

Alfonso Carrafa, cardinal, nephew of the above-mentioned.

Mario Carrafa.

Paolo d'Arezzo, cardinal of the order of the Theatine Fathers, whose canonization is being considered now in Rome.

Anibal di Capua, noble Neapolitan, son of the duke of Termini.

Alfonso Cardinal Gesualdo, noble Neapolitan, son of the prince of Venosa.

Ottavio Cardinal Acquaviva, noble Neapolitan, son of the duke of Atri.

Detio Cardinal Carrafa, noble Neapolitan.

Francesco Cardinal Buoncompagno, son of the duke of Sora and nephew of Gregory XIII (1572-1585).

Ascanio Cardinal Filomarino, noble Neapolitan.

Iñigo Cardinal Caracciolo, noble Neapolitan, who governs the church of Naples at present.

We have gathered this series of Bishops of Naples from what Don Camillo Tutini of Naples recorded of them in a *General History of the Bishops and Archbishops of this City.*

CARDINALS FROM THE CITY AND KINGDOM OF NAPLES

Dauferio, born in Benevento, monk and abbot of Monte Cassino, was made cardinal by Nicholas II in 1061.

Odorifero, son of the count of Marsi, monk and abbot of Monte Cassino, was made cardinal in the same year by the same pope.

Aldemario, born in Capua, cleric of this church and secretary to the prince of Capua, after becoming a monk of Monte Cassino, was elected abbot by those there where he lived a very holy life, and was made cardinal by Alexander II in 1073.

Teodino, son of the count of Marsi, monk of Monte Cassino, was made cardinal in 1073.

Leone Marsicano, monk of Monte Cassino and

Giovanni Gaieta, born in the city of Gaeta and also a monk of Monte Cassino, were both made cardinals by Urban II (1088-1099).

Gregorio da Ceccano, born in Aquino, was made cardinal by Paschal II (1099-1118).

Odorisio di Sangro, a monk of Monte Cassino, and

Rossemanno Sanseverino, a monk of Monte Cassino, were both made cardinals by Paschal II in 1105.

Pietro Ruffo, noble Neapolitan, was made cardinal by Gelasius II in 1118.

Giovanni Dauferio of Salerno was made cardinal by Calixtus II in 1122.

Alberico Tomacello, noble Neapolitan, was made cardinal by Pope Honorius II in 1125.

Rainaldo of the counts of Marsi, monk and abbot of Monte Cassino, was made cardinal by Innocent II in 1140.

Giovanni Pizzuto, noble Neapolitan of an extinct family, canon regular of St. Victor of Paris, was elected cardinal together with

Alberto Morra, noble Beneventan, by Hadrian IV in 1155 and 1158.

Berardo, born in the city of Benevento, was made cardinal by Alexander III in 1178.

Giovanni, born in Salerno, was made cardinal in 1191 by Celestine III.

Roffrido, born in Isola in the diocese of Sora, and

Pietro Capuano, nobleman of Amalfi, were made cardinals in 1193 by Celestine III.

Pietro Morra, noble Beneventan, was made cardinal by Innocent III in 1195.

Tomaso of the noble family of Capua, was made cardinal in 1212 by Innocent III.

Pietro di Capua was made cardinal by Honorius III in 1221.

Bernardo Caracciolo, noble Neapolitan, was made cardinal by Innocent IV in 1244.

F. Pietro of the city of Aquila, monk of Monte Cassino, was made cardinal by Celestine V in 1294.

Landulfo Brancaccio, noble Neapolitan, was made cardinal by the same pope in the same year.

Fr. Nicolò Caracciolo, noble Neapolitan, of the Order of Preachers,

Guglielmo di Capua, son of the count of Altavilla,

Ludovico di Capua,

Gentile di Sangro,

Filippo Carrafa della Spina, and

Stefano Sanseverino, all noble Neapolitans, were made cardinals by Urban VI in the first appointment in 1378.

Marino del Giudice, noble Amalfitano,

Landulfo Maramaldo, and

Pietro Tomacello, noble Neapolitans, were made cardinal by the same pope in the third appointment in 1381.

Francesco Carbone,

Marino Vulcano,

Rinaldo Brancaccio,

F. Angelo d'Anna, a Camaldoli monk, all four noble Neapolitans, together with

Giovanni Garbone, and

Francesco Castagnola, Neapolitan, were made cardinals by the same Urban in the fourth appointment in 1384.

Arrigo Minutolo, noble Neapolitan, was made cardinal by Pope Boniface IX in 1389.

Cosmo de' Migliorati of the city of Sulmona was made cardinal by Boniface IX in 1390.

Baldassar Cossa, noble Neapolitan, was made cardinal by the same pope in the third appointment in 1402.

Corrado Caracciolo, noble Neapolitan, was made cardinal by Innocent VII in 1405.

Ludovico Brancaccio, noble Neapolitan, was made cardinal by Gregory XII in 1408.

Tomaso Brancaccio, noble Neapolitan, was made cardinal by John XXIII in 1411.

Guglielmo Carbone, noble Neapolitan, was made cardinal in the same year.

Nicolò Acciapaccia, nobleman from Sorrento, was made cardinal by Eugenius IV in 1439.

Astorgio Agnese, noble Neapolitan, was made cardinal by Nicholas V in 1449.

Rinaldo Piscicello, noble Neapolitan, was made cardinal by Calixtus III in 1456.

Oliviero Carrafa, noble Neapolitan, was made cardinal by Paul II in 1464.

Giovanni of Aragon, Neapolitan, son of King Ferdinand I, was made cardinal by Sixtus IV in 1478.

Federico Sanseverino, noble Neapolitan, was made cardinal by Innocent VIII in 1489.

Ludovico of Aragon, noble Neapolitan, was made cardinal by Alexander VI in 1496.

Tomaso da Vio of the city of Gaeta, general of the Preaching Friars, was made cardinal by Leo X in 1517.

Ferdinando Ponzetto, Neapolitan, was made cardinal in the same year by the same pope.

Antonio Sanseverino,

Giovanni Vincenzo Carrafa, noble Neapolitan, and

Andrea Matteo Palmieri, Neapolitan, were, in 1527, made cardinals by Clement VII.

Marino Caracciolo, noble Neapolitan, was made cardinal in 1535 by Paul III.

Giovanni Pietro Carrafa, noble Neapolitan, was made cardinal by the same pope in 1536.

Pietro Paolo Parisio of the city of Cosenza in Calabria and

Fr. Dionisio Laurerio of the city of Benevento and prior general of the Order of the Servites were made cardinals in 1539 by the same pope.

Giovanni Vincenzo Acquaviva of Aragon, noble Neapolitan, was made cardinal by the same pope in 1542.

Giovanni Michele Saraceno, noble Neapolitan, was made cardinal in 1551 by Julius III.

Carlo Carrafa and

Diomede Carrafa, noble Neapolitans, were made cardinals by Paul IV in 1555.

Alfonso Carrafa, noble Neapolitan, was made cardinal by the same pope in 1557.

Girolamo Seripanno, noble Neapolitan, general of the Order of Hermits of St. Augustine,

Iñigo d'Avalos of Aragon, noble Neapolitan, and

Alfonso Gesualdo, noble Neapolitan, were made cardinals by Pius IV in 1561.

Aniballe Bozzuto, noble Neapolitan, was made cardinal by the same pope in 1565.

Guglielmo Sirleto, of the city of Stilo in Calabria, was made cardinal by the same pope in 1565.

Antonio Carrafa, noble Neapolitan, was made cardinal by Pius V in 1568.

Giulio Antonio Santoro of the city of Caserta, was made cardinal by the same pope in 1570.

Paolo d'Arezzo of the city of Itri, regular Theatine cleric, was made a cardinal in the same year by the same pope.

Giulio Acquaviva of Aragon, noble Neapolitan, was also made a cardinal by him in the same year.

Vincenzo Lauro of the city of Tropea in Calabria, was made cardinal in 1583 by Gregory XIII.

Ottavio Acquaviva of Aragon, noble Neapolitan, was made cardinal in 1591 by Gregory XIV.

Lutio Sasso, Neapolitan, was made cardinal by Clement VIII in 1593.

Cesare Baronio of the city of Sora, of the Congregation of the Oratorio, famous author of the *Ecclesiastical Annals,* was made cardinal by the same pope in 1596.

Filippo Spinello, noble Neapolitan, was made cardinal by the same pope in 1604.

Detio Carrafa, noble Neapolitan, was made cardinal by Pope Paul V in 1611.

Ladislao d'Aquino, noble Neapolitan, was made cardinal by the same pope in 1616.

Lutio Sanseverino, noble Neapolitan, was made cardinal in 1621 by Gregory XV.

Francesco Maria Brancaccio, noble Neapolitan, was made cardinal by Pope Urban VIII in 1633.

Ascanio Filomarino, noble Neapolitan, was made cardinal by Pope Urban VIII in 1641.

Pier Luigi Carrafa, noble Neapolitan, was made cardinal by Innocent X on March 6, 1645.

Ottavio Acquaviva, noble Neapolitan, was made cardinal by Innocent X on March 2, 1654.

Carlo Carrafa, noble Neapolitan, was made cardinal by Alexander VII on January 14, 1664.

Iñigo Caracciolo, noble Neapolitan, was made cardinal by Alexander VII on March 7, 1667.

POPES FROM THE KINGDOM AND CITY OF NAPLES

S. Telesforo, born in the ancient city of Turia in Calabria, today called Terranova, was elected pope in 139.

St. Dionysius I, born in the same city of Turia in Calabria, called Magna Graecia, was elected pope in 261.

St. Felix IV, Beneventan, was elected pope in 526.

Boniface V, Neapolitan, was elected pope in 617.

John VII, born in the city of Rossano in Calabria, was elected pope in 706.

Victor III, son of the prince of Benevento, first called Desiderius as a Benedictine monk, was elected pope in 1086.

Gelasius II, born in Gaeta, was raised from a monk of Monte Cassino to the papacy in 1118.

Gregory VIII, from the noble Morra family of Benevento, was elected pope in 1187.

St. Celestine V, first named Pietro, founder of the monastic order called the Celestines, born in the city of Isernia in the Contado di Molise, was elected pope in 1294.

Urban VI, Neapolitan of the house of Prignano, from archbishop of Bari was elected to the papacy in 1378.

Boniface IX, noble Neapolitan, called Pietro Tomacello, was elected pope in 1389.

Innocent VII, born in the city of Sulmona, first called Cosmo de'Migliorati, was elected pope in 1404.

John XXIII, noble Neapolitan, first called Baldassar Cossa, was elected pope in 1410.

Paul IV, noble Neapolitan, first called Giovanni Pietro Carrafa, founder of the order of the Theatine Fathers, was elected pope in 1555.

ECCLESIASTICAL TRIBUNALS

The first is the ordinary Tribunal of the Archbishopric, the major church of this most faithful city, which has the most eminent cardinal with his most reverend vicar, with a lawyer and prosecutor, judges, master of acts and clerks.

Second, there are two tribunals of the most Holy Inquisition, or of the Holy Office, one for the city of Naples, which resides in the same archbishopric; and the other for all the kingdom with judges, consultants, prosecutors, and master of acts, which resides in the house of the Inquisitor.

The third is the tribunal of the most illustrious and reverend monsignor nuncio, which has its auditors, lawyers and prosecutors, with a master of acts, and clerks.

The fourth is the tribunal of the holy building of S. Pietro, which extends throughout the kingdom and has cognizance over the cases of the pious legate. It also has its judges of the first, second and third cases, who are royal ministers chosen by the lord viceroys of the kingdom, who serve a set term, with his secretary, prosecutor, master of acts, and clerks.

The fifth is the tribunal of St. John of Jerusalem, called the Knights of Malta, which also has its judge, with a prosecutor and master of acts.

Churches Free of the Jurisdiction of the Ordinary

The venerable church of S. Maria Incoronata was submitted to the jurisdiction of the reverend prior of the Certosa of S. Martino of Naples, which recognizes all the priests who serve in it, in civil as well as criminal cases.

There is also the venerable church of S. Antonio, similarly free from the ordinary jurisdiction of the archbishop.

There is also the jurisdiction of the venerable church of S. Giacomo degli Spagnoli. The priests of this church are subject to the major chaplain.

ARCHIEPISCOPAL AND EPISCOPAL ORGANIZATION OF THE KINGDOM OF NAPLES

In the Kingdom of Naples there are 148 cities, in which there are 21 archbishoprics and 127 bishoprics, and of these, our lord the king has the right of presenting eight archbishoprics and sixteen bishoprics granted by Pope

Clement VII to the most invincible Charles V on June 29, 1529. The archbishoprics are Brindisi, Lanciano, Matera, Otranto, Reggio, Salerno, Trani, and Taranto. The bishoprics are Ariano, Acerra, Aquila, Cotrone, Cassano, Castellamare di Stabia, Gaeta, Gallipoli, Giovenazzo, Motolla, Monopoli, Pozzuoli, Potenza, Trivento, Tropea and Ugento.

The archbishop of Naples has these suffragans: the bishop of Nola; the bishop of Pozzuoli, who is royal; the bishop of Cerra, who is royal; the bishop of Ischia; and the bishop of Aversa, who is free.

The archbishop of Capua has these suffragans: the bishop of Triano; the bishop of Calvi; the bishop of Caserta; the bishop of Caiazza; the bishop of Carinola; the bishop of Sessa; the bishop of Venafro; the bishop of Isernia; the bishop of Aquino; the bishop of Monte Cassino, who is the abbot of this place of the order of St. Benedict, ordained so by Pope John XXII in 1334 and is free; and the bishop of Fondi, who is free.

The archbishop of Salerno is royal and has these suffragans: the bishop of Campagna, the bishop of Capaccio, the bishop of Policastro, the bishop of Nusco, the bishop of Sarno, the bishop of Marsico Novo, the bishop of Nocera de'Pagani, the bishop of Acerno, and the bishop of Cava, who is free.

The archbishop of Amalfi was made archbishop in the time of Pope Sergius and has these suffragans: the bishop of Lettere; the bishop of Capri; the bishop of Minori; the bishop of Scala, who is united with Ravello and is free; and the bishop of Ravello, who is united with Scala.

The archbishop of Sorrento, ordained by Sergius III, has these suffragans: the bishop of Vico, the bishop of Massa (Lubrense), and the archbishop of Castellamare di Stabia, who is royal.

The archbishop of Consa has these suffragans: the bishop of Muro; the bishop of Cangiano; the bishop of Satriano, who is united with that of Campagna; the bishop of Monteverde; the bishop of Cedonia; the bishop of S. Angelo dei Lombardi; and the bishop of Bisaccia, who is one with that of S. Angelo.

The archbishop of Acerenza has these suffragans: the bishop of Matera, at present united with him, made archbishop and is royal and is called Archbishop Acheruntinus and Materanus; the bishop of Venosa; the bishop of Anglona, who is transferred to Tursi; the bishop of Potenza, who is royal; the bishop of Gravina; and the bishop of Tricarico.

The archbishop of Taranto is royal and has these suffragans: the bishop of Motolla, who is also royal; and the bishop of Castellaneta.

The archbishop of Brindisi was united with that of Oria and today Oria has its own particular bishop, is royal and has this suffragan: the bishop of Ostuni, also royal.

The archbishop of Otranto is royal and has these suffragans: the bishop of Castro; the bishop of Gallipoli, royal; the bishop of Ugento, royal; the bishop of Lecce; the bishop of Capo di Leuco, united with that of Alessano; and the bishop of Nardo, who is free.

The archbishop of Bari has these suffragans: the bishop of Bitonto; the bishop of Molfetta; the bishop of Giovenazzo, who is royal; the bishop of Ruvo; the bishop of Salpe; the bishop of Polignano; the bishop of Mondorvino; the bishop of Lavello; the bishop of Conversano; the bishop of Bitetto; the bishop of Andria; the bishop of Bisceglia; and the bishop of Buda in Slavonia is also suffragan of Bari.

The archbishop of Trani is royal and has these suffragans: the bishop of Montepeluso, who is exempt; and the bishop of Alessano, who is united with that of Capo di Leuco.

The archbishop of Siponto, or of Monte Gargano, which today is called Monte S. Angelo, and of Manfredonia, metropolitan of Apulia has these suffragans: the bishop of Vieste, today suffragan, although in other times free; the bishop of Rapolla, united with that of Melsi, who is free; the bishop of Monopoli, who is royal and free; the bishop of Troia, who is free; and the bishop of San Severo, who is free.

The archbishop of Benevento has these suffragans: the bishop of Nocera d'Apulia, who, according to Frezza, is suffragan of Trani, called also di S. Maria; the bishop of Ascoli; the bishop of Firenzuola; the bishop of Telese; the bishop of S. Agata dei Goti; the bishop of Monteverde; the bishop of Montemarano; the bishop of Avellino, who has united the bishop of Frecenti; the bishop of Vico della Baronia; the bishop of Ariano, who is royal; the bishop of Boiano; the bishop of Bovino; the bishop of Turribolense; the bishop of Dragonara; the bishop of Volturara; the bishop of Larino; the bishop of Canne; the bishop of Termoli; the bishop of Lesina; the bishop of Trivento, who is royal and free; and the bishop of Guardia Alfiera.

The archbishop of Rossano has no suffragan bishops.

The bishop of Bisignano is free.

The archbishop of Cosenza has these suffragans: the bishop of Martorano; the bishop of S. Marco, who is free and is still so; and the bishop of Mileto, who is one with that of Montelione.

The archbishop of Reggio is royal, is titled the count of Bova and has these suffragans: the bishop of Nicastro; the bishop of Taverna, who is united with that of Catanzaro; the bishop of Amantea, who is united with that of Tropea; the bishop of Cotrone, who is royal; the bishop of Oppido; the bishop of Castellamare della Bruca; the bishop of Cassano; the bishop of Tropea, who is royal; the bishop of Geraci; the bishop of Squillace; the bishop of Nicotera; and the bishop of Bova.

The bishop of the Lipari Islands is one with that of Parenza, and they are suffragans to the archbishop of Messina.

The archbishop of S. Severina has these suffragans: the bishop of Umbriatico; the bishop of Belcastro; the bishop of Sitomense; the bishop of Isola; the bishop of Cerenza, who is united with that of Cariati; the bishop of Strongoli; the bishop of Cariati, who is united with Cerenza; and the bishop of Monteleone, who is united with Cerenza.

The archbishop of the city of Chieti has these suffragans: the bishop of the city of Penna, who is united with that of Atri; the bishop of Sulmona, also called Valva; the bishop of Campli; the bishop of Ortona a Mare; the bishop of Sora; the bishop of Teramo, free, who is entitled the prince of Teramo, count of Bisennio, and when performing as a bishop he is armed in white; the bishop of Aquila, who is royal and free; and the bishop of Marsi, who is free.

The archbishop of Lanciano has no suffragans.

18. PORTA CAPUANA DISTRICT. FROM BARATTA PLAN.
Castel Capuana (R), S. Caterina a Formiello (62), SS. Annunziata (bottom L).

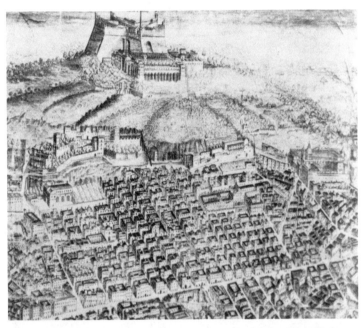

19. CASTEL S. ELMO AND S. MARTINO. FROM BARATTA PLAN.
Montecalvario (grid, center) and Via Toledo (bottom L to R).

THE RULERS OF NAPLES

After the Roman Empire was transferred to Greece and after that majesty began to lose its power, Italy and that part that today is called the Kingdom of Naples was assaulted by different barbarian nations, such as the Goths, the Ostrogoths, the Vandals, the Saracens, and other similar nations, of whose dominion there remains no trace. Narses, captain of the Emperor Justinian I (527-565), after he had defeated the Goths was ungratefully cast aside by the Emperor Justin II (565-578), who succeeded his uncle in 565. Narses, therefore, called the Lombards, under King Alboin, from Pannonia to Italy. Alboin was killed by his wife (Rosamund) in 571.

Cleph succeeded him, and he ruled for a year and a half and was killed in 572. The Lombards no longer wished a royal government and elected thirty-six dukes, among whom they divided their whole empire. Among these was that of Benevento. Under these dukes they lived for the span of ten years; later they appointed Authari, son of Cleph, as their king (584-590), in the year 584. He overran Italy as far as Reggio Calabria, where he established the boundary of the kingdom of the Lombards. Returning from there to Benevento, he was received with honor by Duke Zottone (590-594). He, therefore, gave him Lucania and Calabria, and whatever he might have acquired in these provinces that are included in the Kingdom of Naples.

To his successors several counts of the same nations were obedient, such as those of Chieti, Penna, Aquino, Calvi, Carinola, Carazza, Fundi, Sora, Telese, Termoli, Traietto, Venafro, Alife, Boiano, Isernia, Larino, Molise,

Teano, Acerenza, Conza, Celano, Sangro, Pietra Abundante, Valva, and Marsi, and other similar ones. However, there remained there some lands and cities in Apulia and Calabria that were obedient to Greece. This Duchy of Benevento was afterwards divided into three principalities: of Benevento, Salerno, and Capua, which came to an end after the king was chosen by the Normans, as we will discuss next.

The greater part of the following chronology of dukes and princes of Benevento was communicated by Camillo Pellegrino (1598-1663), gentleman of Capua, drawn from his *History of the Lombards,* which I have in my hands, where he has particular knowledge of them and their deeds.

DUKES OF BENEVENTO

Zottone, elected Duke of Benevento in the year 571, to whom succeeded:

Arechi I, in the year 591, to whom succeeds

Aione I, his son, in the year 640, to whom succeeds

Radoaldo, son of the duke of Forli (Friuli), in the year 642, and to him

Grimualdo I, his brother, in the year 647, who, having been made king of the Lombards, made duke

Romualdo I, his son, in the year 662, to whom succeeds

Grimualdo II, his son, in the year 677, and to him succeeds

Gisulfo I, his brother, in the year 686, to whom succeeds

Romualdo II, in the year 703, who was expelled, and to him succeeded

Gisulfo II in 729, who was expelled, and to him succeeded

Andoaldo (Andelao), in the same year, and to him succeeded

Gregorio, nephew of King Liutprand, in 732, to whom succeeded

Godescalco in the year 738, who was killed, and to him succeeded

Gisulfo II, again, in the year 742, to whom succeeded

Liutprand in the year 750.

PRINCES OF BENEVENTO

Arechi II, in the year 753 succeeded the above-mentioned Liutprand, who because of his ample dominion was not satisfied with the ducal title and wanted to be called Prince, and so had himself anointed and crowned to the royalty (758) by the hand of the bishop of Benevento. His wife was Adelperga, the daughter of King Desiderius, and with her he ruled.

Romualdo, his last son, in the year 777, who died during the life of his father, and after the death of Arechi, succeeded

Grimualdo III, his son, in the year 788. He had as his wife Eirene, the niece of the Emperor of Constantinople, and because he did not leave sons to him succeeded

Grimualdo IV, prince of the same name, and his treasurer, in the year 806. Because of his greed and desire to dominate, he fostered discord among his barons, and he was killed, and to him succeeded

Sico (di Aurenza), in the year 818, who was an exile of Spoleto, to whom succeeded

Sigardo, his son, in the year 832. His wife was Adelchisia, but for being too dissolute with carnal pleasures he was killed, and to him succeeded

Radelchi I, his treasurer, in the year 839. He exiled from Benevento Dauferio, the son of the dead prince, Sigardo, along with Gauferius and Maione his sons and other Beneventani. For fear of war these retreated to Salerno and joined with Landolfo Guastaldo of Capua and with other Beneventani, Salernitani and Amalfitani, procured the freedom of Siconulfo the brother of Prince Sicardo, who by order of his brother had found himself imprisoned at Taranto. Coming to Salerno, they appointed him prince in the year 840. Therefore different wars between Radelchi and Siconulfo took place, which was the main reason for calling the Saracens to their aid, who after a while troubled those provinces. Finally, through the efforts of Emperor Louis, in the year 851 the principality was divided, turning over to Radelchi that of Benevento and to the Siconulfo that of Salerno. After the death of Radelchi there succeeded to the principality of Benevento:

Radelgario, his son, in the year 851; to him succeeded

Adelchi, his brother, in the year 854, and to him succeeded

Gaideriso, his son, in the year 878, and to him succeeded

Radelchi II, the son of Adelchi, in the year 881, who was expelled, and then there was chosen

Aione II, his brother, in the year 884, to whom succeeded

Urso, his son, in the year 890. In his time the Greeks occupied Benevento in 891, and there governed through the Greek Empire, one after the other:

Sambaticio Stratigo in the year 891, and after him

Georgio Patritio, in the year 893 to 896, and he was expelled by Guido, marquis of Spoleto.

Guido, marquis of Spoleto also of the Lombards, expelling the Greeks of Benevento, made himself prince in 896 and afterwards succeeding to the emperor of Italy, left the principality to

Radelchi II, mentioned above, who was driven from the state in 898. After two years he was again driven out by the Beneventani; and Atenolfo, count of Capua, was chosen prince.

Atenolfo I, the Count of Capua, driven from Benevento by Radelchi, was elected prince in the year 900 and wished to entitle himself prince of Benevento and of Capua, after his death (in 910) succeeded by

Atenolfo II (911-940) and

Landolfo I (910-943), his sons, in the year 910, and after the death of Atenolfo, Landolfo ruled alone another three years until 943, and to them succeeded

Atenolfo III (933-943) and

Landolfo II (940-961), and to him succeeded

Pandolfo I, called Iron Head, in the year 943. After this prince, who died in the beginning of the year 981, there is the greatest obscurity regarding other princes succeeding up to around the year 1000. It is again the princes of Salerno and Capua in the same years. Nevertheless, the following princes of Benevento are noted, rediscovered in history:

Pandolfo II, in the year 981, to whom succeeds

Landolfo V in the year 1015, to whom succeeds

Pandolfo III in the year 1033, to whom succeeds

Landolfo VI in the year 1059. He held the principality until 1077, in whose person the princes terminate, and Benevento passed to the Roman Church.

But Platina said (sic) that during the life of Gregory X Benevento had passed to the Roman church under the pontificate of this pope, who was elected in the year 1049 and lived until 1055. It was given to him by the Emperor Henry II in satisfaction for the feudal duty that he gave to the Roman church for the church of Bamberg given by Emperor Henry I to Pope Benedict VIII.

PRINCES OF SALERNO

Siconulfo, son of Sicone, prince of Benevento, was elected prince against Radelchi in 840, on account of the work of the Beneventani, Salernitani, and Amalfitani with the help of Landolfo, count of Capua. After many subsequent wars between them, they made peace by dividing the principality, leaving to Radelchi that of Benevento and to Siconulfo that of Salerno. This division was confirmed by Emperor Louis (the Pious) in 851 as in the *Chronicle of Cassino,* Book I, chapters 24 and 28. To him succeeded

Sicone, his son, left a young boy under the tutelage of Pietro, his godfather, in 851. Because he aspired to rule, he sent Sicone to King Louis to learn, as he told him, the behavior of court, and he as much held the state for Ademario his son. When Sicone afterwards was returning to his state in Capua, one night he was killed through the work of Ademario.

Ademario, son of Pietro, in 852, after he took the state from Sicone and had him killed, and was unleashed from fear, gave himself over to tyranny, allowing his wife Guaimaltruda many evils. Therefore in 861 he was imprisoned by the Salernitani, and in his place was chosen

Dauferio, son of Maione, brother-in-law of the above Siconulfo, in 861. But because this election was carried out by some young Beneventani, without the consent of the Salernitani, it was not approved, and he was deposed through the work of Guaifaro, his uncle, who aspired to rule.

Guaifaro, uncle of Dauferio and brother of Maione, who were the sons of Dauferio the Mute, deposed his nephew and sent him into exile in Naples. He was chosen prince in 861, and at the end of his life he became a monk of Cassino (880). His wife was Landelaica, daughter of Landone, count of Capua. To him succeeded

Guaimario I, his son, who was taken as a partner in the principality of his father in the year 877. He was such a cruel man, that he wished that Guido, marquis of Spoleto, would renounce the principality of Benevento, while he coveted it. The Beneventani did the work, so that he was imprisoned in Avellino, as it happened, by Alferio, lord of that place. After Marquis Guido insisted that he free him, which he could not obtain, he was forced to lay siege to Avellino. Finally to remove himself from that pressure, Alferio had Guaimario blinded and sent him back to the marquis. From there he went to Salerno, and persisting in the same life, was by force made to withdraw to the monastery of S. Massimo of Salerno, leaving the administration to Guaimario II, his son, whom he had by the Princess Iota, sister of Marquis Guido, and there he died around 899.

Guaimario II, son of the first, was taken by his father as a partner in the principality in 893. He married Gaitelgrima, the daughter of Atenolfo, prince of Benevento and Capua. He died in 946, and to him succeeded

Gisulfo, his son, who was three years old when his father had him invested in 934. And he found himself ruling until 975. At the request of his mother, Landolfo, his uncle, with his four sons, who had been expelled from Capua, were called to Salerno. Made great and powerful, one night they imprisoned him, and they took the state. His wife was Gemma.

Pandolfo I, son of Prince Pandolfo Iron Head, was adopted by Prince Gisulfo into the principality in 959. From the Privileges in Montecalvario.

Landolfo, the father, and

Landolfo, the son, having taken the state from Gisulfo, had themselves acclaimed princes, and they held the principality of Salerno from 975 to 984, in which year Prince Giovanni succeeded. It is said that Prince Landolfo, the son, became a monk of Cassino. As for Prince Landolfo, the father, there is no memory of him up to today, except that some conform in saying that he was expelled by the above-mentioned Prince Pandolfo, who ruled until 981.

Giovanni I (981-983) is considered the son of Prince Gisulfo, named above. There is no certainty as to how he might have regained the state. His (Giovanni II) principality began in 984, and he lived until 994, dying in the arms of one of his concubines on the night that the eruption of Vesuvius occurred, as Cardinal Peter Damian says. And the same cardinal says that this was that Giovanni who was the grandfather of Prince Guaimario who was killed in Salerno. His wife was Sicilgaita, by whom he had

Guido, taken by him as a partner in the principality and dying during the lifetime of his father. In his place his other son Guaimario was taken as partner in 988.

Guaimario III, called the Bold, son of Giovanni, was in 988 taken by his father as a partner in the principality. After he had ruled for 42 years he became a monk in the monastery of Santissima Trinità della Cava in 1029, as Protospata says. He died in the same year. His wife was Gaitelgrima, and he left

Guaimario IV, who was taken by his father as a partner in the principality in 1019. He was also prince of Capua in 1038, and he ruled it for nine years. He was killed in Salerno with thirty-six wounds in 1052, the thirty-fourth year of his principality and his eleventh year as prince. He left his son Gisulfo by his wife Purpura.

Gisulfo, the second of this name and the last of the Lombards, who was taken by his father as a partner in the principality in 1042, had Gemma for a wife, by whom he had many sons. He was expelled in 1074 by Robert Guiscard, his brother-in-law. Others say this happened in 1076.

*

Robert Guiscard, son of the Norman Tancred, was duke of Apulia, Calabria, and Sicily in 1074 or 1076. He held the principality of Salerno from Gisolfo, his brother-in-law. He had for a wife Sykelgaita, sister of Prince Gisolfo, and by her he had Roger. He died in 1085, although he had another wife (Alberada) with whom he had Bohemond, prince of Antioch, who went on crusade with Baldwin.

Roger (Borsa), son of Robert, succeeded his father in 1085. He had as a wife Adelaide, the daughter of Robert the Frisian, count of Flanders. He died in 1111 and to him succeeded

William, his son, who has as a wife Gaitelgrima, daughter of Roberto, count of Airola. He died in 1127 without leaving sons, and to him succeeded

Roger II, count of Sicily, his uncle, son of Count Roger of Sicily, brother of Duke Robert Guiscard, who was made king of Sicily in 1130.

*

Charles, son of Charles I (of Anjou), was made prince of Salerno by the king, his father, in 1269. After the death of his father he succeeded to the crown, and he was called Charles II.

Charles, the first son of Charles II, while king of Hungary, was prince of Salerno in 1292.

PRINCES OF SALERNO
FROM NON-ROYAL FAMILIES

Giordano Colonna, brother of Pope Martin V (1417-1431), was made prince of Salerno and duke of Venosa in 1419 by Queen Giovanna II. To him succeeded

Antonio Colonna, his son, in 1423, and he held the principality until 1432.

Raimondo Ursino, count of Nola and grand justiciar of the kingdom, was made prince of Salerno by King Alfonso I. He died in 1458, and to him succeeded

Felice Ursino, his son, who was deprived of the principality by King Ferrante I in the war that he had with the barons in 1460. He gave this city to

Roberto Sanseverino, count of Marsico and grand admiral of the kingdom. He had as a gift from King Ferrante I the city of Salerno with the title of prince in 1463. To him succeeded

Antonello Sanseverino, his son, in 1477. He came into discord with King Ferrante; he was removed from the state and died in Sinigaglia in 1497.

Roberto Sanseverino, son of Antonello, after the Catholic King (Ferdinand of Spain) had acquired the kingdom, had the principality of Salerno and all his paternal estate. He married Donna Maria of Aragon, niece of the same Catholic King, to whom succeeded

Ferrante Sanseverino, his son, who lost the state in 1552 through rebellion, and by the king it was sold to

Nicolò Grimaldo, Genoese duke of Eboli, making him prince of Salerno in 1558 after that city became a royal domain, so he lives there today under the wings of the king, our lord.

COUNTS AND PRINCES OF CAPUA

Trasmondo, count of Capua.

Mictula, count of Capua.

Landolfo, count of Capua in 820 (840-842), to whom succeeded

Landone I, his son, count of Capua in 856 (842-861), and to him succeeded

Landone II, his son, in 861, and he was expelled by his uncle.

Pando (Marepahis), having expelled his nephew, was count of Capua in 862, and to him succeeded

Landolfo II (862-879), his brother, who was bishop of Capua, and to him

Landone III (882-885) and to him succeeded

Pandenolfo (885-887), his brother, to whom succeeded

Atenolfo I (887-910), who being count of Capua, was elected prince of Benevento by the Beneventani in 900, after he expelled Prince Radelchi. He also wished to entitle himself prince of Capua, and to him succeeded

Atenolfo II (911-940) and

Landolfo III (901-943), his sons, who were princes in 910, and after the death of Atenolfo, Landolfo ruled alone until 943, and to him succeeded

Atenolfo III in 943 (933-943). To whom succeeded

Landolfo IV in 961 (940-961), and to him succeeded

Pandolfo I, called Iron Head, in 969. To whom succeeded

Landolfo V in 981 (959-968), and to him succeeded

Landenolfo II in 982. To whom succeeded

Laidolfo in 993, and to him

Ademario in 1000, chosen by the Emperor Otto (III), the he was expelled, and chosen was

Landolfo VI, called di S. Agata, in the same year, and to him succeeded

Pandolfo II in 1007 and with him also ruled

Pandolfo III, prince of Benevento, from 1009, who with

Pandolfo IV, son of the above-mentioned Prince Pandolfo of Benevento, ruled from 1015 up to 1022, and expelled by the emperor (Henry II),

Pandolfo V (1020-1022), formerly count of Teano, was chosen, and expelled in 1022

Pandolfo IV, son of the prince of Benevento, mentioned above, was chosen in 1025 (1026-1038). After he was expelled by the emperor

Guaimario IV, prince of Salerno, was chosen in 1038, and he held
  it for nine years and after returned it to his brother-in-law
Pandolfo IV, mentioned above, and he was prince for the third time
  in 1047. He was also duke of Naples, and to him succeeded
Pandolfo VI (sic), his son, in 1047, and to him
Pandolfo VII, the last of these people in 1058.
Richard the Norman, count of Aversa, was expelled from the state.
  Landolfo (VIII, 1047-1062), prince of Capua, took this
  principality in 1058. He took as a partner in government his son,
  Giordano.
Giordano, son of Richard, was taken by his father as partner in
  1038 and after his death in 1078, he remained alone, and to him
  succeeded
Richard II, in 1090, who was expelled by the Capuani, and
Landone, Lombard, count of Teano, was chosen in 1091. He was
  expelled by

*

Richard II of Aversa, named above, who recaptured the state in
  1098, and in the siege of Capua a miracle of St. Bruno occurred.
  Bruno woke Count Roger, who came to the aid of Prince
  Richard, by making him cautious of treason plotted against him,
  to who succeeded
Robert, his brother, in 1107, and to him
Richard III (of Aversa) in 1120, to whom succeeded
Giordano II in 1120 and to him
Robert II in 1127, who was expelled by King Roger II, who
  appointed
Anfusio, his son, in 1135, who was expelled by
Robert II, prince named above, who recaptured the state in 1137,
  who, expelled again by the king,
Anfusio returned again in 1137, and to him succeeded
William, his brother, in 1144 who was later king of Sicily.
Robert II recaptured the state a third time in 1155.
Robert, son of King William, was made prince of Capua by the
  king, his father, in 1158. After his death the king of Naples
  retained the title of the prince of Capua for himself up to King
  Charles III (of Durazzo), who gave it to Francesco Bottilo
  Prignone, nephew of Urban VI, and later by Queen Giovanna II
  given to Rinaldo, son of King Ladislas, her brother, and after to
  Braccio da Montone and thereafter to Sergio Caracciolo. Finally
  since King Ferrante II's father was Alfonso II, duke of Calabria,
  he was himself prince of Capua, after which it always remained
  part of the royal crown.

DUKES OF NAPLES

Theodoro, consul and duke of Naples, from whom descended the family of dukes, built in Naples the church of SS. Pietro e Paolo under the empire of Constantine, the fourth indiction, which was 316 according to Falco, Capaccio, and Summonte.

N., consul and duke. Mention is made of this duke without name in the life of S. Patrizia c.361 AD

N., consul and duke. Mention is made of this duke in the life of S. Severo, bishop of Naples, in 383 AD, in the miracle done by him who asked to pay the debt to death.

Maurentio, consul and duke. St. Gregory mentions him in letter 70 of Book 7 in 593 AD, writing to him that the bishop of Naples was annoyed by Vectano, count of Miseno, over the question of twenty barrels of wine, and he ordered it to be given to him for that one time so that he would not annoy him.

Gundino, consul and duke. St. Gregory mentions him in letter 5 of book 12 around 602.

Constantino, elected duke and consul by Pope St. Gregory in 604. Indiction 7, letter 24.

John Campsino. When he died, Giovanni, exarch of Ravenna, occupied Naples in 615 and after he went to Ravenna and took the exarchate in 619, he remained in Naples.

N., duke and consul in 619, who is not mentioned by name, to whom succeeded

Theodoro II, duke and consul, and to him

Sergio Crispano in 661, to whom succeeded

Theocrito, duke and consul in 685 under Pope Benedict II. During his time the eruption of Vesuvius occurred.

Giovanni II, surnamed Cumano, for having taken that city from the hands of the duke of Benevento. He was elected duke and consul in 717, and to him succeeded

Exhilerato, duke and consul, and adherent to Emperor Leo the Isaurian. He tried to kill Pope Gregory II, according to Baronio in volume 9, in the year 726, and he was killed by the Romans, and to him succeeded

Pietro, who was chosen consul and duke and master of the knights in 726. Following the footsteps of his predecessor he was killed, as claims Anastasio, librarian. To him succeeded

Stefano, chosen consul and duke in 732, and after ten years, from his dukedom of Laico, he was chosen bishop of Naples in 744.

Cesario, son of Stefano, was taken by his father as a partner in the dukedom in 770 and died during the life of his father.

Theofilo II (794-801), the husband of Euprasia, daughter of Stefano, was chosen duke and consul in 787.

Antichimio (Antimo, 801-818) was chosen consul and duke at the time of Pope Leo III around 795.

Theotisto was chosen duke and consul after Antimo, after a controversy arose over the election of the new duke. He was sent to Sicily by this Theotisto, who was chosen duke and master of the knights.

Theodoro III, Prothospatario, was chosen duke after Theotisto, but being of wicked habits was expelled alive by the Neapolitans; and they elected

Stefano III (821-832), duke and master of the knights, who was nephew of the first Stefano, against whom, in 817 came Sicone, prince of Benevento, to lay siege to Naples. Not able to obtain it, Sicone turned to deceit. As if negotiating for peace, his ambassadors entered the city to surrender and killed him. Then there was chosen

Bono (832-834), one of the ambassadors, who was the murderer. He died in 820, and to him succeeded

Leone, son of Bono, who was elected duke (in 834). After six months he was expelled by Andrea, his father-in-law, from the dukedom.

Andrea II (834-840). After he expelled his son-in-law, Leone, from the dukedom, he was made duke in 820. Sicardo, prince of Benevento, came against him to lay siege to Naples in 837 under the pretext that he denied him tribute. He had recourse to the help of the Saracens and made peace. Andrea was also duke of Sorrento and Amalfi.

Contardo, captain of the Emperor Lothair (840-855), who came to Naples to help Andrea, found Sicardo dead in 837. Andrea gave him his daughter Euprasia as a wife, formerly the wife of Leone, who out of a desire to rule killed Andrea and took the state in 837. Because he did evil he was killed after three days (in 840) by the Neapolitans.

Sergio I (840-860), from the line of the dukes of Amalfi, was chosen duke, consul and master of Neapolitan knights in 837. By his wife, Drosa, he had Gregorio; Attanagio, bishop of Naples, who was included among the saints; Stefano, bishop of Sorrento; and Cesario.

Gregorio III (864-870) succeeded Sergio, his father, in the dukedom in 844. He had two sons, Sergio and Attanagio, bishop of Naples, who succeeded to the bishopric of his above-mentioned uncle.

Sergio II (870-877), son of Gregorio, was taken by his father as a partner and succeeded at the death of his father. He kept a close friendship with the Saracens, who lived in Garigliano. Hating the holy admonitions of his uncle Attanagio, he imprisoned him and for that was excommunicated by the pope. Afterwards he was expelled from the state in 878 by his brother Attanagio, who succeeded to the bishopric of Naples through the death of his uncle.

Attanagio (877-898), brother of Sergio, was bishop of Naples through the death of Bishop S. Attanagio, his uncle in 878. He expelled his brother from the state, and he blinded him and held the state until 914, as in the decretal letters of Pope John VIII (872-882).

Gregorio IV (898-915) was elected duke and master of the Neapolitan knights in 914. He allied with Giovanni, duke of Gaeta; Guaimario, prince of Salerno; Atenolfo and Landolfo, princes of Benevento; with the Greeks, the Apulians and the Calabresi, and together with the pope and Marquis Alberico, they expelled the Saracens from Garigliano (in 915).

Giovanni II (915-919) was duke and master of the knights in 944, as Leone Hostiense writes in book 1, chapter 59. He was also duke of Sorrento. He died in 993 in the eruption of Vesuvius, according to Cardinal Peter Damian, letter 5, chapter 13. To him succeeded

Marino I (919-928), his son, whom he had taken as a partner, and was duke, consul and master of the knights with his father, in the twenty-ninth year of (Byzantine Emperor) Constantine (VII, 913-959), and the twenty-sixth of Emperor Romanus (I, Lecapenus, 920-944), which was 947 of the Christian era, as in a donation he made to the monastery of S. Vincenzo in Voltuno, a Neapolitan church in Piazza di Forcella; and in another of 638 he made to the same monastery, according to Giovanni, where mention is made of Duke Marino II (968-975), his son.

Oligamo Stella, consul, and duke, is mentioned by Francesco Elio Marchese in the families of Naples under Pope Sergius IV (1009-1012) who took the seat in 1009, if we wish to lend credence to him.

Giovanni III (928-968), son of Marino I, was duke, consul and master of the knights in 1018, as in a donation made to the monastery of S. Severino of Naples.

Sergio IV (1002-1027), son of Giovanni IV (999-1002) is found as duke and master of the cavalry in 1027 under (Byzantine Emperor) Basil (II, 976-1025), in the fifth year of Constantine (VIII, 1025-1028). Mention is made of him and of his son Giovanni in 1034 under the fifth year of the Emperor Romanus (III, Argyrus, 1028-1034) in a donation made to the monastery of S. Sebastiano, of which he was a monk.

Giovanni V (1036-1050), son of Sergio, was duke in 1034, as in the donation mentioned above.

Sergio V (1050-1082), son of Giovanni, who was the son of Sergio, was duke in 1053, as in a donation made to the monastery of S. Sebastiano, Sergio e Bacco, of the fishery in Torre di S. Vincenzo, in the eleventh year of the Emperor Constantine IX (1042-1055). This Sergio was expelled from the state by Pandolfo, prince of Capua. After three years he regained it, and he is found in 1071 in the consecration of the church of Monte Cassino.

Pandolfo, prince of Capua, was also duke of Naples after he expelled Sergio around 1047, and he remained there three years.

Giovanni VI (1097-1120), son of Sergio VI (1082-1097), was taken as a partner by his father, who had regained the state, and is found as duke in 1090, the ninth year of Emperor Alexius (I Comnenus), as is read in a donation made to the monastery of S. Liguoro of Naples, through Duke Sergio, his father, as much for himself, as for his son, Giovanni. His wife was Eba, daughter of Goffredo, duke of Gaeta.

Sergio VII (1120-1137), son of Giovanni VI, had a long war with King Roger (II), of whom he made himself subject in 1137, and he died in 1139, on account of which King Roger acquired Naples.

*

Roger I (II), king, entitled himself also the duke of Naples, on account of which he made few dukes afterwards.

Anfusio, his son, as Falco of Benevento, an author of these times, says.

Alierno Cutuno, is found at the time of King Tancred (of Lecce, 1190-1194), consul and duke in 1190 in the privilege conceded to him from the coast of Amalfi.

PREFECTS, COUNTS AND LATER DUKES OF AMALFI

The city of Amalfi was built by the Romans in 339 AD, which at the time of Prince Sicardo was in total power over the seas. Since Sicardo feared this, he plotted with some Amalfitani the destruction of the city, promising them the greatest gifts, but these refused to commit such an impiety against their land. He united with other Amalfitani, whom he found agreeable to him, and with his Lombards and the Salernitani, at night they took it and destroyed it, carrying off all the citizens to live in Salerno. But they secretly united and set fire to the houses and the farms of the Salernitani, and they returned to their homeland in 829, electing their governors, calling them "Prefects," who were the following, although the list is interrupted:

Pietro was the first prefect in 819. To him succeeded

Scripo, son of Count Costanzo in 819. To him succeeded

Mauro in 831, after whom they choose two prefects every year. The series of them is not perfect because many are missing. Nevertheless, we found the following without any dates.

Marino, and after him

Urso, after whom they elected two prefects.

Urso II, count, and

Sergio, count, to whom succeeded

Leone, count, and

Tauro, count, to whom succeeded

Lupino, count, and

..., count, to whom succeeded

Urso III, count, and

Sergio II, count, and after them they returned to one, who was

Andrea, who was also duke of Naples and Sorrento, and after him

Sergio, son of Gregorio, duke of Naples, and after many years interval, because of not having any information, succeeded

Marino II, son of Luciano Pulchiar, who ruled with

Sergio III, his son of 14 years, and Marino, blinded, was sent into exile in Naples, and succeeded

Mauro, son of Marco Cunnacio, nephew of Marco, to whom succeeded

Sergio IV, son of Count Pietro, nephew of Marco Antonio Vicario, and to him succeeded

Marino III, who ruled four years and to him succeeded

Urso IV, son of Count Marino, son of Count Panteleone, son of Marco Cunnacio, expelled after six months, and they elected

Urso V, Calastante, son of Giovanni Salvo Romano Vitale, who was expelled after six months, and they proclaimed

Marino II (I, 859-873), the Blind, who was in exile in Naples with

Pulchero (874-883), his son, of whom Pope John VIII (872-882) makes mention in 877 in a letter of decretal lamenting that he had made league with the Saracens, and to him succeeded

Sergio V (di Leonato, 883-884), son of Sergio Eunato, with

Pietro, bishop, son of Urso, who ruled for one year, and Sergio (di Turco, 884-889) remained alone, who ruled five years, and to him succeeded

Mansone (890), nephew of Sergio I, son of Lupino I, nephew of Marco Vicario Antiocheno, and deposed after ten years, they elected

Leone II, Neapolitan, son of Marino (II, 890-896), nephew of Leone.

Mansone II Fusolo (897-914), son of Urso in 862. He held the dukedom for 16 years and became a monk, and to him succeeded

Mastallo (I, 914-952), son of Mansone Fusole, in 908. He held the dukedom for 40 years, joined with Giovanni.

Giovanni (939-947) his son, to whom succeeded

Mastallo II (950-958), his brother, with Androsa, his mother. He was killed and chosen was

Sergio VI (of Amalfi, I, 958-966), imperial noble, son of the said count. He held the dukedom seven and a half years from 952, and to him succeeded

Mansone III (I, 958-976), imperial noble, who ruled for 24 years from 959 and was expelled from the state by his brother and after imprisoned.

Alfeno (Adelferio, 984-988), after he imprisoned his brother, was made duke in 976 and to him succeeded

Sergio VII (II, as co-ruler, 984-988), his son, to whom succeeded

Mansone III (I, again, 988-1002), his uncle. Restored, he held the dukedom for 16 years and to him succeeded

Giovanni III (I, 1004-1007), called Perella, his son, imperial noble. He died after three years and to him succeeded

Sergio VIII (III, 1002-1014), his son, who ruled with

Giovanni III (II, 1014-1030), his son, for 15 years. To him succeeded

Sergio IX (IV, 1030-1034), in the year 1019, to whom succeeded

Mansone IV (II, 1034-1038), his son, with Maria his mother (1039), ruled for 44 years and 3 months from 1035.

Giovanni IV (II, 1039), having expelled Mansone, his brother, deprived him of his eyes, and confined him in the Sirenusa Islands, called de Galli, made himself duke.

Guaimario I (1039-1042), prince of Salerno, after he expelled Giovanni, he had the dukedom of Amalfi in 1039, and he held it for five years and six months.

Mansone IV (II, again, 1043-1052), mentioned above, thus blind, regained the dukedom, and stayed there ten years until 1054 and then returned

Giovanni IV (II, 1052-1069), his brother from Constantinople. The Amalfitani expelled Mansone and reinstated Giovanni and he ruled another 16 years. To him succeeded

Sergio X (IV, 1069-1073), his son, in 1070. He ruled for 16 years and with him succeeded

Giovanni V (III, 1069-1073), who was shortly afterward expelled by Robert Guiscard.

Robert Guiscard, duke of Apulia, acquired Amalfi in 1085, and the other dukes of Apulia held it in succession. Then under the king of Naples it was possessed by the barons Sanseverino, Ursino and Piccolomini. At present it is under the royal state.

DUKES OF SORRENTO: AN INTERRUPTED CHRONOLOGY

Andrea, duke of Naples, was also duke of Sorrento and Amalfi in the year 836, as we read in Eremperto in the peace made with Sicardo, prince of Benevento.

Giovanni, duke and consul of Naples and Sorrento, in 933, as Leone Hostiense says.

Guaimario IV (I of Amalfi), prince of Salerno and duke of Sorrento in 1039, of which he was invested.

Guidone, his brother, who is found duke in 1052.

Sergio, duke of Sorrento, attended the consecration of the church of Monte Cassino in 1071.

Sergio, son of Duke Sergio, is seen in the privileges granted by Duke William of Apulia at the Cavense monastery in 1117 where he signed "Prince of Sorrento." He was father-in-law of Giordano, prince of Capua.

DUKES OF GAETA, WHO ARE REMEMBERED

Giovanni, the great noble, was in 731 at the time of Pope Gregory III (731-741).

Docibile, duke of Gaeta, made a truce with the Saracens in 878, as we see in the decretal letter of Pope John VIII (872-882) and collected in Leone Hostiense in book 1 chapter 42. Pandolfo, prince of Capua, having demanded Gaeta from the pope in 883 and obtained it, displeasing Docibile, made league with the Saracens, who were in Agropoli, and he led them to Garigliano.

Giovanni Tipato I (877-933), son of Docibile I, lived in 914 at the time of Gregorio IV, duke of Naples, and he was made imperial patrician by the Greek emperor.

Alfedanio Bello gave his daughter Eba as a wife to Sergio (IV), duke of Naples, around 960.

Athenolfo d'Aquino (1045-1058), brother of Landone, count of Aquino, was taken by Landolfo, count of Theano, near Theano, and given into the power of Guaimario (IV), prince of Salerno. Upon which the counts of Aquino with the help of the Normans went to overcome Theano, but they were barred by (Frederick) the abbot of Cassino. But, falling into their hands, the abbot was held. For his liberation Guaimario returned Athenolfo, and the

Gaetani, through their disdain of Guaimario, named Athenolfo their duke. Because of this, Guaimario went against Athenolfo, overcame him, made peace and confirmed himself duke of Gaeta.

*

Richard and Giordano, father and son, (Norman) princes of Capua (and Aversa), acquired Gaeta in 1059, the second year of their principality. A document has been found where it is noted the seventh year of the principality of Capua and the sixth of the dukedom of Gaeta, which would be 1064, while they acquired Gaeta in 1058. After Prince Richard died, although he did not possess Gaeta, Prince Giordano retained for himself the title of duke with everything else as long as he lived, while at the same time are found the following dukes:

Lando (1064-1065), count of Traietto, was duke of Gaeta, as is gathered from a donation made to the Cassino monastery of how much he concerned himself with the good fathers and mothers under the Abbot Odoriso in the eighth year of Pope Gregory (Alexander II, 1061-1073) and the eighth of Emperor Henry IV, which would have been the year 1064.

Goffreddo Ridello, the Norman, also named Loffredo, was duke of Gaeta in 1072 (1068-1086). He gave to the monastery of S. Benedetto the church of S. Erasmo of Gaeta in the seventeenth year of the principality of Richard and Giordano, from which they seem to be subjects of the prince of Capua.

Ugone is mentioned as the duke of Gaeta in a donation made to the monastery of Cassino of the church of S. Erasmo, from whom was born

Giovanni and

Marino, brothers, who were dukes of Gaeta.

Jonatas, duke of Gaeta (1113-1121), is seen as duke in 1116 with the date of the fourth year of his dukeship, the beginning of which would then have been in 1112.

Andrea (dell'Aquila, 1111-1113), consul and duke of Gaeta, is found around 1114 in the *Chronicle of Cassino,* Book 4, chapter 72.

Roger II, king of Sicily, duke of Apulia (1113-1121), prince of Capua, and duke of Gaeta, with similar titles, is honored in a writing of 1153, the twenty-fourth year of his reign and dukedom, so that he acquired the dukedom in 1129.

THE COUNTS AND THE DUKES OF APULIA AND CALABRIA, FROM WHOM THE KINGS OF NAPLES DESCENDED

William, a Norman, called Iron Arm (1042-1046), son of Tancred, count of Hauteville in Normandy, after he and his brothers had expelled the Greeks from Apulia, had himself made count, and he died in 1046, and to him succeeded

Drogo, his brother, in (1046-)1051, who was killed by his god-father, and to him succeeded

Humphrey, his brother, who died in 1056, and to him succeeded

Robert Guiscard, his brother, which in the Norman tongue means bold and shrewd. Since he was count, he was made duke of Apulia and Calabria by the pope (Nicholas II), making him a vassal of the Roman Church in 1059. He died in 1085, and to him succeeded

Roger (Borsa), his son, who died in 1101, and to him succeeded

William (1111-1127), his son, who died in 1127 without sons, and to him succeeded

Roger, count of Sicily, who was the first king of Naples in 1130, the son of Roger, count of Sicily, brother of Robert Guiscard.

ROYAL CATAPANS, STRATEGOI, PATRICIANS AND CAPTAINS UNDER THE GREEK EMPEROR

Belisarius, patrician, after he had expelled the Goths from Italy, governed for the Emperor Justinian from 538 to 545. Source: *The Compendium of the Kingdom.*

Conone succeeded Belisarius until he was expelled by Totila, king of the Goths, when he took Naples in 545. Biondo.

Narses, patrician of the Persian nation, was a eunuch of the imperial palace and captain of the Emperor Justinian. He governed from 566 to 568. *The Compendium.*

Sabarto, Neapolitan gentleman, governed for the Emperor Constans II in 660. *The Compendium* and the *Lives of the Emperors.*

Gregorio, stratego and bailiff, governed Apulia for the Emperor Basil I (867-886) in 875. Lupo Protospata.

Cassano, patrician, governed with the title of duke for the Emperor Basil in 879. Eremperto.

Giovanni Candida, stratego and captain, governed for the Emperor Basil in 879, after Cassano. The same Eremperto.

Tradezi, stratego, governed for the Emperor Leo VI and Alexander in 886. Protospata.

Constantine, patrician steward of the emperors mentioned above, governed in 887. Eremperto.

Sambaticio, stratego, governed for the same emperors in 891. Protospata.

Giorgio, patrician, governed for the same emperors in 893. Eremperto.

Nicephorus Phocas, grandfather of the Emperor Nicephorus II, governed in 896 through the same emperors. Fazello (Tommaso, 1498-1570).

Melisano, stratego, governed for the same emperors in 900. Protospata.

Eustasio, steward and courtier of the Emperor Constantine VII (913-959), son of Leo, who began to rule in 909, governed for the same. Fazello.

Giovanni Mazzalone governed after Eustasio for the same Constantine and was killed by the Calabresi. Fazello in the second decade, Book 6, Chapter 1.

Cosmo Tessalonicense, stratego, governed for the same emperor after Giovanni. Fazello, as above.

Crinito Caldo, catapan, governed for the same emperor after Cosmo, and he was removed from it through his avarice. Fazello.

Ursino, stratego, governed for the same emperor in 921. Protospata.

Pascale, governed for the same emperor in 937. Fazello.

Imogalapto, stratego, governed in 940 for the emperors Alexander (912-913) and Constantine (VII, 913-959). Protospata.

Mariano Antipato, patrician catapan and stratego of the Greeks of Apulia and Calabria, governed for the same emperors in 955. Prototspata.

Manucio or Emanuele, patrician, governed for the Emperor Nicephorus II (963-969) in 965. Protospata.

Chalocharo, patrician, governed for the emperors Basil II (976-1025) and Constantine VIII (1025-1028) in 982. Protospata.

Romano, patrician, governed for the same emperors in 985. Protospata.

Giovanni, patrician, called Ammirapolo, governed for the same emperors in 989. Protospata.

Gregorio Tratamora, captain, governed for the same emperors in 999. Protospata.

Xyphea, catapan, governed for the same emperors in 1006. Protospata.

Curcua, or Cursira, patrician, governed for the same emperors in 1008. Protospata. He died in 1010, and to him succeeded

Basil, catapan, called Misordoviti, in 1010 governed for the same emperors. As in the *Annals of the Duke of Andria,* which called him Miserdovito.

Turnichio, catapan, governed for the same emperors in 1017. Protospata and Apuliense.

Basil Bogiano, or Bolano, catapan, governed for the same emperors in 1018. Protospata, Apuliense and Hostiense.

Vulcano, catapan, governed for the same emperors in 1027. Protospata.

Oresti Chretoniti governed for the same emperors in 1028. Protospata.

Christofaro, catapan, governed for the Emperor Romanus III (1029-1034) in 1029. Protospata.

Pothone, catapan, governed for the same emperor in the same year after Christofaro left. Protospata.

Constantino Protospata, called Opo, catapan, governed for the same emperor in 1033. Protospata.

Michael, patrician and duke, called Sfrondil, governed for Emperor Michael IV Paslagone (1034-1041) in 1038. Protospata.

Niceforo Dulciano, catapan, governed for the same emperor in 1039. Protospata.

Michael Protospata Dulciano governed for the same emperor in 1041. Protospata, the *Duke of Andria,* and Apuliense.

N., son of Budiano, catapan, governed for the same emperor Michael in 1041. *Duke of Andria.*

Ducaliano, captain of the Roman emperor in 1041. Hostiense, Chapter 67, Book 2, if he is not the above-mentioned Michael.

Giorgios Maniace, or Malocco, governed for the emperors Michael V Calatate (1041-1042) and Constantine IX Monomachus (1042-1055) in 1042. He had himself called emperor. Protospata, Apuliense, Hostiense, and the *Compendium.*

Pando, patrician, was killed by Maniace in 1046. Protospata.

Theodoro Cane, catapan, succeeded Maniace after expelling him from Italy. He governed for the same emperors in 1044. Protospata.

Palatino, catapan, governed for the same emperors in 1046. Protospata.

Argiro, patrician and duke, son of Melo, governed for the same emperors in 1052. Protospata.

Trombi, patrician, governed for Emperor Isaac I Comnenus (1057-1059) in 1058. Protospata.

Mabrica, captain of the Greeks, governed for the Emperor Constantine X Ducas (1059-1067) in 1066. Protospata and Apuliense.

Ciriaco governed for the Emperor Romanus IV Diogenes (1067-1071) around 1068. *The Compendium,* Biondo and Riccio.

THE NORMAN KINGS OF THE KINGDOM OF NAPLES WHO RULED FOR SIXTY-FIVE YEARS

Roger II, Norman count of Sicily, son of Count Roger, brother of Duke Robert Guiscard, both sons of Tancred, count of Hauteville in Normandy, after the death of his nephew, William, duke of Apulia, who died without sons, succeeded to him in the dukedom of Apulia and principality of Salerno, and with that to rule of Sicily. Since it did not seem to him a title appropriate to his status, he wished to be called King of Sicily, Apulia, and Calabria, and he had himself invested with it by Anacletus (II), antipope, in 1130. But when Pope Innocent II attacked him as a supporter of Anacletus, he (Innocent) did battle with Roger and ended in prison. But after he made peace, he confirmed the royal title for him in 1139, as Falco of Benevento says. Roger had three wives. Elvira bore him Roger, duke of Apulia; Anfusio, prince of Capua; William, prince of Taranto; and Henrico, who was made prince of Capua after the death of his brother. The second was Sibilla, sister of the duke of Burgundy, and he did not have any sons with her; the third was Beatrice, daughter of the count of Rethel, by whom he had Constance, who by King William II, her nephew, seeing that he did not have sons, was given as a wife to (Emperor) Henry VI, king of Germany, son of the Emperor Frederick I Barbarossa. Roger died in 1154 at 59 years of age, having reigned for 24 years.

William (I, the Bad), prince of Taranto, was chosen as a partner in the kingdom in 1150 by his father King Roger, after the other brothers died, and he had him crowned in Palermo, and he reigned with him for four years. When his father died, he, who was called "the Bad" because of his bad habits, reigned until 1166 and died on May 15th. His wife was Margaret, daughter of Garcia (VI), king of Navarre, by whom he had Roger, duke of Apulia; Robert, prince of Capua; William; and Henry.

William II (the Good), son of King William the Bad, since his two older brothers had died, succeeded to his father in the kingdom in 1166. He was called "the Good" to differentiate him from his father, and he made peace with the Emperor Frederick Barbarossa in 1185. He gave his aunt Constance as a wife to Henry (VI), king of Germany, son of the emperor. He died in 1189 without leaving any sons by Joan, daughter of Henry (II), king of England.

Tancred, count of Lecce, son of Roger, duke of Apulia, first son of King Roger II, born by a daughter of Robert, count of Lecce, after the death of King William II, swore fealty to Queen

Constance. He was later proclaimed by the barons in Palermo, and he was crowned king in January 1190; but the barons of Apulia refused to swear fealty to him and proclaimed Henry VI king.

Tancred, therefore, when he understood this, proceeded with his army and took the whole kingdom. When Emperor Frederick died, King Henry, his son, proceeded to Italy in 1191 and was crowned emperor in Rome by Pope Celestine. From there he proceeded into the kingdom with the empress. He laid siege to Naples (1191) and sent the empress to Salerno. But when he became ill and wished to return to Germany with his wife, the Salernitani refused to give her up, and she was sent to King Tancred in Sicily. In 1192, at the intercession of the pope, she was returned to the emperor; although others say that King Tancred received his aunt with honor and sent her back to the emperor. Tancred's wife was Sibilla, by whom he had Roger and William (III) and three other sons. He died on February 20, 1194.

Roger, first-born son of Tancred, was crowned while his father was living in 1191, having taken for his wife Urania (Irene), daughter of Isaac (II), the emperor of Constantinople. In a popular uproar in Palermo he was wounded, from which he died in 1194(3). King William also made his father swear fealty to him and crown him king; and a little while after his father Tancred died of sorrow.

William, the third of this name, son of Tancred, with Alteria, Constance and Modonia, his sisters, after a long war, surrendered to the Emperor Henry VI with an agreement to renounce the kingdom, as they did in 1195(4). Henry gave him the principality of Taranto and to his mother that *contado* (province) of Lecce. But having imprisoned and castrated him, he let him die in a miserable prison (Hohenems in Voralberg), as the Anonymous Cassinese recounts.

THE SWABIANS (HOHENSTAUFEN) KINGS OF THE KINGDOM OF NAPLES WHO RULED FOR SEVENTY-ONE YEARS

Henry VI, Swabian emperor, son of the Emperor Frederick I Barbarossa, through reason of Constance, his wife, daughter of the first King Roger, came two times to take the kingdom, and finally obtained it in 1195(4), having imprisoned King William. He died on September 28, 1197, excommunicated (1192) by Pope Celestine III (1191-1198).

Constance, empress, remained with Frederick (II), her son, queen and king of the kingdom from 1197 after the death of Emperor Henry. Empress Constance died on November 27, 1190. King Frederick, being a child, remained under the guardianship of the pope, who sent his legates to govern the kingdom.

Frederick II, son of Emperor Henry, succeeded in the kingdom in 1197 to his father and in 1198 to his mother. He had three wives: Constance, the sister of the king of Castile; Yolande, the daughter of John of Brienne, king of Jerusalem; and Isabella, the daughter of the king (John) of England. With them he had Henry (VII), Conrad and another Henry (titular king of Jerusalem). He had illegitimate sons, Enzo, king of Sardinia; Manfred, prince of Taranto, Federico and others. He died on December 13, 1250, after 53 years as king and 52 years as emperor, and to him succeeded

Conrad (IV), his son, in 1250, finding that his older brother had died, came there from Germany for the conquest of the kingdom. In August 1251 he took Naples, and he fell ill in Apulia and died there in April (May 1254) not without suspicion of poison that was inside an enema given to him by the order, as they say, of Manfred. He left in Germany a small son named Conrad, born by (Elizabeth) the sister of the duke of Bavaria.

Conrad II (V), named Conradin, found himself in Germany with Manfred, his uncle, in possession of the kingdom after the death of King Conrad, his father. Manfred governed it as *balio* (regent) for his nephew from 1254.

Innocent IV, pope, when he knew of the death of King Conrad, led an army into the kingdom, which was already assigned to the church for the excommunication into which Frederick and Conrad, his son, had fallen. In June 1254 he reached Naples, where he died in December 1254. He was buried in the archbishopric of Naples. When Alexander IV was elected, he proceeded from there to Rome. Manfred, who had first sworn fealty to the papacy, in its absence and with the help of the Saracens, took the kingdom for Conradin, his nephew, as he governed as regent.

Manfred, while he ruled the kingdom as regent for his nephew, arranged false news to come from Germany of the death of Conradin, and he took the kingdom for himself in 1258 and held it until 1266. He was killed by King Charles I. By Beatrix (of Savoy), daughter of the duke of Saxony, his wife, he had Constance, whom he married to King Peter (III) of Aragon, and another (daughter), who was the marchesa of Saluzzo.

THE ANGEVIN KINGS OF THE KINGDOM OF NAPLES WHO RULED FOR ONE HUNDRED SEVENTY YEARS

Charles I, count of Anjou and Provence, brother of St. Louis, king of France, was invested by Pope Clement IV with the kingdom of Naples, so that he expel Manfred from it, who had occupied it, and for which he had been excommunicated. For this purpose Charles, after gathering a powerful army, proceeded into the kingdom and fought with Manfred, killed him, and took the kingdom in 1266. But he was attacked in 1268 by King Conradin, and after various events of fortune Charles remained victorious. Once he had this King Conradin in his hands, he had him publicly decapitated with other lords in the Piazza del Mercato in Naples. This king, Charles, died in 1285, at the age of 54 in the nineteenth year of his reign. His wife was Beatrice, countess of Provence.

Charles II, son of the above king, succeeded to the kingdom in 1284(5) and held it until 1309, in which year he died. As a wife he had Mary, queen of Hungary, who succeeded to that kingdom; and by her he had Charles, who was king of Hungary (1290-1295); Louis, bishop of Toulouse, who was a saint; Robert, duke of Calabria, who was later king of Naples; Philip (I), prince of Taranto; Giovanni, prince of Morea and duke of Durazzo; Tristano; Raimondo; Berlingiero; Pietro, count of Gravina; Clementia, wife of Charles, dauphin of France, who was later queen; Blanche, wife of King James (II) of Aragon; Eleanor, wife of Frederick of Aragon, king (Frederick II) of Sicily; Marie, wife of the king of Majorca; and Beatrice, wife of the marquis d'Este. He lived 70 years and reigned for 24.

Robert III, son of King Charles II, after a great argument before the pope with Charles, king of Hungary, his nephew, son of Charles his brother, succeeded his father in the kingdom. He married Yolande of Aragon, daughter of the king of Aragon, with whom he produced Charles, duke of Calabria, also called Carlo senza Terra, who died (1328) during the lifetime of his father. His second wife was Sancia of Aragon (Sancia of Majorca), sister of the king of Majorca, who died blessed, without children. She became a nun after the death of Robert. He lived for 64 years, having reigned for almost 34. He died in 1343.

Giovanna I, daughter of Charles, duke of Calabria, succeeded King Robert, her grandfather, in 1343. She had four husbands: Andrew, son of the king of Hungary; Louis, prince of Taranto, both her cousins, who had the title of king; James (III), the infante of Majorca; and Otto, duke of Brunswick. Since she did not have children, she adopted Louis, duke of Anjou, son of the king of France, against (the claims of) King Charles III, who came against her. She died at 55, strangled by King Charles in 1381(2).

Andrew, first husband of Queen Giovanna, died after two years and eight months as king, strangled in Aversa through the agreement of some barons, not without the complicity of the queen, his wife. He left a small son named Carlo, who survived a short time.

Louis, named Tarentino, lived 15 years as the husband of Giovanna, namely five first and then ten after he was crowned king. He died in 1362 at the age of 42, and he was buried at the monastery of Monte Vergine.

Lewis, king of Hungary, at the time of this Giovanna, proceeded with an army into the kingdom in a vendetta for the death of King Andrew, his brother, and put to flight the queen with her husband Louis. They travelled to their estate in Provence, and Lewis made himself lord of the kingdom. He ruled three years (1347-1350), after which the kingdom was regained by Queen Giovanna. She held it until 1381, when she was murdered by King Charles III (1382).

Charles III, named Durazzo, son of Louis, duke of Durazzo – who was fathered by John, prince of Morea – was invested with the kingdom by Pope Urban VI (Roman line, 1378-1389), because Queen Giovanna adhered to the election of Clement VII, the antipope (Avignon line, 1378-1394), who with the help of the king of Hungary, came to take the kingdom in 1381, where he had Giovanna killed (1382) in revenge for King Andrew. Charles disavowed Louis of Anjou, adopted by Giovanna, who had come against him with an army. He married Margaret, his cousin, who bore three children, Giovanna (II), Ladislas, and Maria, who died a little girl. Called to the succession of the kingdom of Hungary (1385), Charles went there and was killed through the work of the old queen (Mary of Hungary) in 1386. He reigned in Naples for four years (1382-1386) and lived 23.

Ladislas, son of Charles, succeeded his father to the kingdom (1386). Louis II of Anjou, son of the first, came against him twice with his army to take the kingdom, and he was repelled. Ladislas had three wives. The first was Costanza of Chiaro-monte, a Sicilian, daughter of Manfredi, count of Modica. He repudiated her and gave her as a wife to Andrea di Capua. The second was Maria, sister of the king of Cyprus; and the third was Maria d'Engenio, contessa of Lecce and princess of Taranto, widow of Raimondo Ursino. He had children by none of them. After he had ruled for 29 years, being 40 years old, he died in

1414, leaving an illegitimate son, Rinaldo, who was prince of Capua.

Giovanna II, sister of Ladislas, succeeded to her brother in the kingdom. She had as a husband James, count of La Marche in Provence, who, against the wishes of his wife, entitled himself king. Previously, while her brother (Ladislas) was still alive, she married William, archduke of Austria. Troubled by (the claims of) Louis III of Anjou, she adopted as a son Alfonso (V), king of Aragon. Once they had begun to quarrel, she revoked the adoption and adopted Louis III in opposition to Alfonso. Louis died in Calabria (1434). The queen died on February 2, 1435 at the age of 65, having reigned 21 years. She left as heir René, brother of Louis III.

René of Anjou, made heir of Queen Giovanna, was proclaimed by some barons in Naples, but finding that he was a prisoner of the duke of Burgundy, he sent his wife Isabella there in 1436, and she was received in Naples as queen. He was later freed and came to Naples on May 19, 1438 and remained there four years (1438-1442) in continuous war with King Alfonso, by whom he was driven out in 1442.

THE ARAGONESE KINGS
OF THE KINGDOM OF NAPLES
WHO RULED FOR FIFTY-EIGHT YEARS

Alfonso I of Aragon was adopted by Queen Giovanna II to the succession of the throne in opposition to Louis III of Anjou. But later deprived of the adoption by the queen, he took the realm by arms against René. His wife was Maria, daughter of the king of Castile, his cousin, and he did not have sons. He died in 1458 at the age of 66 after he ruled for 24 years.

Ferrante I, illegitimate son of King Alfonso, was legitimized by him (in 1440) and qualified to the succession of the kingdom through the dispensation of the pope (Pius II, 1458-1464). In the beginning of his rule he was troubled by the barons, who called in Jean, duke of Anjou and Calabria, son of King René, for the kingdom (1459), whom he repelled (1465). Ferrante had two wives: Isabella, daughter of Tristan of Clermont, count of Cupertino and sister of Giovanni Antonio Ursino, prince of Taranto, by whom he had Don Alfonso (II), duke of Calabria; Don Federico (IV), prince of Altamura; Don Giovanni, cardinal; Don Francesco, duke of S. Angelo; Donna Beatrice, wife of Mattias, king of Hungary; and Donna Eleanor, duchess of Ferrara. By the second wife, who was Giovanna, sister of King Ferdinand of Aragon, called the Catholic King, he had Giovanna, who was the wife of King Ferrante II, his nephew. He also had some bastards, among them Don Ferrante, duke of Montalto; Don Enrico, marquis of Geraci; and others. He ruled for 36 years, having lived for 70, and died on January 25, 1494.

Alfonso II, son of King Ferrante I, succeeded his father in the kingdom in 1494, but when he understood that King Charles VIII of France was preparing to attack him, he was moved by his conscience that bit him because of the lack of love of his subjects, who had been maltreated by him. He renounced the kingdom to Ferrante (II), his son, on January 29, 1495. He had as a wife Ippolita Maria Sforza, daughter of Francesco, duke of Milan, who bore to him Don Ferrante, Don Pietro, and Donna Isabella, duchess of Milan. He also had illegitimate children: Don Alfonso, duke of Biseglia; Don Cesare, count of Caserta; Donna Sancia, wife of Don Goffredo Borgia, prince of Squillace. He ruled one year and one day.

THE FRENCH KINGS OF THE KINGDOM OF NAPLES WHO RULED FOR TEN YEARS ALTHOUGH IN CONTEST WITH THE ARAGONESE AND WITH THE CATHOLIC KING

Charles VIII, king of France, gained the kingdom of Naples on February 21(2), 1495, after he expelled King Ferrante II, and he held it for one year. And with the swiftness with which he took it he lost it, on July 7, 1495.

Ferrante II of Aragon, after having denied King Charles VIII the kingdom of Alfonso, his father, was attacked by Charles and obliged to withdraw with his father to Messina. But he was recalled at once by the Neapolitans; and with the help of the Catholic King (Ferdinand) through the means of el Gran Capitán (Gonsalvo de Cordoba), he took the kingdom. He enjoyed it for a little while, since he died on October 7, 1496. To him succeeded Don Federico, his uncle, through Donna Giovanna, his aunt, since he did not leave any sons.

Federico of Aragon, prince of Altamura, son of King Ferrante I, succeeded his nephew in the kingdom in 1496. But when Louis XII, king of France, and Ferdinand, the Catholic King of Spain, made an alliance against this Federico, they expelled him from the kingdom in 1501 and sent him to France. From the king (Louis XII) he received as a gift the dukedom of Anjou with a provision of 30,000 ducats. Here (at Tours, in 1504), he died, unhappy. He had as a wife Isabella del Balzo, daughter of Pietro, prince of Altamura, by whom was born Don Ferrante, duke of

Calabria, and others. Federico ruled for four years and five months.

Louis XII, king of France, after he allied himself with the Catholic King, gained a part of the kingdom, after he expelled King Federico from it in 1501, and Naples fell to Louis. He held the kingdom until May 1503.

THE SPANISH KINGS
OF THE KINGDOM OF NAPLES

Ferdinand, king of Aragon, called the Catholic, because he expelled the Moors from Granada, was the son of King John (II), the brother of King Alfonso I. He expelled the French from the kingdom through means of el Gran Capitán. He remained absolute lord of it in 1503. Ferdinand had as a wife Isabella, queen of Castile, by whom was born Don Juan who died (1497) during the lifetime of his father; Donna Isabella, queen of Portugal; Donna Joanna, wife of Philip, archduke of Austria; Donna Maria, also queen of Portugal; and Donna Caterina, queen of (Henry VIII of) England. Ferdinand died in 1516 at 64 years of age and after 13 years of lordship of Naples.

THE AUSTRIAN (HAPSBURG) KINGS
OF THE KINGDOM OF NAPLES
WHO HAPPILY RULE AT PRESENT

Charles V, emperor, son of Philip, archduke of Austria, and of Joanna, succeeded through his mother to the realm of Naples. He had by Isabella, daughter of the king of Portugal, King Philip (II); Don Ferrante; Donna Maria, married to Maximilian, king of Bohemia; and Donna Joanna, queen of Portugal; in addition to Donna Margaret, duchess, first of Florence, and later of Parma; and Don Juan (of Austria), both illegitimate. After he lived for 57 years, seven months and 21 days, he died in 1558 after holding the empire for 39 years and the kingdom of Naples for 43 years.

Philip II, king, son of Charles V, so named in respect for the Archduke Philip, his grandfather, who was king of Castile. He had four wives: Maria of Portugal; Mary (Tudor), queen of England; Elisabeth (Valois) of France; and Anne of Austria. By the first was born Don Carlo; the second did not have children; by the third was born Donna Isabella (Clara Eugenia), and Donna Catarina; by the fourth Don Diego, Don Ferrante and King Philip III. He died on September 13, 1598.

Philip III, king, was born on April 27, 1578. He was proclaimed king in Naples on October 11, 1598. His wife was Donna Margarita of Austria, who bore Don Filippo; Don Carlo; and Don Ferrante, cardinal deacon of the titular church of S. Maria in Portico; Donna Anna, wife of Louis XIII, king of France; Donna Maria, wife of Ferdinand, king of Hungary and emperor; and another daughter. King Philip died on March 31, 1621, after he ruled for 22 years, five months and 18 days, at the age of 44.

Philip IV, king, succeeded to his father in 1621. He had two wives: Donna Isabella, daughter of Henri IV, king of France and sister of Louis XIII; and Donna Maria Anna of Austria, daughter of Emperor Ferdinand III. The first bore to him Don Baldassaro and Donna Maria Teresa, wife of Louis XIV, at present king of France. The second bore him Don Prospero, Don Carlo, and Donna Margarita Teresa, wife of Emperor Leopold I, who is still living. King Philip IV died at the age of 60 on September 17, 1665 after he ruled for 44 years, five months and 17 days.

Charles II, king, the second (Hapsburg) by this name, who at present rules, succeeded to his father in 1665 at the age of four. He lives under the tutelage and rule of Donna Maria Anna, his mother.

CAPTAINS GENERAL AND VICEROYS WHO HAVE GOVERNED THE KINGDOM OF NAPLES

After the Emperor Lothar (II) and Pope Innocent II came against King Roger I (in 1132), they obliged him to retire to Sicily. Once they had the kingdom, the emperor and the pope fell into a dispute about who ought to chose the governor. Finally Count Rainulf (d'Alife) was chosen duke and governor by the pope in 1137. He lived until 1139. Source: Falco of Benevento.

Anfusio, prince of Capua, and Roger, duke of Apulia, sons of King Roger II, were sent by their father with an army into the kingdom in 1140(39). Once they gained it he also came, and after he recovered it, he left Anfusio to govern the principality of Capua and Roger to govern Apulia, and he himself returned to Sicily. Falco of Benevento.

Simone Siniscalco was the nephew of Admiral Maio (of Bari) the favorite of King William the Bad. He governed for this king in 1150. Fazello.

Romualdo Guarna, archbishop of Salerno, with Queen Margaret (of Navarre), the mother of King William the Good in 1164. *Chronicle of the Guarna Family.*

Giliberto, count of Gravina, governed for William the Good, around 1167. Fazello.

Riccardo, count of Cerra, brother-in-law of King Tancred, governed for this king in 1190. Richard of S. Germain.

Henrico Testa, marshall of the empire, captain of Emperor Henry VI, governed in 1190 for this emperor. Richard of S. Germain and the Anonymous Cassinese.

Riccardo, count of Calvi, was left by King Tancred as governor and general of his armies in the kingdom in 1191 against the imperialists. Falco of Benevento.

Muscancervello, castellan of Capua; Diopolto Alamano, castellan of Arce, who was later count of Cerra; and Corrado of Merleii, castellan of Sorella, captain of Emperor Henry VI, governed that part that obeyed the emperor in 1191 while they fought a war with Tancred. Richard of S. Germain.

Bertoldo, captain of Emperor Henry VI, governed in 1191. Richard of S. Germain.

Diopolto Alamano was made count of Cerra through the death of Count Riccardo by the Emperor Henry VI. Adhering to Markward (of Anweiler), marquis of Ancona, regent for Frederick, he governed for him in 1199. Having later rebelled against the Emperor Frederick II, he called into the kingdom Emperor Otto (IV in 1200), by whom he was made duke of Spoleto. He governed the kingdom for him in 1209. Richard of S. Germain.

Markward, marquis of Ancona, as regent of Frederick II, entered the kingdom in 1198. *The Compendium* and Richard of S. Germain.

Geraldo, cardinal of S. Adriano, and, after him,

Gregorio of Galganis, cardinal of S. Maria in Portico, legates of Pope Innocent III, governed the kingdom as tutors of Frederick, after they expelled Markward from there, until the king was of age. *The Compendium*

Tomaso d'Aquino, count of Cerra, was viceroy for the Emperor Frederick II in 1220. Costanzo (Angelo di, 1507-1591) and Ammirato (Scipione, 1531-1601).

Henrico of Morra was left as viceroy and captain general by the Emperor Frederick II in 1226 when he proceeded to Lombardy. Richard of S. Germain.

Riccardo Alamano, son of the duke of Spoleto, was viceroy for Frederick II in 1228. *The Compendium,* Biondo, Fazello and the *Lives of the Emperors*.

Tomaso of Aquino, count of Cerra, mentioned above, was left as viceroy in 1231 by Emperor Frederick II. Richard of S. Germain.

Angelo della Marra, viceroy of the kingdom for Frederick II in 1239, as in a unique register of the emperor in the Royal Archives of the Mint of Naples.

Henry (VII), son of Emperor Frederick, being a young boy, was left by his father in 1246 as his lieutenant in the kingdom, who gave him many barons as advisers. *The Compendium.*

Manfred, illegitimate son of Frederick, as of Taranto, was regent of the kingdom for Conrad I, his brother in 1250, who found himself in Germany when the death of Frederick occurred. *The Compendium.*

Richard Filangiero governed Naples after the death of Frederick II in 1251. Under his name the contracts were published that are still used today. Archives of the Monastery of S. Sebastiano of Naples and of S. Severino.

Arrigo the old, count of Rivello, governed for Conrad after he had occupied Naples in 1253. *The Compendium.*

Bartolino Tavernario was governor in 1254 for Pope Innocent IV, whose brother-in-law he was. *The Compendium.*

Richard Filangiero, mentioned above, governed Naples again for the church in 1255. Archives of the Monastery of S. Sebastiano.

Ottaviano Ubaldino, Florentine cardinal, was legate in Naples for Pope Alexander IV in 1255 and remained there until 1261. *The Compendium.*

Manfred, son of Frederick II, was again governor of the kingdom on account of the absence of Conradin, as his regent after the death of King Conrad, until he held the kingdom for himself.

Rinaldo d'Aquino, count of Caserta, viceroy in the times of Manfred, as Summonte says in his life of this king.

*

Charles (the Lame), prince of Salerno, governed the kingdom with the title of viceroy for King Charles I, his father, in 1282 when he went to France. *The Compendium* and the Registers of the Royal Archive of the Mint.

Gerardo, cardinal of Parma, legate of Pope Martin IV; and Robert, count of Artois, cousin of King Charles, were in the governance of the kingdom while Charles II was imprisoned by the Aragonese from 1284 to 1288. *The Compendium,* Biondo, and Giovanni Villani.

Charles, king of Hungary and prince of Salerno, first son of King Charles II, was viceroy in 1292 in the name of his father. From the Royal Registers of the Mint.

Robert, duke of Calabria, third son of King Charles II, was viceroy of his father in 1308. From the Royal Registers of the Mint.

Charles, duke of Calabria, son of King Robert, remained to govern the kingdom when his father was called to the rule of Genoa in 1318. On account of his prudence he was given the administration of the kingdom by his father from the time of his adolescence. Constanzo and the Royal Registers of the Archive of the Mint.

103

Brother Roberto of Hungary (of Mileto), of whom Petrarch says so much bad in his letters, governed the kingdom for Queen Giovanna I and King Andrew of Hungary in 1343 after the death of King Robert.

Americo of Cuardia, French cardinal apostolic legate, governed the kingdom in 1344 for Queen Giovanna I. From the Royal Registers of the Mint.

Charles, duke of Durazzo, who was left by Queen Giovanna I to govern the kingdom in 1348 when she fled to Provence with Louis her husband because she feared King Lewis of Hungary. *The Compendium* and Biondo.

Corrado Lupo (a mercenary captain of the Free Companies) was viceroy for King Lewis of Hungary after he had expelled Queen Giovanna I in 1348. *The Compendium.*

Fra Morreale (another mercenary captain) governed for the same king of Hungary, who went to Rome for the Jubilee in 1350. *The Compendium.*

Roberto, prince of Taranto, older brother of King Louis, governed the kingdom while the king and Queen Giovanna were in Sicily for the war in 1357. Costanzo.

Galeazzo Malatesta, lord of Rimini, was viceroy for the same king in 1362. *Annals of Aquila.*

Otto, duke of Brunswick, fourth husband of Queen Giovanna I, governed Naples in the name of his wife at the time that King Charles III entered the kingdom in 1381. History of Corio.

Queen Margaret was left by King Charles III, her husband, to govern the kingdom when he went to seize the possessions of the king of Hungary in 1385, where he was killed. She remained governess and regent of King Ladislas, her son. From the Royal Registers of the Mint and *The Compendium.*

Tomaso Sanseverino, count of Montescaglioso, was viceroy for Louis II of Anjou in 1386 after he expelled King Ladislas from Naples. Costanzo and Ammirato.

Cecco of Borgo, named count of Montederisi by Cozzo, marquis of Pescara, was viceroy for King Ladislas after his coronation in Gaeta in 1390. *Annals of the Duke of Monteleone* and Ammirato.

Monsieur de Montjoie proceeded from Provence to Naples with the armada with the title of viceroy for Louis II of Anjou in the same year, 1390. *The Compendium.*

Angelo Acciaiolo, Florentine cardinal, governed the kingdom during the infancy of King Ladislas, as apostolic legate in 1392. From the Royal Registers of the Mint.

Floridasso Capecelatro was viceroy for King Ladislas when he had recovered the city of Naples from the hands of King Louis II in 1406. *Annals of Monteleone.*

Maria of Cyprus, second wife of King Ladislas, was left by her husband as viceregent in the kingdom, which she governed with the counsel of the archbishop of Conza, Gurello Aurilia, Gentile de Merolinis and Leonardo d'Afflitto in 1404, when Ladislas proceeded into Hungary. From the Royal Registers of the Mint of the same year.

Mello of Alvero, archbishop of Conza; Gurello Origlia (Aurilia), great protonotary of the kingdom; Leonardo d'Afflitto, lieutenant of the great chamberlain; and Francesco Dentice, called Naccarella, marshall of the kingdom, were elected viceroys of the kingdom by King Ladislas on March 26, 1408 when the king went to the war of Tuscany and Rome. In 1409, he added to them Benedetto Acciaiolo, count of Ascoli. From the register of 1410, fol. 137. After the death of Gurello Origlia, which followed in 1412, Bernardo Zurlo, count of Montuori and grand seneschal, was chosen in his place, and they governed until 1414, when the king died.

Giovanna, sister of King Ladislas, who was called archduchess of Austria, governed the kingdom at the time that her brother found himself waging war abroad in 1413. Costanzo.

Pandolfello (Piscopo) Alopa, the favorite of Queen Giovanna II, after he was made count and treasurer by her, was also governor for her in the kingdom in 1414. *The Compendium,* Corio, and others.

James (II), count of Le Marche, husband of Queen Giovanna II, after having Pandolfello killed, governed the kingdom in the name of his wife. *The Compendium.*

Alfonso, king of Aragon, adopted by Queen Giovanna II (in 1421) and made duke of Calabria, governed the kingdom as viceroy of the queen.

Braccio di Fortibraccio of Perugia, most famous (mercenary) captain, was employed by King Alfonso and Queen Giovanna with the title of viceroy and grand constable of the kingdom, giving to him the city of Capua in 1421. *The Compendium* and the Annals of Aquila.

Don Pedro of Aragon, called Infante, remained to govern Naples in place of King Alfonso, his brother, when he was obliged to proceed to Spain in aid of Don Enriquez, his brother, in 1423. *The Compendium* and others.

Egidio Sasitera, viceroy for King Alfonso. From the tomb of Mariella Minutola, his wife, inside the chapel of the Castel Nuovo of Naples.

George of Germany, count of Pulcino, was viceroy for Queen Giovanna II and for Louis III of Anjou in 1423 until 1425. The *Annals of Monteleone* and Ammirato.

Ser Giovanni Caracciolo, count of Avellino and grand seneschal of
the kingdom, most favorite of Queen Giovanna II, governed the
kingdom for her in 1425 until he was killed in 1433(2). *The
Compendium* and the *History of the Caracciolo Family.*
Louis III of Anjou, adopted by Giovanna II, being duke of
Calabria, governed for this queen.
Raimondo Ursino, count of Nola; Baldassare della Ratta, count of
Caserta; Giorgio della Magna, count of Pulcino; Perdicasso
Barrile, count of Montederisi; Ottino Caracciolo, count of
Nicastra and grand chancellor; Gualtiero and Ciarletta, both
Caracciolo; Indico d'Anna, named the Monk, grand seneschal;
Urbano Cimino; Giovanni Cicinello; Tadeo Gattola; with five
other lords totaling sixteen were left to govern the kingdom by
Queen Giovanna II in 1435 in the name of René, established by
her as heir. They (a *balia* of 20) governed until 1436(5), when
Queen Isabella came to take possession of it in the name of René,
her husband. In the instruments that were made at that time it
says "sub regimine gubernatorum relictorum per clarae memoriae
serenissimam reginam Ioannam secundam."
Queen Isabella, wife of King René of Anjou, took possession of the
kingdom for him and remained there as governess in 1436,
finding her husband imprisoned by the duke of Burgundy. *The
Compendium* and supplement to *De claris mulieribus* of
Boccaccio (Giovanni, 1313?-1375).
Giacomo Fiesco, Genoese, was left as viceroy in Naples for King
René when in 1438 he went from there to the siege of Sulmona.
Summonte and Book 4 of Costo in the *Life of Hadrian V.*
Arnoldo Sanz, Catalan, castellan of the Castel Nuovo of Naples,
governed for King Alfonso that part of Naples that submitted to
him when it was taken from King René in 1438. Costanzo.
Alano Cibo, Genoese, father of Pope Innocent VIII, was viceroy
for René in 1438, and because of his good administration he was
confirmed by King Alfonso after he took Naples in 1442.
Bartolomeo Fazio (1400-1457).
Antonio Caldora, after the death of his father Giacomo. King René
granted him the privilege of viceroy for all that part of the
kingdom that submitted to him in 1439. Costanzo and the *Annals
of Monteleone.*

*

Don Ferrante of Aragon, duke of Calabria, remained to govern the
kingdom when King Alfonso, his father, brought war to the
Florentines and went to defend the liberty of Milan, after Duke
Filippo (Maria Visconti) died in 1447. Fazio.
Queen Isabella (of Clermont), wife of King Ferrante I, governed
Naples at the time when her husband went out against the

rebellious barons from 1459 until 1463. *The Compendium,* Costanzo, supplement to *De claris mulieribus* of Boccaccio.

Gilbert, count of Monpensier, dauphin of Auvergne and archduke of Sessa, was viceroy for King Charles VIII when he took Naples and the kingdom in 1494, and he was expelled from it by King Ferrante II. *The Compendium* and others.

Don Federico of Aragon governed Naples for King Ferrante II, his nephew, who waged war in Apulia with the French in 1497. Guicciardini (Francesco, 1483-1540), *History of Italy.*

Don Ferrante of Aragon, count of Nicastro and Arena, and later duke of Montalto, son of King Ferrante I, was made viceroy of Naples and Terra di Lavoro in 1500 by his brother King Federico. Cancelleria.

*

Louis of Armagnac, duke of Nemurs, was viceroy of Naples for Louis XII, king of France, after the division of the kingdom made between King Louis and the Catholic King (Ferdinand of Spain) in 1502. Guicciardini.

*

Gonsalvo Ferrante di Cordoba, duke of Terranova and S. Angelo, named el Gran Capitán, who had expelled the French from the kingdom, remained as viceroy for the Catholic King (Ferdinand of Spain) in 1502 until 1506. *Comp. Privil.* of Naples.

Don Antonio di Cardona, marquis of Padula, was left in Naples as lieutenant for the kingdom by el Gran Capitán when he left. Registers of the Cancelleria.

Don Juan of Aragon, count of Ripacorsa, was left as viceroy of Naples by the Catholic King when he left there, taking with him el Gran Capitán on June 8, 1507. *The Compendium* and the same.

Don Antonio de Guevara, count of Potenza, was left as lieutenant in Naples by the count of Ripacorsa, having been called to Spain by the Catholic King on October 8, 1508. *Annals of Passaro.*

Don Raimondo di Cardona, count of Alveto, became viceroy in Naples for the Catholic King in 1509. *The Compendium.*

Don Francesco, cardinal Remolines, archbishop of Sorrento, was lieutenant in Naples when Cardona went with the army to Lombardy in 1511, when the destruction of Ravenna followed. *The Compendium.*

Don Berardo Villamario was lieutenant after the cardinal of Sorrento through the absence of Cardona on February 23, 1512. *The Compendium.*

Don Raimondo di Cardona was again lieutenant in Naples in February 1516. Cancelleria.

Don Carlo di Lannoy, viceroy for the Emperor Charles V in March 1522. *The Compendium.*

The Royal Collateral Council governed in 1523 on account of the absence of Lannoy when he went with the army to Lombardy. Cancelleria.

Andrea Carrafa, count of S. Severina, was lieutenant in February 1525 because Lannoy went to Milan. From that followed the defeat and capture of the King Francis I at Pavia. *Annot.*

The Royal Collateral Council, and for it Don Giovanni Carrafa, count of Policastro, and then Ludovico Montalto, Sicilian regent, governed the kingdom in 1527 because of the absence of Lannoy. Cancelleria.

Don Ugo di Moncada, knight of Jerusalem, was viceroy on account of the death of Lannoy in September 1527. *The Compendium.*

Philbert de Châlons, prince of Orange and viceroy in July 1528, who brought the army from Rome when Lautrec went to besiege Naples. And there Don Ugo died in the sea battle. *Annot.*

Pompeo Colonna, cardinal, was lieutenant in September 1529 when the prince of Orange went to the war in Tuscany.

Don Pedro di Toledo, marquis of Villafranca, was viceroy from July 1532 to 1553. *Annot.*

Don Luis di Toledo, son of Don Pedro, was lieutenant when his father went to the war of Siena in April 1553, where he died. *The Compendium.*

Don Pedro Pacheco, cardinal Saguntino, viceroy in 1553 for the Emperor Charles V. He was reconfirmed by King Philip II when his father invested him with the kingdom of Naples, and the marquis of Pescara took possession of it on November 15, 1554. *Annot.*

Don Bernardino di Mendozza, when the above-mentioned cardinal departed, was lieutenant in May 1555 until the duke of Alba arrived.

Don Fernando Alvarez di Toledo, duke of Alba, became viceroy in Naples in February 1556. *The Compendium.*

Don Federico di Toledo, son of the duke of Alba, remained as lieutenant when his father went to Spain on October 29, 1557.

Don Juan Manriquez was lieutenant after Don Fernando from June 6, 1558.

Cardinal Bartolomeo della Cueva became viceroy in September 1558. *The Compendium. & Annot.*

Don Perafan of Ribera, duke of Alcalà, became viceroy on June 12, 1559. *The Compendium. & Annot.*

Don Antonio Perrenot, cardinal of Granvelle, viceroy on April 19, 1571. *Addition to the Compendium.*

Don Diego Simanca, bishop of Badaxo, of the Council of State, was lieutenant on account of Granvelle's departure in September 1571, when he went to Rome for the election of Gregory XIII. He returned to Naples on May 19, 1572. Cancelleria.

Don Iñigo di Mendozza, marquis of Mondegiar, viceroy from July 10, 1575. Costa's *Addition to the Compendium.*

Don Juan di Zuñiga, named the commander major of Castile and prince of Pietreperzia, became viceroy on August 11, 1579. *Addition to the Compendium.*

Don Pedro Girón, duke of Ossuna, viceroy in December 1581. *Addition to the Compendium.*

Don Juan di Zuñiga, count of Miranda, nephew of the commander major, became viceroy in April 1586. *Addition to the Compendium.*

Don Enriquez de Guzman, count of Olivares, became viceroy in July 1595.

Don Fernandez Ruiz de Castro, count of Lemos, became viceroy in February 1599.

Don Francesco de Castro remained lieutenant of his father when he went to Rome in March 1600 to give obedience to the pope in the name of the new king. After the death of this count, his father, which followed on September 20, 1601.

Don Juan Alfonso Pimentel, count of Benevento, became viceroy in April 1603.

Don Pedro Fernandez de Castro, count of Lemos, first son of the above-mentioned count of Lemos, became viceroy in May 1610.

Don Francesco de Castro, count of Castro and duke of Taurisano, was lieutenant on account of the departure of his brother in June 1616.

Don Pedro Giron, duke of Ossuna, became viceroy on July 27, 1616. He was nephew of the above-mentioned duke of Ossuna.

Don Gaspar of Borgia and Velasco, cardinal of the titular church of S. Croce in Gerusalemme, brother of the duke of Gandia, became lieutenant and viceroy on June 3, 1620.

Don Antonio Zapata, archbishop of Burgos, cardinal of the titular church of S. Sabina, became viceroy on December 12, 1620. On the last day of January 1621 he went to Rome in the creation of Gregory XV.

Don Pietro di Leva, general of the galleys of Naples, became lieutenant after Cardinal Zapata went to Rome on January 30, 1622.

Don Antonio Alvarez di Toledo, duke of Alba, knight of the Golden Fleece, became viceroy on December 24, 1622.

Don Perafan (Fernando Afan) de Ribera Enriquez, duke of Alcalà, remained viceroy on August 17, 1629.

Don Manuel di Zuñiga and Fonseca, count of Monterey and Fuentes, being ambassador in Rome, became viceroy on October 27, 1631.

Don Ramiro Filippez de Guzman, duke of Medina de las Torres and of Sabioneta, and prince of Stigliano, became viceroy on November 13, 1637.

Don Juan Alfonso Enriquez de Cabrera, admiral of Castile and duke of the city of Medina de Riosecco, became viceroy on May 7, 1644.

Don Rodrigo Ponze de Leone, duke of Arcos, became viceroy on February 11, 1646. And since at the time of his rule, which was in the year 1647, the revolution (of Masaniello) occurred in Naples, to quell it Philip IV sent with the title of viceroy and plenipotentate Don Juan of Austria, his illegitimate son, who entered with a naval armada on October 1, 1647. He did not succeed in removing Arcos from the government. Then to the same effect on March 2, 1648, when he had come to Rome, where he was ambassador, Don Iñigo Velez de Guevara y Tassis, count of Oñate and Villamediana, left the government to the duke of Arcos, replacing the title of viceroy for that of Oñate.

Don Iñigo Velez de Guevara y Tassis, count of Oñate and Villamediana, became viceroy on March 2, 1648.

Don Beltrano of Guevara y Tassis, was lieutenant for four months of 1650 when the count of Oñate, his brother, went to the enterprise of Portolongone.

Don Garcia d'Haro y Avellaneda, count of Castrillo, became viceroy on November 20, 1653.

Don Gaspar Bracamonte y Guzman, count of Peñaranda, became viceroy on January 11, 1659.

Don Pasquale of Aragon, cardinal of the titular church of S. Balbina, became viceroy on September 8, 1664.

Don Pedro Antonio of Aragon, brother of the same cardinal, became viceroy on April 3, 1666, and governs at present.

THE SEVEN OFFICES OF THE KINGDOM

A long discourse, and not a brief discussion, would be needed to narrate the preeminence and prerogatives of the seven offices of the kingdom. But, because this work does not permit that, we are restricted to the following compendium. When the kings are staying in Naples the kingdom is governed by the following seven officials, in peacetime just as in wartime; through them all the royal orders are executed. Assisting these people who are close to the person of the king – besides the great revenues they have here – the burden that they bear is divided among subordinate officers; although today they also have their lieutenants, who have the full administration of things pertaining to them. Nonetheless, for their public functions they have their determined places, as if the person of the king were there.

The first of these is the Grand Constable to whom (previously) was commended all the land army of the kingdom. He carried the bare sword before the king in cavalcade, and he sat on the right side of the king. Today his jurisdiction resides in the person of the viceroy. The Grand Constable draws 2190 ducats in income each year.

The second is the Grand Justiciar, under whose guardianship the Great Court is governed, extending its jurisdiction not only over civil and criminal cases, but also over feudal cases. All the titled persons of the kingdom are under this jurisdiction. His lieutenant is the Regent of the Vicaria, which was created by the viceroy. Today he draws 2180 ducats in revenue and sits on the left side of the king.

The third is the Grand Admiral, who is captain general of the entire sea militia. He has a limited jurisdiction because he takes cognizance of all the matters of persons who practice sea warfare, except those who are in the service of the Galleys of Naples, who are overseen by their generals. This office has a particular tribunal with its lieutenant judge and notary with the prisons; he has power to create vice-admirals for all the navies of the kingdom; he holds the authority to delegate fifty men who are able to go armed night and day with both offensive and defensive arms, even those prohibited by the royal bans. He has provisions of 2190 ducats and sits on the right of the king, to the side of the Grand Constable.

The fourth is the Grand Chamberlain, who has care of the royal patrimony. Today his jurisdiction resides in the lieutenant of the Camera della Summaria, which is chosen by the king with his presidents. He has provision of 2150 ducats, which are drawn from the *ius tapeti,* from the *capitanie* of the state-owned lands, from the feudal reliefs from the barons, from (excises on) salt and sugar. He sits near the Grand Justiciar.

The fifth is the Grand Protonotary, namely the first notary, or the secretary of the king. In the public parliaments he was the first to speak, and he received the answers of the others. He preserved the royal writings. Today he has a lieutenant, who is the president of the Summaria Camera and vice protonotary; and he has the authority to create the notaries for the kingdom. He draws an income for this office of 2190 ducats and sits near the Grand Admiral.

The sixth is the Grand Chancellor, whose charge was to seal all the privileges and writings of the kingdom. Today his jurisdiction is practiced by the regents of the Cancelleria and by the secretary of the kingdom. He has full authority over the college (University of Naples), where doctors earn degrees, and he delegates the vice chancellor not only at the college of law but also at those of theology and medicine. He has the master ledger of his acts and university porters, and he confers licenses on those who are made doctors. He draws an income of 2160 ducats and sits near the Grand Chamberlain.

The seventh and last office is the Grand Seneschal, who is the prefect or master of the house of the royal palace, who has care of all the royal ornaments and apparatus and of providing all the necessities of the palace of the king. He also has care of the breeds of horses, of the forests, and of the hunting reserves for the king. His jurisdiction today is divided partly between the horseman and the master of the hunt. He has provision of 2190 ducats and sits at the feet of the king.

But to give a sense to the reader of those who have had these seven offices, we have made the following catalog of those who are known not only from different authors but also from different writings in the public archives.

CONSTABLES

Roberto, count of Loritello, nephew of Roger, first king of Naples.
Count Radoperto Scaglione was constable at the time of Roger.
Mario Borrello was constable under King William the Bad.
Manfred, prince of Taranto, brother of King Conrad.
Giordano d'Angione, count of Sanseverino, a relative of King Manfred.
Guillaume Stendard at the time of Charles I.
Guillaume Stendard, another one, was made constable by Charles II in 1302.
Giovanni Ianvilla under the same king.
Arrigo Sanseverino, made constable by King Robert in 1313.
Tomaso Sanseverino, count of Marsico, was grand constable at the time of Queen Giovanna I.
Gianotto Protoiodice, count of Cerra, was constable in 1381 under Charles III.
Alberico da Barbiano, count of Cunio Milano, under the same king.
Tomaso Sanseverino, under the reign of Louis of Anjou.
Sforza, count of Cotignola and prince of Capua, under the reign of Giovanna II.
Andrea Braccio of Perugia, count of Montoria, at the time of the same queen.
Giacomo Caldora, duke of Bari, was grand constable at the time of King René.
Giovanni Antonio Ursino, prince of Taranto, at the time of Alfonso I and Ferrante I.
Pirro del Balzo, prince of Altamura, at the time of King Ferrante I.
Gonsalvo Ferrante di Cordoba, duke of S. Angelo, of Sessa, and of Terranova, under the Catholic King in 1507.
Fabrizio Colonna, duke of Tagliacozzo, was grand constable under Charles V.
Ascanio Colonna was grand constable at the time of Emperor Charles V in 1535.
Marc'Antonio Colonna under Philip II.
Marc'Antonio Colonna II under Philip III.
Don Filippo Colonna, prince of Sonnino and Manupelli, duke of Tagliacozzo and Paliano, marquis of Atessa, count of Albi, grand constable under Philip IV.
Federico Colonna, prince of Butera, duke of Tagliacozzo, and grand constable under the same king.

Marc'Antonio Colonna, duke of Tagliacozzo, prince of Castiglione, and grand constable under the same king.

Lorenzo Colonna, duke of Palliano and Tagliacozzo, prince of Sonnino and Castiglione, grand constable under the same Philip IV and at present under the present king Charles II.

GRAND JUSTICIARS

Mario Borrello was grand justiciar under William I.

Rogiero, count of Andria, grand justiciar under William II.

Ritturo Montenegro, grand justiciar at the time of Emperor Frederick II.

Tomaso d'Aquino, count of Cerra, grand justiciar in 1222 under Frederick II.

Arrigo di Morra, grand justiciar in 1223 under Frederick II.

Federico d'Arena, grand justiciar at the time of King Manfred.

Beltramo del Balzo was also grand justiciar under King Charles I in 1269.

Ottone da Tuzziaco was grand justiciar under Charles II in 1292.

Ermignan de Sabran, count of Ariano, relative of the king, grand justiciar under Charles II in 1301.

Roberto da Cornar, soldier, grand justiciar at the time of King Robert in 1313.

Hugo de Imbellinis, count of Slavonia, grand justiciar under the same king in 1334.

Bertrando del Balzo, count of Monte Scaglioso, grand justiciar at the time of Queen Giovanna I in 1345.

Roberto Riccio was made grand justiciar at the time of the last years of Queen Giovanna I.

Carlo Ruffo, count of Mont'Alto, grand justiciar under Charles III in 1381.

Rogiero Acclociamuro, grand justiciar under the same king.

Roberto Ursino, soldier, grand justiciar under Ladislas in 1390.

Nicolò Celano, count of Celano, grand justiciar under the same king.

Monsieur de Montjoie, grand justiciar for King Louis II of Anjou.

Baldassarre della Ratta, count of Caserta, grand justiciar at the time of King René.

Raimondo Ursino, prince of Taranto and count of Nola, grand justiciar under Alfonso I.

Gilbert of Bourbon, count of Montpensier, dauphin of Auvergne and archduke of Sessa, grand justiciar in 1495 for Charles VIII, king of France.

Antonio Piccolomini, duke of Amalfi, grand justiciar under Ferdinand I in 1480.

Don Alfonso Piccolomini, duke of Amalfi, son of the above-mentioned, was grand justiciar in 1493.

Don Ferdinando Gonzaga, prince of Molfetta, grand justiciar at the time of Charles V.

Don Cesare Gonzaga, prince of Molfetta, grand justiciar under Philip III.

Don Ferdinando Gonzaga, prince of Molfetta, grand justiciar under Philip III.

Tomaso Francesco Spinello, marquis of Foscaldo, grand justiciar under Philip IV.

Giovanni Battista Spinello, marquis of Foscaldo, grand justiciar under the same king and living at present under King Charles II.

ADMIRALS

Belcamuer in 1128 under the rule of King Roger.

George of Antioch in 1131 under the same king.

Maio da Bari in 1156 under William I, called the Bad.

Margaritone in 1189 under the rule of King Tancred.

Arrigo di Malta, count of Marino, in 1222 at the time of Emperor Frederick I.

Alessandro in 1236 under the same emperor.

Nicolò Spinola in 1239 under the same.

Ansaldo de Mari in 1241 under the same Emperor Frederick.

Andreolo de Mari in 1247 under the same.

Filippo Cinardo in 1263 at the time of King Manfred.

Guillaume Stendard in 1263, appointed by Charles I.

Guillaume de Belmont in 1269 at the time of the same king.

Filippo di Tuzziaco in 1270 at the time of the same king.

Narzone di Tuzziaco in 1272 under the same king.

Arrigo de Mari in 1282 at the time of the same king.

Rinaldo d'Avelta was appointed by Charles II in 1294.

Rogiero Doria in 1303, under the same Charles II.

Sergio Siginulfo in 1305 at the time of the same king.

Bartolomeo Siginulfo in 1306 under the same king.

Filippo, prince of Acaia and Taranto, son of Charles II, was made admiral by his father in 1307.

Odoardo Spinola in 1309 was made admiral by King Robert.

Corrado Spinola, son of the above, in 1313 under the same king.

Ademaro Romano was admiral under Robert in 1317.

Tomaso Marzano under the same king in 1327.

Ludovico di Tocco was admiral of the same King Robert and also of Queen Giovanna I.

Goffredo Marzano, count of Squillace, made admiral by Queen Giovanna I in 1342.

Pietro Cossa, or Salvacossa, at the time of the same queen in 1354.

Rinaldo del Balzo under the same queen in 1356.

Roberto Matzano, count of Squillace and duke of Sessa, under the rule of the same queen in 1370.

Giacomo Marzano, son of the above, count of Squillace, made admiral by Charles III in 1381.

Giovanni Antonio Marzano, duke of Sessa, made admiral in 1404 by King Ladislas.

Battista Fregoso, admiral for Louis II of Anjou.

Artale di Luna, made admiral by Queen Giovanna II in 1423.

Marino Marzano, prince of Rossano and duke of Sessa, made admiral by Alfonso I in 1453.

Roberto Sanseverino, prince of Salerno, made admiral by Ferdinand I in 1463.

Antonello Sanseverino, prince of Salerno, under the same king.

Francesco Coppola, count of Sarno, under the same king in 1486.

Federico of Aragon, prince of Altamura, son of King Ferrante I, was made admiral by his father in 1487.

Giovanni Polo under the same king in 1488.

Berardino Sanseverino, prince of Bisignano, made admiral by King Ferdinand in 1497.

Filippo d'Aloves and of la Marche, made admiral by Louis XII, king of France and Naples in 1507.

Don Bernardino Villamarino, count of Bosa and Capaccio, made admiral in 1522 by the Catholic King.

Guillaume de Croy, duke of Sora, was made admiral by Emperor Charles V in 1510.

Don Raimondo di Cardona, count of Alvito, under the same emperor in 1520.

Don Ferrante di Cardona, duke of Somma, under the same emperor.

Gonsalvo Fernando di Cordoba and Cardona, duke of Sessa, admiral under Philip II in 1572.

Don Francesco Carrafa under the same king.

Don Antonio Carrafa, marquis of Corata, in 1584 under the same king.

Matteo di Capua, prince of Conca, admiral in 1597, under Philip II.

Antonio Carrafa, under Philip III in 1607.

Giulio Cesare di Capua, prince of Conca, in 1608 under the same king.

Don Luigi Fernando di Cordoba and Cardona, duke of Sessa, admiral under Philip IV.

Don Antonio Fernandez di Cordoba and Cardona, duke of Sessa, admiral under the same king.

Don Francesco Fernandez of Cordoba and Cardona, duke of Sessa, admiral under the present King Charles II.

CHAMBERLAINS

Adenolfo Mansella was grand chamberlain at the time of King Roger and William I.

Manfredi Maletta, count of Mileno and Frequento, and lord of Monte S. Angelo, grandfather of King Manfred, was grand chamberlain in 1264.

Pietro de Belmont, count of Monte Scaglioso, was chamberlain at the time of Charles I in 1269.

Pietro Caracciolo under the same king in 1279.

Giovanni Monforte, count of Squillace, chamberlain in 1292 under Charles II.

Berardo Caracciolo under the same king in 1305.

Diego della Ratta, count of Caserta, was chamberlain at the time of King Robert in 1310.

Carlo Artus, count of S. Agata, was chamberlain in 1345 at the time of Queen Giovanna I.

Arrigo Caracciolo, count of Geraci, chamberlain in 1348 at the time of the same queen.

Raimondo del Balzo, count of Spoleto, grand chamberlain at the time of the same queen.

Giacomo Arcucci, count of Minorvino, was made chamberlain by this queen in 1375.

Giordano Marzano, count of Alisi, grand chamberlain at the time of Charles III in 1381.

Francesco Prignano in 1400 under Ladislas.

Berlingiero Cantelmo, count of Arce, chamberlain in 1407 at the time of the same king.

Giacomo Cantelmo, count of Arce, under the same king.

Pandolfello Alopa was made chamberlain by Queen Giovanna II.

Ruggiero Gaetano, grand chamberlain under the same queen.

Lorenzo Colonna, count of Albi, by the same queen.

Francesco d'Aquino, count of Loreto and Satriano, was grand chamberlain under Alfonso I.

Girolamo Sanseverino, prince of Bisignano, grand chamberlain under King Ferdinand I.

Iñigo d'Avalos, marquis of Pescara, made chamberlain by Ferdinand I.

Alfonso d'Avalos, marquis of Vasto, was grand chamberlain at the time of Charles V.

Ferrante Francesco d'Avalos, son of the above, and marquis of Pescara, was grand chamberlain under Philip II.

Don Alfonso d'Avalos, marquis of Vasto and Pescara, was grand chamberlain under the same king.

Don Iñigo d'Avalos, marquis of Pescara and Vasto, was grand chamberlain under Philip III.

Don Cesare d'Avalos was grand chamberlain under the same king.

Don Ferrante Francesco Maria d'Avalos of Aquino and Aragon, marquis of Vasto and Pescara, prince of Francavilla, grand chamberlain under Philip IV.

Don Ettorre Pignatello of Aragon, duke of Monteleone and Terranova, marquis of Vaglio, prince of Noia, grand chamberlain under the same king and also at present under Charles II.

PROTONOTARIES

Nicolò under King Roger in 1133.

Rogiero da Taranto in 1173.

Abbot N. in 1195 under Emperor Henry VI.

Alberto N. was protonotary under the same emperor in 1196.

Matteo N. was protonotary under the empire of Constanza in 1198.

Arrigo N. in 1219 was protonotary under Emperor Frederick II.

Giovanni di Lauro under the same emperor in 1220.

Giacomo da Catania under the same emperor in 1224.

Pietro delle Vigne was protonotary under the same emperor in 1226.

Filippo di Matera under the same emperor in 1229.

Procopio da Matera under the same emperor in 1232.

Giovanni d'Alise was protonotary under King Manfred in 1263.

Roberto da Bari was protonotary under Charles I in 1266.

Sparano da Bari under the same king in 1279.

Bartolomeo di Capua under the same king in 1284.

Giacomo di Capua was protonotary under Charles II in 1207.

Ruggiero Sanseverino, archbishop of Bari, was protonotary of Giovanna I in 1343.

Ligorio Zurulo was protonotary at the time of the same queen in 1346.

Landolfo Caracciolo, archbishop of Amalfi, was protonotary at the time of the same queen in 1348.

Napoleone Ursino was protonotary at the time of Louis and Giovanna, mentioned above, in 1352.

Ugo Sanseverino, count of Potenza, protonotary at the time of the same queen in 1370.

Giovanni Ursino, count of Manupello, protonotary under Charles III in 1381.

Gualtieri d'Engenio, count of Cupertino, protonotary under the same king in 1383.

Berardo Zurlo was protonotary under King Ladislas in 1390.

Napoleone Ursino II, count of Manupello and S. Valentino, under the same king.

Leone Giordano Orsino, count of Manupello, was protonotary under the same king.

Gurello Origlia was protonotary in 1406 under King Ladislas.

Francesco Zurlo, count of Montuoro, was protonotary in 1415 at the time of Giovanna II.

Christofaro Gaetano, count of Fundi, in 1420 under the rule of the same queen.

Honorato Gaetano, count of Fundi, protonotary in 1442 at the time of Alfonso I.

Honorato Gaetano II, count of Fundi and duke of Traietto, at the time of Ferdinand II in 1469.

Pier Berardino Gaetano, count of Moscone, protonotary in 1484 under the same king.

Goffredo Borgia, prince of Squillace and count of Cariati, in 1494 under the same king.

Ferrante Spinello, duke of Castrovillari, protonotary in 1525 under Charles V.

Henry, count of Nassau, protonotary in 1536 under the same emperor.

Andrea Doria, prince of Melfi, protonotary under the same emperor.

Giovanni Andrea Doria, prince of Melfi, protonotary in 1555 under Philip II.

Andrea Doria, prince of Melfi, protonotary in 1606 under Philip III.

Giovanni Andrea Doria, prince of Melfi, protonotary under Philip IV.

Andrea Doria, prince of Melfi, protonotary under the same King Philip IV and at present under Charles II.

CHANCELLORS

Maione da Bari was grand chancellor at the time of King Roger.

Asclettino was chancellor under William I, called the Bad.

Matteo Bonello, chancellor under William II, called the Good.

Gualterio, bishop of Troia, was grand chancellor under Emperor Henry VI in 1195.

Gualterio de Paleariis, chancellor under Emperor Frederick II in 1206.

Gualterio d'Ocree, grand chancellor at the time of King Manfred.

Maestro Geoffrey de Belmont, chancellor under Charles I in 1269.

Pietro de Belmont, count of Monte Scaglioso and Alba, was chancellor under the same king.

Simon of Paris, chancellor under the same king in 1270.

Adamo de Dussiaco, archbishop of Cosenza, was chancellor under Charles II in 1292.

Guglielmo Longo da Bergamo was grand chancellor under the same king and then cardinal.

Pietro de Ferraris, archbishop of Arles in France, was chancellor under the same Charles II in 1300.

Ingerano Stella, archbishop of Capua, was grand chancellor under King Robert in 1320.

Filippo, bishop of Cavillona, was grand chancellor at the time of Queen Giovanna I in 1344.

Nicolò Alunno was grand chancellor at the time of the same queen.

Honorio Savello, grand chancellor under Charles III in 1382.

Giovanni Tomacello, prince of Altamura, duke of Orvieto and Spoleto, count of Sora, Minornino, and Nocera; chancellor under Ladislas in 1392.

Filippello Tomacello was chancellor under the same king in 1400.

Marino Boffa, count of Alise and Bovino, was grand chancellor at the time of Queen Giovanna II in 1416.

Ottino Caracciolo, count of Nicastro, chancellor at the time of the same queen in 1419.

Algiasio Ursino, chancellor at the time of the same queen in 1421.

Orso Orsino was grand chancellor under Alfonso I.

Ugo d'Alagno, count of Burrello, chancellor under the same king.

Giacomo Caracciolo, duke of Cagnano and count of Brienza, chancellor under Ferrante I in 1479.

Petricone Caracciolo, duke of Martina and count of Buccino, chancellor under the same king in 1488.

Mercurio Gattinara, count of Castro, grand chancellor under Charles V in 1535.

Battista Caracciolo, duke of Martina, chancellor under the same emperor in 1550.

Cosmo Pinelli, duke of Acerenza, chancellor under Philip II in 1557.

Don Iñigo d'Avalos was grand chancellor under Philip II in 1562.

Don Cesare d'Avalos was chancellor under the same king.

Tiberio Pignatello was grand chancellor under Philip III.

Camillo Caracciolo, prince of Avellino, grand chancellor under the same king.

Marino Caracciolo, prince of Avellino, grand chancellor under Philip IV.

Francesco Marino Caracciolo, prince of Avellino, grand chancellor under the same King Philip IV and at present under Charles II.

SENESCHALS

Riccardo, son of Count Drogo, was seneschal at the time of King Roger.

Ugolino di Tocco, seneschal in 1195 under Henry VI.

Geoffrey Sanguineto, made seneschal by Charles I in 1269.

Giovanni d'Apia, grand seneschal, appointed by Charles II in 1292.

Carlo della Leonessa, seneschal under the same king in 1302.

Goffredo di Milliaco, seneschal under the same king in 1303.

Ugo del Balzo, made seneschal by the same king in 1307.

Leone Regio, seneschal at the time of King Robert.

Roberto de Cabani, count of Eboli, grand seneschal at the time of Queen Giovanna I in 1345.

Christofaro de Costanza, seneschal at the time of the same queen in 1352.

Nicolò Acciaiolo, count of Melfi, grand seneschal under the same queen in 1360.

Angelo Acciaiolo, count of Melfi, grand seneschal under the same queen in 1366.

Marsilio de Carrara, seneschal under Charles III in 1382.

Salvatore Capece Zurlo, seneschal under King Ladislas.

Gabriello Ursino, duke of Venosa, seneschal in 1409.

Artuso Pappacoda, seneschal under the same king in 1410.

Giovanni Scotto, seneschal at the time of Louis II of Anjou.

Pietro d'Andrea, count of Troia, seneschal of Queen Giovanna II.

Sergianni Caracciolo, duke of Venosa and count of Avellino, grand seneschal at the time of the same queen in 1425.

Arrigo d'Anna, called the Monk, grand seneschal at the time of the same queen.

Francesco Zurlo, count of Nucera and Montuori, made grand seneschal by Alfonso I in 1442.

Francesco d'Aquino, count of Loreto, seneschal under the same king.

Pietro de Guevara, marquis of Vasto, grand seneschal under Ferrante I in 1470.

Stefano Bicesi, lord of Beaucaire, seneschal and grand chamberlain of King Louis XII in 1501.

Carlo de Guevara, count of Potenza, seneschal at the time of Charles V in 1535.

Alfonso di Guevara, count of Potenza, seneschal under Philip II.

Don Iñigo de Guevara, duke of Bovino, seneschal under Philip III.

Don Giovanni de Guevara, duke of Bovino, seneschal under the same king.

Don Iñigo di Guevara II, duke of Bovino, grand seneschal under King Philip IV.

Don Carlo di Guevara, duke of Bovino, grand seneschal under the same king and also under Charles II.

ROYAL TRIBUNALS

The first tribunal is the one called the Council of State, or of War, which consists of many lords chosen by the Catholic Master, with whom the regents of the Royal Cancelleria intervene. The head is his Excellency the Lord Viceroy, and it resides in his palace.

The second tribunal is the Collateral Council, which consists of five regents from the Royal Cancelleria, two Italians and three Spaniards, and one secretary named by the crown, which holds jurisdiction above its subjects in the Royal Cancelleria.

The third tribunal is the Council of Capuana, at first named S. Chiara, which consists in a president and 24 counsellors who dispense justice in four rotas in four courtrooms, and in each one of these rotas, there is one head and two of these counsellors. Ordinarily they dispense justice in the Criminal Vicaria.

The fourth tribunal is the Royal Camera of the Summaria, which consists in one lieutenant, the head of them, and eight presiding, learned judges, three Italians and five Spaniards, and three presidents called *idioti* (uneducated people) which are usually two Italians and one Spaniard, and it has a lawyer and a fiscal procurer and secretary with 24 *rationali* (audit officials).

The fifth tribunal is the Grand Court of the Civil and Criminal Vicaria, in which there is a regent named by the Vicaria as head. It is divided into six civil judges, which consist of two rotas in two courtrooms; and another six criminal judges, which also usually number eight or more, according to the will of the lord viceroys of the kingdom who govern at the time. The Criminal Vicaria also has a lawyer and fiscal prosecutor with the *percettore,* who waits to collect the proceeds of the civil and criminal courts.

The sixth is the Tribunal of the grand admiral commonly called the Admiralty Court, which is ruled by the judge chosen by the grand admiral. In criminal cases the fiscal lawyer of the Vicaria intervenes.

The seventh tribunal is that of S. Lorenzo, which is ruled by the elected officials who govern this most faithful city, who usually refer cases to the consulting learned judges to decide.

The eighth is the tribunal of the Piazze, attended by the five or six knights who settle the differences that arise among the knights, from which no blood is spilt.

The ninth tribunal of this city is the tribunal of the counts, called that of Revision, and that of brick, water and fortification.

The tenth is the Tribunal of the Immortal College of Doctors of Naples, which consists of a vice chancellor and thirty ordinary doctors called collegiates, with civil and criminal jurisdiction for whatever concerns the doctors of law.

And in respect to the medical doctors the same vice chancellor intervenes with the medical doctors.

The eleventh is the Tribunal of the Major Chaplain, who has jurisdiction in the royal chapel and its chaplains. Above these students he has his Consultants, who are usually royal ministers. They judge the cases of this tribunal with his approval.

The twelfth is the Tribunal of the Protonotary, which has jurisdiction over all the notaries and judges of contracts in the kingdom, above which the Visitor presides.

The thirteenth is the Tribunal of the Royal Mint, which establishes the weights and measures and has its own judge. From him one appeals to the Sacred Council. This court has twenty-four Masters of the Measures, which are chosen by the lord viceroys who are currently in office.

The fourteenth is the Tribunal of the Bailiff, named S. Paolo, which has jurisdiction over damages and small claims, and it renders its own privileges. From this tribunal one appeals to the fore-mentioned Tribunal of the Royal Mint.

The fifteenth is the Tribunal of the Silk-Makers Guild, which has its consultant or judge with three counsels.

The sixteenth is the Tribunal of the Wool Guild, with its judge and counsels.

The seventeenth is the Tribunal of the Giustintiero, which presides over of the disputes and has its prosecutor and master of acts.

The eighteenth is the Tribunal of the Master Portolan with civil jurisdiction over those who have public practice. It has its consultant, or judge, and master of acts.

The nineteenth is the Tribunal of the Major Fondaco or Royal Exchequer of Naples, which extends throughout the whole kingdom under the jurisdiction of the royal Chancellor of the Exchequer.

The twentieth is the Tribunal of the Prostitutes with its judge, prosecutor, and master of acts.

The twenty-first is the Tribunal of the Chief Physician, the jurisdiction of which extends above all the subjects of the kingdom.

The twenty-second is the jurisdiction of the Post Master General over all its carriers.

MILITARY TRIBUNALS

The twenty-third is the Tribunal of the Royal Galleys, with its learned auditor general, who presides over the cases of his subordinates.

The twenty-fourth is the Tribunal of the Clerk of Rations who keeps the stamp of all the soldiers, which are done with many officials and clerks.

The twenty-fifth is the Royal Treasury, which has jurisdiction of all subjects.

The twenty-sixth is the Tribunal of the Auditor General of the Camp, who is a jurist and has jurisdiction over all the professional soldiers of the kingdom, Spanish and Italian, and above those in the new militia, called the Battalions.

The twenty-seventh is the Tribunal of the Spanish Tercios which has jurisdiction over cases of the Spaniards of this city of Naples.

The twenty-eighth are the Tribunals of the Royal Castles: Nuovo, dell'Ovo, and S. Elmo, in each one of which there is a judge called the auditor.

The twenty-ninth is the Tribunal of the *Razza*, or Royal Cavalry.

The thirtieth is the jurisdiction of the Hunt.

The thirty-first is the jurisdiction of the Royal Arsenal.

The thirty-second is the jurisdiction of the secretary of the kingdom over the subjects in the Royal Cancelleria.

The thirty-third is the jurisdiction of the wine tax, which is governed by its *arrend*.

The thirty-fourth is the jurisdiction of the gambling tax.

The thirty-fifth is the jurisdiction of the consuls of goldsmiths or silversmiths.

The thirty-sixth is the jurisdiction of the Giudeca (Jewish quarter) with four consuls, which has for a judge a delegated a counsellor.

The thirty-seventh is the jurisdiction of the consuls of the foreign nations, such as the Venetians, Genoese, Florentines, Ragusans, and others.

THE NOBILITY OF NAPLES

PRINCES

Amoroso, of the house of
Loffredo
Angri, Doria
Apici of Tocco
Ascoli, of Leyva
Athena, of Caracciolo
Avella, Doria
Avellino, of Caracciolo
Belmonte, of Ravaschiero
Belvedere, of Carrafa
Bisignano, of Sanseverino
Capistrano is the grand duke of
Tuscany
Caramanico, of Aquino
Cariati, of Spinello
Carovigni, of Serra
Carpignano, of Lanario
Casalmaggiore, of Brancia
Caserta, of Gaetano
Caspoli, of Capua
Cassano of Bari, of Aragona
d'Ayerbo
Cassano of Calabria, of
Pallavicino
Castellaneta, of Miroballo
Castellofranco, of Sersale
Castiglione, of Aquino
Cellamare, of Giudice
Chiusano, of Carrafa
Colle d'Anchise, of Costanzo
Colle, of Somma
Colombrato, of Carrafa
Conca, of Capua
Crucoli, of Aquino

Durazzano, of Gargano
Ferolito, of Aquino
Forino, of Caracciolo
Francavilla, the marquis of
Pescara Avalos
Gallicchio, of Coppola
Gesso, of Capua
Giraci, of Grimaldo
Leporano, of Moscettola
Marano, of Manriquez
Mayda, of Loffredo
Melfi, Doria
Melita, of Silva
Molfetta, of Gonzaga
Monasteraci, of Galeoto
Mondorvino, of Pignatello
Mont'Albano, of Toledo
Monteauto, of Capece
Monteleone, of Capece Galeota
Montemarano, of Marchese
Montemileto, of Tocco
Montesarchio, of Avalos
Nola, of Pignatello
Oliveto, of Spinello
Ottaiano, de'Medici
Pietra Pulcina, of Aquino
Prisiccio, of Bartirotti
Riccia, of Capua
Rocca dell'Aspro, of
Filomarino
Rocca Romana, of Capua
Roccella, of Carrafa
Rossano, of Aldobrandino
S. Agata, of Ferrao

San Martino, of Gennaro
Sanseverino, of Albertino
Sansevero, of Sangro
Santobuono, of Caracciolo
Sanza, of Orefice
Satriano, of Ravaschiero
Scalea, of Spinello
Scilla, of Ruffo
Solofra, of Orsino
Sopino, of Carrafa
Squillaci, of Borgia of Aragon

Squinzano, of Enrinches
Stigliano, of Carrafa
Strongoli, of Campitello
Sulmona, of Borghese
Tarsia, of Spinello
Teramo, its bishop
Torre Nova, of Caracciolo
Torre Padula, of Rocco
Venafri, of Peretti, now Savelli
Venosa, of Lodovisio
Vetrana, of Albrizio

DUKES

Aceranza, of Pinello
Acre, of Buoncompagno
Airola, of Caracciolo
Alessano, the first-born son
    of the prince of Cassano of
    Bari
Aluito, of Gallio
Andria, of Carrafa
Apellosa, of Ricca
Aquaro, the first-born son of
    the prince of Oliveto
Arcella, of Caracciolo
Atri, of Acquaviva
Atripalda, the first-born son
    of the prince of Avellino
Avigliano, the prince of
    Melfi, of Doria
Ayello, the prince of Massa
    Cybò Malaspina
Bagnara, of Ruffo
Bagnoli, of Maiorca
Bagnuolo, Sanfelice
Barrea, of Afflitto
Bellorisguardo, of Pignatello
Belvedere, of Brancia
Bernauda, of Bernaudo
Bisaccia, of Pignatello
Bovino, of Guevara

Cagnano, of Vargas
Caivano, of Barrile
Calabritto, of Tuttavilla
Campo Chiaro, of Mormile
Campolieto, of Carrafa
Cancellara, of Carrafa
Cantalupo, of Gennaro
Cardinale, the prince of
    Satriano
Casacalenda, of Sangro
Castel di Sangro, Caracciolo
Castel Saraceno, of Rovito
Castellonovo, of Brancaccio
Castelluccia, of David
Castro, of Pallavicino
Castrovillari, the prince of
    Cariati
Ceglie, of Lovrano
Celenza, of Caracciolo
Cerisano, the first-born son of
    the prince of Castelfranco
Civita di Penna, the duke of
    Parma, of Farnese
Collepietro, of Carrafa
Crosia, of Mandatoricci
Evoli, of Grimaldi, now
    Doria

Ferrandina, the prince of
  Mont'Albano
Ferrazzano, of Vitagliano
Flumari, of de Ponte
Fragnito, of Mont'Alto
Fuorli, of Carrafa
Girifalco, of Caracciolo
Gravina, of Orsino
Grumo, of della Tolfa
Guardia, of della Marra
Ielzi, of Carrafa
Laconia, the first-born son of
  the prince of Mayda
Laurenzana, of Gaetano of
  d'Aragona
Laurino, of Carrafa
Laurriano, of Sanfelice
Limatola, of Gambacorta
Lizzano, of Clodino
Lustra, of Brancaccio
Macchia, of della Marra
Madaloni, of Carrafa
Marianella, of Barrile
Marsi, of Colonna
Martina, of Caracciolo
Marzano, of Laudato
Miranda, of Crispano
Mondragone, the first-born
  son of the prince of
  Stigliano
Mont'Alto, of Moncada of
  Aragon
Montecalvo, of Gagliardo,
  now Pignatello
Monteleone, of Pignatello
Montenegro, of Bucca of
  Aragon
Montenegro, of Grego
Nardò, of Acquaviva
Nocara, of Loffredo
Nocera, of Carrafa
Noci, the duke of Nardò
Noia, of Carrafa

Orsara, of Franchis
Perdifumo, the prince of
  Rocca d'Aspro
Peschici, di Regina, now
  Pisanello
Popoli, of Cantelmo
Rapolla, now Druzzano, of
  Carrafa
Regina, of Capece Galeota
Rocca, of Caracciolo
Rodi, of Capece
Roscino, of Villano
S. Agapito, of Provenzano
S. Agata, of Cosso
S. Angelo à Fasanella, of
  Capece Galeota
S. Cipriano, of Tufo
S. Donato, of Sanseverino
S. Donato, of Vaez
S. Elia, of di Palma
S. Giovanni, of Cavaniglia
S. Mango, of Chignones
S. Martino, of Leonessa
S. Nicandro, of Caropreso
S. Pietro in Galatina, of
  Spinola
S. Pietro, of Lopez
Salandra, of Revertera
Salza, of Strambone
Saracena, of Pesdara di Diano
Serre, of de Rossi
Sessa, of Cordova and
  Cardona
Sesto, of Spinola
Siano, of Capece Latro
Sicignano, of Caracciolo,
  now of Tocco
Sora, the duke of Arce, of
  Buoncompagno
Speyzano, of Moscettola
Tagliacozzo, of Colonna
Taurisano, of di Castro
Telesa, of Ceva Grimaldo

127

Termoli, the prince of Rocca
Romana
Terranova, the prince of
Giraci
Terrenova, of Pagano
Tocco, of Pinello
Torre Maggiore, the first-
born son of the prince of S.
Severo

Traetto, the prince of
Stigliano
Turano, of Cavalcante
Tursi, the first-born son of the
prince of Avella
Vayrano, of Mormile
Vietri, of Sangro

MARQUISES

Achaia, of delli Monti
Acquaviva, the first-born son
of the duke of Atri
Aieta, of Cosentino
Alfidena, of Bucca of Aragon
Alvignano, of Capece
Amato, of Loffredo
Anzi, the first-born son of the
prince of Belvedere
Arena, of Concublet
Arienzo, the first-born son of
the duke of Madaloni
Atessa, the duke of
Tagliacozzo
Baselice, of Ridolfi
Bella, of Caracciolo
Bellante, the prince of
Caserta
Belmonte, of Tappia
Bervicara, of Gastigliare
Binetto, of Caracciolo
Bitetto, of Carrafa
Bonito, of Pisanello
Bracigliano, of Miroballo
Brancalione, the duke of
Rapolla, of Carrafa
Brìenza, of Caracciolo
Bucchianico, the first-born
son of the prince of S.
Buono
Buonalbergo, of Spinello

Caiazzo, of Corso
Cammarota, of Marchese
Campagna, the prince of
Monaco, of Grimaldi
Campi, of Enriquez
Campolattaro, the prince of
Caspoli
Canna, of Loffredo
Capograssi, of Capponi
Capriglia, of Caracciolo
Capurso, of Pappacoda
Casa d'Arbori, of Caracciolo
Casal Nuovo, of Pignatello
Casobuono, of Pelciotta,
Campitello
Cassano, of Serra
Castelguidone, of Caracciolo
Castelluccio, of Pescara
Castelnuovo, the prince of
Sansevero
Castelpoto, of Castiglia
Castelvetere, the first-born
son of the prince of
Roccella
Ceglie of Bari, de Angelis
Ceglie of Otranto, of Lobrano
Cerchiara, the prince of Noia
Cerella, of Manriquez
Cilenza, of Gambacorta
Cinque Frondi, of Gifoni
Circello, of di Somma

Civita Retengha, of del Pezzo
Civita S. Angelo, of Pinelli
Colle Longo, of Sanesio
Corigliano, of delli Monti
Corleto, the prince of Colle
  d'Anchise
Crispano, of Strada
Cusano, of Barrionuovo
Ducenta, of Folgore
Faicchio now duke of
  Martino
Fuscaldo, of Spinello
Gagliati, of Sanchez
Galatola, the first-born son of
  the duke of Acerenza
Genzano, of del Tufo
Gioia, the first-born son of
  the prince of Giraci
Grassignano, of Lottiero
Grotteria, of Aragona
  d'Ayerbo
Grottola, of Sanchez, now
  Caracciolo
Ilicito, the prince of
  Castellaneta
Introdoco, of Bandino
Laino, of Cardines
Larino, the prince of
  Casalmaggiore
Lauro, of Pignatello
Lavello, of del Tufo
Longobosco, of Iodice
Macchiagodena, of
  Caracciolo
Melito, of Brandolino
Mignano, of Dura
Mirabella, of Naccarella
Missanello, the prince of
  Gallicchio
Misuraca, the first-born son
  of the prince of Scalea
Monacilone, of Alarcon di
  Mendozza

Mont'Agnano, of Vespolo
Monte Falcione, of Poderico
Monte Falcone, of di Martino
Monte Falcone, of Gargano
Monte Forte, of Loffredo
Monte Rocchetto, of Morra
Monte Silvano, of Brancaccio
Montenigro, of Carrafa
Montepiloso, of Grimaldo
Montorio, of Castellet
Morcone, of Baglione
Motola, of Caracciolo
Motta Gioiosa, of Caracciolo
Oria, of Imperiale
Oriulo, of Pignone
Padula, of di Ponte
Padulo, of Carbonespina
Paglieta, of Pignatello
Pentidattilo, of Francopetra
Pescara, the prince of
  Francavilla, of Avalos
Petra Catella, of Ceva
  Grimaldo
Petrella, of Caputo
Pietra Vayrana, of Grimaldo
Pietra, of Lottiero
Pimonte, of Lanario
Pisciotta, of Pappacoda
Pizzoli, of Torres
Polignano, of Radolvich
Polla, of Villano
Ponte Latrone, of Capece
Postiglione, of Franco
Ramagnano, of Lagni
Rapolla, of Braida
Rende, the marquis delle
  Valle
Ripa, of Riccardo
Roggiano, of Macedonio
Rosito, of Brancia
S. Agata, the marquis of
  Trivico
S. Angelo, of di Ponte

S. Angelo, of Salvo
S. Eramo, of Caracciolo
S. Floro, of Zapata
S. Giorgio, of Milano
S. Giovanni, of del Tufo
S. Giuliano, of Longo
S. Giuliano, of Ramirez Montalvano
S. Lucido, of Sangro
S. Mango, of Mastrogiudice
S. Marco, of Cavaniglia
S. Marzano, of Mastrillo
S. Massimo, the duke of Cantalupo
S. Mauro, of Brancia
Sagineto, of Maiorana
Salceto, of Spina
Salice, the prince of Vetrana
Sanseverino, the prince of Avellino
Sorito, of Ardoino
Specchio, of Trani
Spinazzola, the prince of Mondorvino
Spineto, of Imperato

Taviano, of de Franchis
Terza, of d'Azzia
Tiana, of Missanello
Torre di Francolise, the prince of Rocca Romana
Torrecuso, of Caracciolo
Tortora, the marquis of Roggiano
Trivico, of Loffredo
Tufillo, of Lombardo
Turano, of Cafarelli
Turfara, the marquis of Trivico
Valle, of Alarcon Mendozza
Varanello, of Carrafa
Vasto, the prince of Francavilla, of Avalos
Vico di Pantano, of Suarez
Vico, prince of Oliveto
Villa, of Manso
Villamaina, of Tappia
Vinchiaturo, of Longo
Voltorara, of Caracciolo
Zirò, the first-born son of the prince of Tarsia

COUNTS

Acerra, the marquis of Laino
Albi, the duke of Tagliacozzo
Aliano, the prince of Stigliano
Altavilla, the first-born son of the prince of Riccia
Anversa, the prince of Rocca Romana
Biccari, the duke of Airola
Borrello, the duke of Monteleone
Bova, the archbishop of Reggio
Buccino, the duke of Martina

Buonvicino, of Caselli
Campobasso, the prince of Molfetta
Canosa, the marquis of Campagna
Capaccio, the duke of Evoli
Carinola, the prince of Stigliano
Casalduni, of Sarriano
Castagneta, the count of Montella
Castel dell'Abbate, the prince of Rocca dell'Aspro
Castel di Lino, of Vitelli

Castiglione, of Brancaccio
Castro, the first-born son of
the duke of Taurisano
Celano, of Piccolomini of
Aragon
Cerrito, the duke of Madaloni
Chiaramonte, of Sanseverino
Conneianni, of Marullo
Conversano, the duke of
Nardò
Conza, the prince of Venosa
Corvaro, of Mareri
Fondi, the prince of Stigliano
Gambatesa of the house of
Mendozza
Gioia, the duke of Atri
Giovenazzo, the prince of
Molfetta
Giulia Nova, the duke of Atri
Loreto, of Afflitto
Macchia, of di Regina
Mareri, of Colonna
Martorano, the first-born son
of the prince of Castiglione
Misciagne, of Beltrano
Mola, of Vaez
Molise, the prince of
Strongoli
Mont'Aperto, the first-born
son of the prince of Monte
Mileto
Montederisi, the marquis of
Vasto and Pascara
Montella, of Gattola
Montuoro, of di Capua
Muro, the prince of Solofra
Nicotera, the prince of Scilla
Oppido, of Orsino
Palena, the first-born son of
the prince of Conca
Palmerici, of de Matteis
Picerno, of Caracciolo
Policastro, of Carrafa

Potenza, the marquis of
Trivico
Roccarainola, the first-born
son of the duke of
Castelluccia
Ruvo, the duke of Andria
S. Angelo, the count of
Soriano, first-born son of
the duke of Nocera
S. Christina, the first-born
son of the prince of Cariati
S. Giovanni in Fiore, of
Pignatello
S. Maria in Grisone, of
Venato
Saponara, of Sanseverino
Sarno, the count of Mareri
Scala, of Spinello
Schiavi, of Caracciolo
Serra Mazzana, of Braida
Setino, the prince of S. Buono
Simari, the first-born son of
the prince of Squillaci
Sinopoli, the prince of Scilla
Soriano, the first-born son of
the duke of Nocera
Torella, the prince of
Avellino
Trivento, the first-born son of
the duke of Barrea
Ugento, of Pandone
Vaglio, of Salazario
Vasto Meroli, of Tappia

131

NOBLE FAMILIES OF THE *SEGGI* OF THE FAITHFUL CITY OF NAPLES

*Noble Families of
the Seggio of
Porta Capuana*

Aprani
Barrili
Boccapianoli
Bozzuti
Brancia
Buoncompagno
Cantelmo
Capece
Caraccioli del
  Leone
Caraccioli Rossi
Colonna of the
  duke of Zagarola
Crispiani
della Leonessa
della Marra
Dentici
di Silva
di Somma
Filomarini
Franco of the
  Marquis of
  Postiglione
Galeoti
Guindazzi
Lagni

Latri
Loffredi
Maricondi
Mendozza of the
  princes of Melito
Minutoli
Morra
Orsini of the duke
  of Bracciano
Piscicelli
Protonobilissimi,
  called Faccipecori
Sconditi
Seripandi
Tocco
Tomacelli
Zuroli

*Extinct Families of
the Same Seggio*
Acciaioli
Acciapaccia
Agalto
Aiello
Aquilio
Arbusto
Arcella
Ayossi
Baffo
Baraballi
Barrese
Boccafingo
Brancacci
Cadino
Cappasanti
Carboni of the
  marquises of
  Padula
Castrovetere

Catanei
Comino
Comite marone
Cosso
d'Acerris
d'Insola
dall'Aversana
de Diano
de Puteo
della Valle
Forma
Gagliardi
Iovane
Manco
Mansella
Mastaro
Olopesce
Padarano
Pandoni of the duke
  of Boiano
Paparone
Pesce
Proculo
Quintana
Romano
Saccapanno
Sardo
Scaldo
Sicchimanno
Siginolfi of
  Passarelli
Sigismundi
Sincilla
Tortello
Virginio
Vulcani dell'onde
Zaccaria, and others

Noble Families of the Seggio of Nido

Acquavivi
Affliti di Mazzeo
Avalos
Azzia of the
  Marquis of Terza
Berlingieri
Bologna
Brancacci
Cabanigli
Cantelmi
Capani
Capeci
Capua
Cardenas
Carrafa
Cosso
Dentice delle Stelle
Duce
Frezza
Gaetani
Gallucci
Gatta
Gesualdi
Girone of the duke
  of Ossuna
Giudice
Gonsaga of the
  duke of Ferrante
Grisoni

Guevari
Guindazzi
Luna
Mastrogiudice
Milani
Monsolini
Montalti
Orsini of the duke
  of Gravina
Piccolomini
Pignatelli
Ricci
Sangro
Sanseverino
Sarraceno
Sersali
Spina
Spinelli
Tolfa
Tommacelli
Vulcani

Extinct Families of the Same Seggio

Acerra
Agaldi, later
  named, by the
  lords of Corbano,
  di Corbano
Alagno
Aldemorisco
Assanti
Avezzano of the
  lords of Tricarico
Beccaria of Pavia
Capuani
Caraccioli Bianchi
Cardoini
Cardona
Celano
Centeglias of the
  marquis of
  Cotrone

Clignetta of the
  lords of Caiazza
Diazcarlone of the
  counts of Alisi
Ferramosca of the
  count of
  Mugnano
Fontanola
Gallerati
Gattola of Gaeta
Malaspina
Malatesta of the
  lords of Rimini in
  Romagna
Marramaldi
Monforti of the
  lords of Campo
  Basso
Offiero
Palentana of the
  lords of Ravenna
Papiro
Rumbo
Sanframundo of the
  counts of Cerra
  and of Cerreto
Solpitio
Toraldi of the lords
  of Pulignano
Villamarina of the
  counts of
  Capaccio, and
  others

Noble Families of the Seggio of Montagna

Capua
Carmignani
Cicinelli
Coppola of
    Coluccio
Franconi
Maio
Miraballi
Muscettola
Pignoni
Poderico
Ribera of the dukes
    of Alcalà
Rocchi
Rossi
Sancez of the
    marquis of
    Grottola
Sanfelici
Sorgenti
Toledo
Villani of the
    marquis of Polla

*Extinct Families of
    the Same Seggio*
Abissa
Albo
Alneto

Arcamoni
Arco
Arrichinto
Baiano
Balestrieri
Barbati
Boccatorti
Boffi, called
    Stendardi
Bonifacii
Bruto
Buteo
Cafatini
Calandri
Cannuta
Caperuso
Cappansata
Caputo
Cardoini
Chianola
Cicalese
Cicino
Cimbro
Cocchiola
Costanzi
Cotogno
Cozza
Crissi
Cupidini
Curvesieri
Egino
Fagilla
Falce
Falla
Ferrara
Gambacorta
Genutio
Giontula
Graffa
Guarracini
Hercules
Hipanta
Ianaro

Impero
Iulo
Iuntola
Lanzalonga
Maiorana
Mammoli
Mandolino
Mardones
Marogani
Mazza
Moscone
Mugillaro
Mummia
Musetta
Oricchioni
Origlia
Orimini
Paladini
Palumbo
Pappansogna
Piezo
Pigna
Pizzofalcone
Pizzuni
Ponzetti
Porra
Raimo
Retrosa
Rosso del Leone
Sarno
Scannacardillo
Scortiati
Scrignara
Sforza
Sicola
Simia
Soto
Spiccicacaso
Tora
Toso
Trofeo
Verticillo, & others
Yagante

*Noble Families of
the Seggio of
Porto*

Alesandro
Angelo
Arcamoni
Cardona
Colonna d'Ascanio
Dura
Gaeta
Gennaro
Griffi
Inserra
Macedonii
Macedonii of
Maiori
Mele
Origlia
Pagani
Pappacoda
Severini
Stramboni
Tuttavilla
Venati

*Extinct Families of
the Same Seggio*
Aghilar of Cordoba
del Gran Capitán
Aiossa
Albino
Alopa

Aquaria
Arbusto
Arimino
Attratino
Aventino
Cacciaconte
Cammerino
Campeggio
Cappella
Capranico
Castagna
Castagnola
Cicolino
Crasso
Dopnibono
Druso
Eboli
Ferrillo of the count
of Muro
Fiorentino
Fodio
Foglietto
Fregosi
Furio
Fuso
Gennari of the
counts of
Nicotera
Gentili
Genutio
Giptio
Helba
Iacobatio
Iancolleto
Ianvilla
Isalla
La Porta del
Cardinale
Landriano
Latio
Laurentiis
Maczono
Malabranca

Manatis
Manco
Mandagoro
Mansi
Manto
Mileto
Molino
Nissiaco
Noveletto
Oringa
Ossa
Pannizzato
Paparone
Pipino
Podietto
Proculo
Proposto
Quaranta
Rofa
Scalla
Scarso
Scorno
Sparella
Squallato
Viola, and others

*Noble Families of
the Seggio of
Portanova*

Agnese
Aponti of the
   marquis of S.
   Angelo
Capuani
Coppola
Costanzi
Gattoli
Liguori
Miraballi
Mocci
Mormili
Sitica of the duke
   of Altemps

*Extinct Families of
the Same Seggio*
Acerra
Adimario
Alagona
Albertis
Amala
Anna
Annecchina
Arbusto
Arcamone
Arco
Atellano
Basso

Bonifacio of the
   marquises d'Oria
Bosgarelli
Brissio
Bruno
Cafatini
Camerina
Cantelana
Cantelmo
Capassi
Capisucco
Cappella
Caputo
Carlino
Carnegraffa
Casamatta
Castagnola del
   Cardinale
Castellina
Cerva
Cicada
Cicaro
Collalta
Colle de Medio
Corradio
Diano
Edina
Farinola
Fingerio
Flandrino
Fogliano
Franco
Frangipane
Gambatella
Gentile
Gonsaga
Gorvo
Griffina
Lottleri
Manfrone
Massovia
Mastaro
Monforti

Monticello
Montuoro
Moschini
Nardino
Novelletto
Offiero
Ollopesce
Olzina
Omnibono
Oringa
Orlando
Picco of the lords
   of Mirandola
Pittavia
Pozzella
Pulzina
Ravignano
Ronchella
Sannazaro
Sassoni
Scannasorice
Scrignara
Sforza
Siscara of the count
   of Aiello
Stagnasangue
Tora
Toso
Turtello
Valignano, and
   others
Vellone

NOBLEST FAMILIES OF THE CITY OF NAPLES WHO DO NOT BELONG TO A *SEGGIO*

Afflitti of the dukes of Barrera, the counts of Loreto and of Trivento

Aierbi of Aragon, descendents of the royal blood of Aragon, of the marquises of Grotteria, the counts of Simmari, and today princes of Cassano

Aquini of the marquises of Corato, of the princes of Castiglione, of Cruculi, of Santomango, of Ferolito and Pietra Polsina

Azzia of the counts of Noia

Belprati of the counts formerly of Anversa

Beltrani of the counts of Misagne

Blanch of the lords of Oliveto

Bucca of Aragon of the marquises of Alfedena

Castrioti de Scanderbeg, of the marquises of Civita S. Angelo, and others

Castrocucchi of the lords of Alvedona and the ancient lords of Castrocucco

Concobletti of the marquises of Arena, counts of Stilo, and lords of S. Catana

Evolì of the counts of Trivento and the ancient lords of Castropignano

Filingieri of the lords of Pozzuoli, and the counts of Marsico, Nocera, Satriano, Avellino, ancient lords of Pia and of Candida

Franchi of the marquises of Taviano

Galeoti of the princes of Monasterace

Gambacorti of the lords of Pisa, dukes of Limatula, marquises of Cilenza and lords of Frasso

Gargani of the princes of Durazzono and Montefalcone

Leyva of the princes of Ascoli

Marchesi of the marquises of Camerota

Marchesi of the princes of Monte Marano

Medici of the princes of Ottaiano

Mendozza of the marquises of Valle

Messanelli of the marquises

Moncada of Aragon of the dukes of Montalto

Monti of the marquises of Corigliano and of Acaia

Orsini of the counts of Pacento

Pisanelli of the marquises of Bonito

Rossi of the counts of Caiazza and of S. Secondo

Ruffi of the counts of Catanzaro and Montalto, the marquises of Cotrone, the princes of Scillo, the counts of Sinopoli and the dukes of Bagnara

Sanseverino of the dukes of S. Donato and the lords of Calvera

Scaglioni, descendants of the royal blood of the Norman princes, counts of Capitanata and Abruzzo, lords of Contato, Martorano and Pittabella

Sicari of the counts of Aiello

Suardi of the lords of Berbamo, Gambatesa and Airola

Toraldi, lords of Badolato and of the marquises of Polignano

Torelli of the lords of Rugnano

Tufi of Fundatori, and the counts of Aversa, the ancient lords of Tufo, the marquises of Genzano, Lavello and S. Giovanni

Valva, ancient lords of Valva.

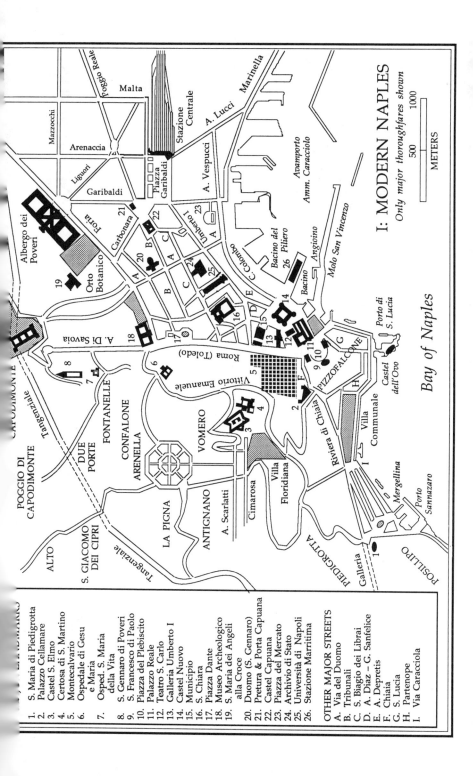

I: MODERN NAPLES

Only major thoroughfares shown

METERS 500 1000

Bay of Naples

1. S. Maria di Piedigrotta
2. Palazzo Cellamare
3. Castel S. Elmo
4. Certosa di S. Martino
5. Montecalvario
6. Ospedale di Gesù e Maria
7. Osped. S. Maria della Vita
8. S. Gennaro di Poveri
9. S. Francesco di Paolo
10. Piazza del Plebiscito
11. Palazzo Reale
12. Teatro S. Carlo
13. Galleria Umberto I
14. Castel Nuovo
15. Municipio
16. S. Chiara
17. Piazza Dante
18. Museo Archeologico
19. S. Maria dei Angeli alla Croce
20. Duomo (S. Gennaro)
21. Pretura & Porta Capuana
22. Castel Capuana
23. Piazza del Mercato
24. Archivio di Stato
25. Università di Napoli
26. Stazione Marrittima

OTHER MAJOR STREETS
A. Via del Duomo
B. Tribunali
C. S. Biagio dei Librai
D. A. Diaz – G. Sanfelice
E. A. Depretis
F. Chiaia
G. S. Lucia
H. Partenope
I. Via Caracciola

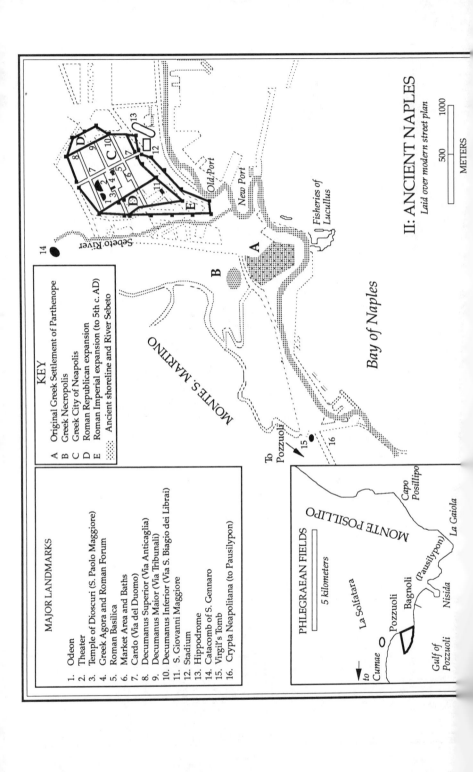

II: ANCIENT NAPLES
Laid over modern street plan

KEY

- A Original Greek Settlement of Parthenope
- B Greek Necropolis
- C Greek City of Neapolis
- D Roman Republican expansion
- E Roman Imperial expansion (to 5th c. AD)
- ⋯ Ancient shoreline and River Sebeto

MAJOR LANDMARKS

1. Odeon
2. Theater
3. Temple of Dioscuri (S. Paolo Maggiore)
4. Greek Agora and Roman Forum
5. Roman Basilica
6. Market Area and Baths
7. Cardo (Via del Duomo)
8. Decumanus Superior (Via Anticaglia)
9. Decumanus Maior (Via Tribunali)
10. Decumanus Inferior (Via S. Biagio dei Librai)
11. S. Giovanni Maggiore
12. Stadium
13. Hippodrome
14. Catacomb of S. Gennaro
15. Virgil's Tomb
16. Crypta Neapolitana (to Pausilypon)

MONTE S. MARTINO

Sebeto River

Bay of Naples

New Port

Old Port

Fisheries of Lucullus

To Pozzuoli

METERS

500   1000

PHLEGRAEAN FIELDS

5 kilometers

to Cumae

La Solfatara

Pozzuoli

Bagnoli

Gulf of Pozzuoli

Nisida

(Pausilypon)

MONTE POSILLIPO

Capo Posillipo

La Gaiola

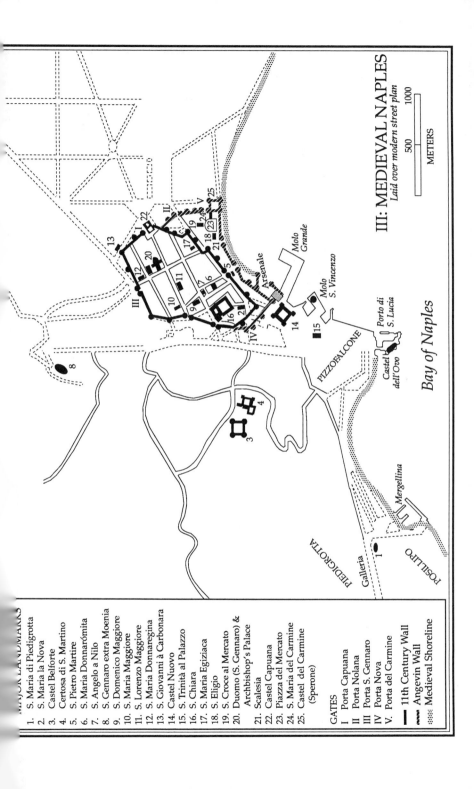

MAJOR LANDMARKS

1. S. Maria di Piedigrotta
2. S. Maria la Nova
3. Castel Belforte
4. Certosa di S. Martino
5. S. Pietro Martire
6. S. Maria Donnarómita
7. S. Angelo a Nilo
8. S. Gennaro extra Moenia
9. S. Domenico Maggiore
10. S. Maria Maggiore
11. S. Lorenzo Maggiore
12. S. Maria Donnaregina
13. S. Giovanni à Carbonara
14. Castel Nuovo
15. S. Trinità al Palazzo
16. S. Chiara
17. S. Maria Egiziaca
18. S. Eligio
19. S. Croce al Mercato
20. Duomo (S. Gennaro) &
    Archbishop's Palace
    (Sperone)
21. Scalesia
22. Castel Capuana
23. Piazza del Mercato
24. S. Maria del Carmine
25. Castel del Carmine

GATES

I   Porta Capuana
II   Porta Nolana
III Porta S. Gennaro
IV   Porta Nova
V   Porta del Carmine

---   11th Century Wall
ⲟⲟⲟ   Angevin Wall
⫶⫶⫶   Medieval Shoreline

III: MEDIEVAL NAPLES
Laid over modern street plan

```
0        500       1000
|____|____|____|____|
      METERS
```

Bay of Naples

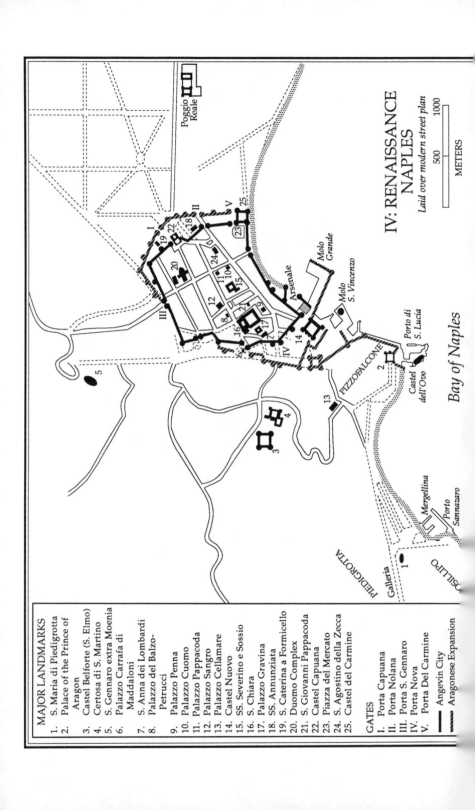

MAJOR LANDMARKS

1. S. Maria di Piedigrotta
2. Palace of the Prince of Aragon
3. Castel Belforte (S. Elmo)
4. Certosa di S. Martino
5. S. Gennaro extra Moenia
6. Palazzo Carrafa di Maddaloni
7. S. Anna dei Lombardi
8. Palazzo del Balzo-Petrucci
9. Palazzo Penna
10. Palazzo Cuomo
11. Palazzo Pappacoda
12. Palazzo Sangro
13. Palazzo Cellamare
14. Castel Nuovo
15. SS. Severino e Sossio
16. S. Chiara
17. Palazzo Gravina
18. SS. Annunziata
19. S. Caterina a Formicello
20. Duomo Complex
21. S. Giovanni Pappacoda
22. Castel Capuana
23. Piazza del Mercato
24. S. Agostino della Zecca
25. Castel del Carmine

GATES

I. Porta Capuana
II. Porta Nolana
III. Porta S. Gennaro
IV. Porta Nova
V. Porta Del Carmine

— Angevin City
░░ Aragonese Expansion

IV: RENAISSANCE NAPLES

Laid over modern street plan

0   500   1000
METERS

Bay of Naples

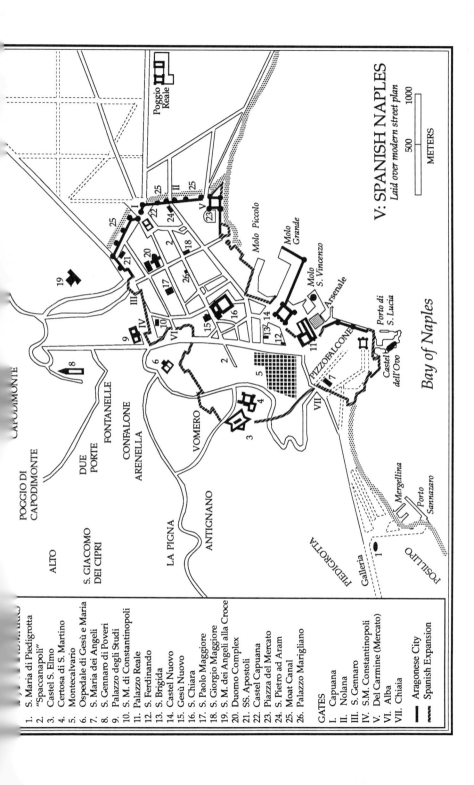

V: SPANISH NAPLES

Laid over modern street plan

1. S. Maria di Piedigrotta
2. "Spaccanapoli"
3. Castel S. Elmo
4. Certosa di S. Martino
5. Montecalvario
6. Ospedale di Gesù e Maria
7. S. Maria degli Angeli
8. S. Gennaro di Poveri
9. Palazzo degli Studi
10. S. M. di Constantinopoli
11. Palazzo Reale
12. S. Ferdinando
13. S. Brigida
14. Castel Nuovo
15. Gesù Nuovo
16. S. Chiara
17. S. Paolo Maggiore
18. S. Giorgio Maggiore
19. S. M. dei Angeli alla Croce
20. Duomo Complex
21. SS. Apostoli
22. Castel Capuana
23. Piazza del Mercato
24. S. Pietro ad Aram
25. Moat Canal
26. Palazzo Marigliano

GATES

I. Capuana
II. Nolana
III. S. Gennaro
IV. S.M. Constantinopoli
V. Del Carmine (Mercato)
VI. Alba
VII. Chiaia

— Aragonese City
~ Spanish Expansion

Bay of Naples

Molo Picolo
Molo Grande
Molo S. Vincenzo
Arsenale
Porto di S. Lucia
Castel dell'Ovo
PIZZOFALCONE

Poggio Reale

CAPODIMONTE
POGGIO DI CAPODIMONTE
ALTO
S. GIACOMO DEI CIPRI
DUE PORTE
FONTANELLE
CONFALONE
ARENELLA
LA PIGNA
VOMERO
ANTIGNANO
PIEDIGROTTA
Galleria
Mergellina
Porto Sannazaro
POSILLIPO

500   1000

METERS

BIBLIOGRAPHY

I. GENERAL WORKS

Blanchard, Paul. *Blue Guide: Southern Italy*. New York: W.W. Norton, 1982.

Braudel, Fernand. *The Mediterranean and the Mediterranean World in the Age of Philip II*. Trans Siân Reynolds. 2 vols. New York: Harper & Row, 1972-73.

Cochrane, Eric. *Italy 1530-1630*. Ed. Julius Kirshner. London & New York: Longman, 1988.

Duckett, Eleanor Shipley. *The Gateway to the Middle Ages: Italy*. Ann Arbor: University of Michigan Press, 1961.

Haskins, Charles Homer. *The Normans in European History*. New York: Norton, 1966.

Hay, Denis & John Law. *Italy in the Age of the Renaissance, 1380-1530*. London & New York: Longman, 1989.

Housley, Norman. *The Italian Crusades*. Oxford & New York: Oxford University Press, 1982.

Larner, John. *Italy in the Age of Dante and Petrarch, 1216-1380*. London & New York: Longman, 1980.

Previté-Orton, C.W. *The Shorter Cambridge Medieval History*. 2 vols. Cambridge: Cambridge University Press, 1966, 1:507-18, 605-15; 2:682-703, 763-82, 860-66, 1083-84.

Runciman, Steven. *The Sicilian Vespers*. Cambridge: Cambridge University Press, 1958.

Wickham, Chris. *Early Medieval Italy: Central Power and Local Society, 400-1000*. Ann Arbor: University of Michigan Press, 1989.

II. WORKS ON NAPLES

Baddeley, St. Clair. *Robert the Wise and His Heirs 1278-1352*. London: W. Heinemann, 1897.

—. *Queen Joanna I*. London: W. Heinemann, 1893.

Bentley, Jerry H. *Politics and Culture in Renaissance Naples*. Princeton: Princeton University Press, 1987.

Caggese, Romolo. *Roberto d'Angio e i suoi tempi*. 2 vols. Florence, 1922-1930.

Bibliography

Capasso, Bartolomeo. *Topografia della città di Napoli nell'XI secolo*. Naples: s.n., 1895.

—. *Napoli greco-romano*. Naples: Società Napoletana di storia patria, 1905.

Cassani, Silvia, Daniela Campanelli, & Fiammetta Chiuazzi, eds. *Napoli: Città d'arte*. Naples: Electra, 1986.

Cautela, Gemma, ed. *Napoli sacra: Realta e proposte per il centro storico*. Naples: Electra, 1986.

Civiltà del Seicento a Napoli. 2 vols. Naples: Electa, 1984.

Cortese, Nino. *Cultura e politica à Napoli del Cinque al Settecento*. Naples: Edizioni scientifiche italiane, 1965.

Croce, Benedetto. *History of the Kingdom of Naples*. Ed. H. Stuart Hughes. Chicago & London: University of Chicago Press, 1970.

Cruciani, Alessandro, ed. *Napoli e Dintorni*. Milan: Touring Club Italiano, 1979.

d'Agostino, Guido. *La capitale ambigua: Napoli dal 1458 al 1580*. Naples: Società editrice napoletana, 1979.

D'Arms, John. *Romans on the Bay of Naples: A Social & Cultural Study on the Villas and their Owners from 150 BC to AD 400*. Cambridge: Harvard University Press, 1970.

De Franciscis, Alfonso, Daniela del Pesco Spirito et al. *Campania*. Trans. Rudolf G. Carpanini et al. Naples: Electa for Banco Nazionale del Lavoro, 1977.

De Seta, Cesare. *Storia della città di Napoli. Dalle origini al Settecento*. Rome & Bari: Laterza, 1973

—, ed. *Atlante cartografico della città di Napoli*. Naples: s.n., 1980(?).

—. *Napoli. La Città nella storia d'Italia*. Rome & Bari: Laterza, 1981.

Doria, Gino. *Storia di una capitale. Napoli dalle origine al 1860*. Naples: Riccardi, 1968.

Galante, Gennaro Aspreno. *Guida sacra della città di Napoli*. Ed. Nicola Spinosa. Naples: Società editrice napoletana, 1985.

Galasso, Giuseppe. *Mezzogiorno medievale e moderno*. Torino: Einaudi, 1965.

—. *Napoli spagnola dopo Masaniello: Politica, cultura, società*. Naples: Edizioni scientifiche italiane, 1972.

Gleijeses, Vittorio. *La storia di Napoli: dalle origini ai nostri giorni*. Naples: Società editrice napoletana, 1974.

— & Lydia Gleijeses. *Giovanna I d'Angio, regina di Napoli*. Naples: Società editrice napoletana, 1978.

—. *Il colle di San Martino a Napoli: il Museo e la Certosa, Castel Sant'Elmo*. Naples: Società editrice napoletana, 1979.

—. *La Guida storica, artistica, monumentale, turistica della città di Napoli e dei suoi dintorni.* 4th edition. Naples: Società editrice napoletana, 1979.

—. *La storia di Napoli.* 3 vols. Naples: Società editrice napoletana, 1981.

—. *Spaccanapoli e il centro storico.* Cava dei Tirreni: Di Mauro, 1983.

Gunn, P. *Naples, A Palimpsest.* London: Chapman & Hall, 1961.

Harsey, Georges L. H. *Renewal of Naples, 1485-1495.* New Haven & London: Yale University Press, 1969.

Labande, Y. & E. R. *Naples and its Surroundings.* Trans. J. H. Shaw. London: Nicholas Kaye, 1955.

Ricerche sul '600 Napoletano. 2 vols. Milan: Edizioni "L&T," 1985-86.

Russo, Giuseppe. *La città di Napoli dalle origini al 1860.* Naples: Società per Risanamento di Napoli, 1960.

—. *Napoli come città.* Naples, 1966.

Ryder, Alan. *The Kingdom of Naples Under Alfonso the Magnanimous: The Making of a Modern State.* Oxford: Clarendon Press, 1976.

—. *Alfonso the Magnanimous, King of Aragon, Naples and Sicily, 1396-1458.* Oxford & New York: Oxford University Press, 1990.

Sabatini, F. *Napoli Angioìna: Cultura e Società.* Naples: Edizioni scientifiche italiene, 1975.

Seward, Desmond. *Naples, A Travellers' Companion.* New York: Athenuem, 1986.

Smith, Denis Mack. *A History of Sicily: Medieval Sicily, 800-1713.* New York: Dorset Press, 1988.

Storia di Napoli. 10 vols. Naples: Società editrice storia di Napoli, 1975-81.

III. SPECIAL STUDIES

Banner, Robert. *St. Louis and the Court Style in Gothic Architecture.* London: Zwemmer, 1965.

Beck, James. "Donatello and the Brancacci Tomb in Naples." In *Florilegium Columbianum: Essays in Honor of Paul Oskar Kristeller.* New York: Italica Press, 1987, pp. 125-45.

Berger-Dittscheid, Cornelia. "S. Lorenzo Maggiore in Neapel, das gotische "Ideal' Projekt Karls I. und seine 'franziskanischen' Modificationem." *Festschrift für Hartmet Biermann.* Weinheim, 1990, pp. 41-64.

Blunt, Anthony. *Neapolitan Baroque and Rococo Architecture.* London: Zwemmer, 1975.

di Stefano, Roberto. *La Cattedrale di Napoli: storia, restauro, scoperte, ritrovamenti*. Naples: Editoriale scientifiche, 1974.

Filangieri, Riccardo. "Report on the Destruction by the Germans, September 30, 1943, of the Depository of Priceless Historical Records of the Naples State Archives." *American Archivist* 7 (1944): 252-55.

—. *I registri della cancelleria angioina*. Naples: Archivio di Stato, 1950-.

Fraschetti, Stanislao. "I Sarcofagi del reali angioini in Santa Chiara di Napoli." *L'Arte* 1 (1898): 385-438.

Gardner, Julian. "A Princess among Prelates: A Fourteenth-Century Neapolitan Tomb and Some Northern Relations." *Römisches Jahrbuch für Kunstgeschichte* 23 (1988): 30-60.

Glass, Dorothy. *Romanesque Sculpture in Campania: Patrons, Programs, and Style*. University Park, PA & London: Pennsylvania State University Press, forthcoming.

Jamison, E. M. "Documents from the Angevin Registers of Naples: Charles I." *Papers of the British School at Rome* 17 (1949): 87-89.

Krautheimer, Richard. *Early Christian and Byzantine Architecture*. The Pelican History of Art. Harmondsworth & New York: Penguin, 1986.

Krüger, Jürgen. *S. Lorenzo Maggiore in Neapel: eine Franziskanerkirke zwischen Ordenideal und Herrschaftsarchitektur*. Franziskanische Forschungen 31. Werl: Dietrich- Ceolde, 1986.

Labrot, Gérard. *Baroni in città. Residenza e comportamenti dell'aristocrazia napoletana, 1570-1734*. Naples, 1979.

Léonard, Émile G. *Les Angevins de Naples*. Paris: Presses universitaires de France, 1954.

Musto, Ronald G. "Queen Sancia of Naples (1286-1345) and the Spiritual Franciscans." In *Women in the Medieval World*. Oxford & New York: Basil Blackwell, 1985, pp. 179-214.

Pane, Giulio. "Pietro di Toledo, Vicerè, Urbanista." *Napoli nobilissima* 14 (1975): 81-95, 161-82.

Pane, Roberto. *Architettura dell'età barocca in Napoli*. Naples: Editrice politecnica, 1939.

—. *Il Rinascimento nell'Italia meridionale*. 2 vols. Milan: Edizioni di comunità, 1975 & 1977.

Petraccone, Claudia. *Napoli dal Cinquecento all'Ottocento. Problemi di storia demografica e sociale*. Naples: Guida, 1969.

Venditti, Arnaldo. "Problemi di lettura e di interpretazione dell'architettura paleochristiana di Napoli." *Napoli nobilissima* 12 (1973): 177-88.

INDEX

149

Index

Index

churches cont.
S. Maria cont.
delle Grazie 53
delle Grazie alle Paludi 29, 30
delle Grazie at Capodimonte
(Caponapoli?) 38
Incoronata 49, 67
della Libera 50
di Loreto a Toleto 54
di Loretto 12
Maggiore (Pietrasanta) lxviii,
lxix, lxxi, 37, 45, 49, 54, 59;
chapel of Santissimo
Sacramento in 44
della Misericordia 38
dei Miracoli 51
di Monserrato 53
del Monte di Carmelo 49
del Monte 51
di Montevergine 53
delli Monti 25, 54
di Nazaret 23
della Neve at Chiaia 38
della Nova lxvii, 46, 50
Ognibene 38, 53
dell'Oliva 51
della Pace (La Pace) 53
del Paradiso (Pergola) a
Posillipo 14, 52
del Parto a Mergellina 15, 53
della Pazienza Cesarea 55
del Pianto lxxxviii
a Piazza 37; well-keepers'
chapel of S. Maria a Forte in
43
di Piedigrotta 16, 52; tombs of
house of Cardona 15
della Pietà dei Turchini 55
Porta Coeli 54
di Portanova, see S. Maria in
Cosmedin
in Portico 101
di Portosalvo of Barcaroli 43
Regina Coeli Mon.(?) 52
Regina di Tutti i Santi 38, 43
Ritonda 37
del Rosario 47
della Salute 50
della Sanità 50
di Scala 37
Scalaceli 23

a Segno 37
delle Scuole Pie alla Duchesca
54
del Soccorso 51
del Soccorso all'Arenella 38
della Speranza 51
della Stella 53
Succurre Miseris 42, 55
dei Vergini 12, 52
della Verità 51
della Vita 52
della Vittoria 54
S. Marta 43; embroidery-makers'
chapel of S. Luca 42
S. Marteo 38
S. Martino lxxiii, 19, 49, 52
S. Nicola a Nilo lxvi
S. Nicola a Tolentino 51
S. Nicola, chapel of S. Maria del
Soccorso 42; innkeepers' chapel
of S. Maria della Catena 43;
musicians' chapel of S. Angelo
in 40
S. Nicolò of Bari 60
S. Paolo Maggiore (Pietro e
Paolo) lxvi, lxviii, lxxvii, 10,
46, 49, 54; staurita of SS. Pietro
e Paolo in 44
S. Patrizia 46, 49, 53
S. Peregrino 46
S. Pietro a Maiella 52
S. Pietro ad Aram 46, 52
S. Pietro in Vincoli de'Spetiali 44
S. Pietro in Vincoli, chapel of
Monte of the city of Massa in 43
S. Pietro Martire lxvii, lxxi,
lxxiii, 49, 50; chapel of Monte
di Cetara in 43; chapel of Nome
di Dio in 41; chapel of S. Maria
del Rosario in 43; chapel of S.
Maria Incoronata in 43
S. Potito 53
S. Restituta xxviii, lxvi, lxx, 3,
37, 59; Principio chapel lxxi; see
also S. Gennaro and Stefania
S. Rocco 50
S. Sabina 109
S. Sebastiano 50
S. Sergio xxix
S. Severino xxix, xxviii, 52

Index

This Book Was Completed on December 19, 1990 at
Italica Press, New York, New York and Was Set
in Times. It Was Printed on 50 lb Acid-
free Glatfelter Natural Paper with
a Smyth-Sewn Binding by
McNaughton & Gunn,
Ann Arbor, MI
U. S. A.
*   *   **
*

OTHER HISTORICAL TRAVEL GUIDES
PUBLISHED BY ITALICA PRESS

The Marvels of Rome
Mirabilia Urbis Romae

Theoderich
Guide to the Holy Land

Pierre Gilles
The Antiquities of Constantinople

William Fitz Stephen
Norman London

The Pilgrim's Guide to Santiago de Compostela
(Codex Calixtinus)
William Melczer
(forthcoming 1991)